HV2430 .L58 2004

0134108898997

Literac
: cult
20

# Literacy and Deaf People

# Literacy and Deaf People

*Cultural and Contextual Perspectives*

Brenda Jo Brueggemann, *Editor*

Gallaudet University Press
Washington, D.C.

Gallaudet University Press
Washington, DC 20002
http://gupress.gallaudet.edu

© 2004 by Gallaudet University
All rights reserved
Published in 2004
Printed in the United States of America

*Interior page design by Stephen Tiano Page Design & Production*

*Cover design by Gary Gore*

Library of Congress Cataloging-in-Publication Data

Literacy and deaf people : cultural and contextual perspectives / Brenda Brueggemann, editor.
   p. cm.
   Includes bibliographical references and index.
   ISBN 1-56368-271-0 (alk. paper)
   1. Deaf--Education. 2. Deaf children--Education. 3. Literacy. 4. Deafness--Social aspects. 5. English language--Study and teaching. 6. Education, Bilingual. I. Brueggemann, Brenda Jo, 1958-

HV2430L58 2004
371.91'2--dc22                                              2004045154

∞ The paper used in this publication meets the minimum requirements of American National Standard for Information Sciences—Permanence of Paper for Printed Library Materials, ANSI Z39.48-1984.

# Contents

Introduction: Reframing Deaf People's Literacy     1
*Brenda Jo Brueggemann*

### Part I
### "Modernizing" Deaf Selves and Deaf Education: Histories and Habits

The Modern Deaf Self: Indigenous Practices     29
and Educational Imperatives
*Tom Humphries*

What Does Culture Have to Do with the Education     47
of Students Who Are Deaf or Hard of Hearing?
*Claire Ramsey*

Double Jeopardy: Women, Deafness,     59
and Deaf Education
*Susan Burch*

Deaf, She Wrote: Mapping Deaf Women's     73
Autobiography
*Brenda Jo Brueggemann*

### Part II: Multicultural and Bilingual Perspectives

The Relationship between Language Experience     91
and Language Development: A Report from Norway
*Elizabeth Engen and Trygg Engen*

Deaf Immigrant and Refugee Children:     110
Institutional and Cultural Clash
*C. Tane Akamatsu and Ester Cole*

Cultural and Linguistic Voice in the Deaf     139
Bilingual Experience
*Lillian Buffalo Tompkins*

Struggling for a Voice: An Interactionist View     157
of Language and Literacy in Deaf Education
*Sherman Wilcox*

English Literacy in the Life Stories of Deaf College   192
Undergraduates
*Kathleen M. Wood*

Contributors   209

Index   211

# Literacy and
# Deaf People

# Introduction: Reframing Deaf People's Literacy

## Brenda Jo Brueggemann

The way that children are trained and schooled is a crucial demonstration of the way that they are perceived and treated in a given society. . . . Discovering who was taught, and when and how, is related far more to the social, political, legislative, economic, and religious forces at work in a society than it is to the unique social and educational needs of disabled persons. At the same time, this history mirrors our progress toward appreciating the basic humanity of all people.
                    Margret Winzer, *A History of Special Education*

Although it is conventional to focus on the disability of deaf children, their inability to hear, an alternative perspective is needed.
                    Claire Ramsey, *Deaf Children in Public Schools*

Deaf people's literacy: This is no new subject. Typically approached as a problem or even a paradox in much of the long-stretching literature, literacy and deaf people have never danced smoothly together. Perhaps because literacy itself is usually defined as (and by) the dominant culture's literacy, bound to standard spoken and written forms of a language and certain skill levels at those standard forms (see Goody 1968; Goody and Watt 1988; Kintgen, Kroll, and Rose 1988), literacy studies have most often defined deaf people as lacking. Yet in the past, deaf studies scholars such as Timothy Reagan (1990) and Donald F. Moores and Kathryn P. Meadow-Orlans (1990) have been concerned about the pathological definitions of deafness that are inherent in the English language itself and embedded in our educational systems. They have sought to explore literacy and deafness from contextual and cultural models that look beyond a sometimes simplistic deficit model that leaves deaf people only and always lacking.[1]

---

1. The debates—and confusion—over when, where, and how to use "Deaf" or "deaf" have been considerable. Some scholars argue that the use of "Deaf" (capitalized) emphasizes

Responding to the context of this deficit model, for example, college writing teacher Lisa Bednar has written of "literacy and the deaf" as a "problematic topic," particularly when it comes to writing. She sees literacy as the "source of difficulty" for deaf students in her college writing classrooms, however, not so much because of *their* deficits but because of the context in which they are asked to acquire literacy.

> In spite of the fact that literacy is not a synonym for the English language, our (hearing) American culture tends to view it as such, ignoring other critical kinds of literacy—in the case of the deaf, for example, the gestural American sign language . . . . Thus the Deaf have been advised—indeed, at times, forced—to become at least marginally skilled in what "hearies" have an easier time mastering, the written English language. (1989, 53)

Likewise, as Donald Moores makes clear in his introduction to *Educational and Developmental Aspects of Deafness* (1990), deaf students' illiteracy is often correlated with—even caused by—a narrow focus on oral- and English-based methods of communication:

> Historically, the priorities of education of the deaf have concentrated on the mastery of grammar and on the production and understanding of speech. Teacher training programs have emphasized these areas at the expense of content subjects such as math, science, literature, social studies and history. In a typical school day, deaf children spend less time on academic subject matter than hearing children. (11)

---

the idea that deaf people have a unique culture and a shared language, whereas "deaf" (lower case) only conveys the medical/audiological designation of a condition. It has become fairly common for scholars in deaf and disability studies to indicate their distinction between "Deaf" and "deaf" in an opening footnote along these lines for almost two decades now. But the fact remains that most of the time, authors—and readers—are still confused about which one is right (or wrong) in any given instance. I have recently written about this continued confusion in an essay, "Think-Between: A Deaf Studies Commonplace Book." Here I choose to use "deaf" (lower case) throughout—unless I am quoting from one of the contributors to this volume who distinguishes between "Deaf" and "deaf." My choice on this matter does not mean that I do not believe—or do not understand—that there is indeed a distinction between "deaf" designated as a medical/audiological "impairment" and "deaf" as a cultural, linguistic way of life and community designation. But since many people who are designated as medically/audiologically deaf are not necessarily culturally deaf—and most of time, I prefer to think broadly and inclusively about both of these groups of people (as well as all the people with hearing loss who are between them), I choose again to just use one term, "deaf."

Thus, as the literature on literacy and deafness has often reported, when they are judged by hearing English literacy standards, deaf high school seniors in the United States have an average reading ability at the 3.6 grade level, and roughly half of those seniors only score between the second- and third-grade level on tests of academic achievement (Lou 1988).

There is no shortage of research studies about the significant discrepancies in functioning literate abilities between deaf and hearing students. But these studies, as some other researchers also note, are framed within a "medical deficit model" where deafness is regarded as a severe handicap and not just a receptive or expressive difference (see Mittelman and Quinsland 1991; Sacks 1988; Lane 1992). Yet there have also been alternative approaches to the study of cognition and literacy skills among deaf students. These studies focus on what deaf students *can do* and consider the fuller context and processes of their thinking, reading, and writing—going beyond offering only a repetitive analysis of the errors in their products. Many of these alternative approaches were collected in editions also published by Gallaudet University Press in the past two decades, including David S. Martin's *Advances in Cognition, Education, and Deafness* (1990) and Donald F. Moores and Kathryn P. Meadow-Orlans's *Educational and Developmental Aspects of Deafness* (1990). Likewise, a significant number of literacy and composition studies in the past two decades have turned the focus to capabilities, contexts, cultures, and processes for literacy among deaf literacy learners instead of attending to only their deemed deficits. (See, for example: Ahlgren and Hyltenstam 1994; Batson 1989; Bednar 1989; Brueggemann 1999; Gregory and Hartley 1991; Higgins and Nash 1996; Humphries and MacDougall 2000; Moores and Meadow-Orlans 1990; Padden 1990; Paul 1988; Ramsey 1997; Ramsey and Padden 1998; Strong 1988; Webster 1986.)

This volume follows in that trend by locating the study of deaf people's literacy within their various cultural constructs and specific contexts. In such locations, deaf literacy learners may still indeed present a problematic topic. As Bednar once noted and Carol Padden echoed in her 1990 pamphlet, *Deaf Children and Literacy: Literacy Lessons*, "Deaf children come from all races, classes and backgrounds, but as a group they have a hard time learning to read and write" (1). While there are surely "still many deaf people whose lives are economically or socially constrained by an inability to use written English effectively" (Mittelman and Quinsland 1991), we have come to understand more the contexts that create (and constrain) deaf people's literacy. In exploring these literacy-learning contexts and the various cultural landscapes in which they occur, we might come to understand the "problematic" of "deafness and literacy" as one that is socially constructed. And if we consider deaf people's literacy as socially constructed and context bound, then we must critically consider at least three overlapping areas: our entire education system's accountability in constructing "deaf people's literacy" in the first place, the specific contexts in which deaf people become literate (or not), and the specific situation and skills of each individual child/person/literacy learner.

As Claire Ramsey argues in *Deaf Children in Public Schools* (1997), it has been "conventional to focus on the disability of deaf children, their inability to hear" when thinking about and seeking to understand their relationship to literacy. Taken together, the nine essays in this volume are unconventional in that they offer—as Claire Ramsey has urged educators and literacy scholars to offer (see the epigraph above)—an alternative perspective. This alternative perspective frames deaf people's literacy in contextual and cultural ways.

The idea for this collection grew out of a conference held in October 2000, The 15th Annual Conference on Issues of Language and Deafness, sponsored by Boys Town National Research Hospital in Omaha, Nebraska.[2] Six of the authors collected here gave keynote addresses or workshops at this conference. It is from the frame of their remarks at this turn-of-the-century event that this collection takes shape. This collection seeks to flesh out Tom Humphries' ideas about the connection between "the modern Deaf self" and recent changes in deaf education and literacy learning, as expressed at this conference.

## MODERNIZING DEAF SELVES AND DEAF EDUCATION— HISTORIES AND HABITS

The first section of this volume offers four essays centered on exploring the histories and habits, the contexts and cultural backdrops, for "modernizing" deaf people and deaf education. Written by scholars from four different academic disciplines—Humphries in both teacher education and

---

2. Mary Pat Moeller was the chief organizer of this conference, and the genesis of this volume should go to her credit. Indeed, when the idea for this book began to develop, Moeller was urged to be a co-editor but declined because of her own schedule and demands for finishing her dissertation. Her presence is, I hope, still strong in each of these chapters.

communication, Ramsey in both special education and communication disorders, Burch in history, and Brueggemann in both English and comparative studies—these four essays map different, but sometimes overlapping, terrains. Moreover, they also exhibit how different methodologies are useful for exploring the relationships between literacy and deaf people. In outlining the historical construction of "the modern Deaf self," Humphries works at least three different ways: employing theories around the development of self-identity and group/cultural consciousness; attending to close readings of texts and contexts delivered by American deaf people since the 1950s; and engaging discourse analysis and sociolinguistic studies to illuminate the actual "teacher talk" in two different deaf educational settings. Ramsey embraces dense anthropological theories surrounding the (still unsettled) question of "culture," while she also moves effectively between personal narrative (telling stories about her own educational experience as both student and teacher, for example) and pointed polemic. Burch makes use of the historian's tools, supporting her argument about how deaf women were held in "double jeopardy" in regards to American deaf education as it developed at the turn of the last century by using carefully researched historical "facts." Brueggemann combines rhetorical analysis, a method of constructing and interpreting persuasive discourse that is two-and-a-half millennia old, with the newer capabilities of critical autobiographical studies that have been in force mostly since the second half of the twentieth century in order to create a preliminary map for critically approaching deaf women's autobiography.

In "The Modern Deaf Self: Indigenous Practices and Educational Imperatives," Tom Humphries first explores the development of "the modern Deaf self" (since the 1950s) and the connections between this newly developed deaf self-identity and changes in deaf education over the past forty years. He argues "for bilingual education, second language teaching, Deaf identity development among Deaf school children, and a greater and more controlling presence of Deaf people in schooling decisions and management." Humphries marks how the disappearance of the concept (and term) *deaf-mute* in the 1960s and the ways that deaf people began in the 1960s to "adopt a modern sensibility of self as people of culture" and to discover that "the new discourse of 'ASL' and 'Deaf culture' was so close to [their] idea of themselves that they began to create greater and greater distance between themselves and the ideas of others about them." The development of this modern deaf self was motivated by four dominant themes that he briefly outlines: (1) "an ideal of completeness and a concept of wellness"; (2) "distance from rather than solidarity with hearing people"; (3) greater "control of their own institutions, destiny, and image"; and (4) "economic imperatives . . . in their push for more participation in the professional world." Finally, he lists a fifth cultural imperative arising from the development of the modern deaf self over the past forty years and names it as the focus of his chapter—"the efforts to re-organize and operationalize education of Deaf children in ways that fit the new Deaf consciousness."

Having established the connection between the development of a modern deaf self and changes in deaf education over the past forty years as his theme, Humphries moves then to specific examples and "analysis of interviews and dialogue among teachers, parents, and others, as well as direct observation" in order to "reveal how once closely held perceptions in the Deaf community, increasingly made public, have reorganized views of Deaf children's development, teacher training practice, and classroom practice." Humphries roughly establishes each decade from 1950 to 1980 as a different key phase in the development of the modern deaf self: (1) *maintenance* of deaf people's identity contradictions as they often "'accommodated others' beliefs but [also] asserted the 'normalcy' of being Deaf" in the 1950s; (2) *telling the story (and having it told back)* to them by hearing people who began, increasingly, to "probe the lives of Deaf people and translate what they learned from Deaf people into scientific texts" in the 1960s; (3) *the emergence of a self-conscious discourse of culture* by the mid-1970s when there arose a "questioning of the new Deaf self" along with "a self-conscious discourse of culture," which created "a discourse of boundaries and margins"; (4) *a projection into public policy* during the 1980s. It was here, in this projection and the fourth phase, Humphries argues, that deaf people "began to insist that education address newly imagined development patterns for Deaf children with increased emphasis on bilingualism and first and second language development." The examples he offers of this projection into public policy—especially around the education of deaf children—come from "'teacher talk' in real instruction time" as they discuss the literacy learning of the deaf children they instruct.

From this teacher talk, Humphries concludes his essay with interesting and specific sociolinguistic features in an attempt "to understand how teachers make connections between English and ASL in natural ways during instruction." Such connections are literacy lessons in and of themselves. For example, the use of "chaining," fingerspelling, and English-initialized signs among these teachers is studied within the context of the educational setting—a residential school where ASL and English are used alongside each other, with each remaining intact, and a public school district where "signing is strongly influenced by English in various ways." As Humphries concludes (in an argument that is central to this entire volume), schools—and especially schools where deaf children are taught—"are the product of ideologies about teaching, about how Deaf children learn, and about the relationship of ASL and English." And in these ideologies, the modern deaf self continues to evolve and emerge, tightly connected to the contexts of specific educational settings and bound to the concepts of culture and language that teachers and students carry with them as they go about literacy learning.

Claire Ramsey also concerns herself with *contexts* and *culture* as the controlling concepts in modern deaf education in "What Does Culture Have to Do with the Education of Students Who Are Deaf or Hard of Hearing?" Although "the narrowness of everyday definitions of culture [have] become especially apparent in education," she argues that there is value in "seriously thinking about culture in deaf education," especially since "it is becoming apparent that Deaf cultural ways, especially ways of using language, contribute to learning." Just as Humphries outlines the unique double identity that characterized American deaf people before 1960, Ramsey actually acknowledges that a fair amount of this double consciousness probably still exists in deaf children today.

> In the United States, deaf education presents a more elaborate set of cultural problems, in part because at least two sources of culture exist for deaf children—the culture of their families, and the culture of American Deaf people. . . . Many deaf children become expert border dwellers as they grow up, with knowledge of their family's cultural ways, as well as those of Deaf people. (47–48)

Borrowing on the work of cultural anthropologist Tomasello, Ramsey first historically outlines the evolution and transmission of culture among humans, and she illuminates the ways we become, and are, "fish in the water of culture." She works to ground the theoretical work of Tomasello and others on the subject of culture to the specific case of deaf people. For example, she discusses the "three kinds of time" that delineate cultural evolution and transmission—phylogenetic time (from biological inheritance), historic time, and ontogenetic time (developmental time in individuals)—with more specific examples centered on deaf people, especially with regards to language learning.

Ramsey asserts that "the circumstances of deaf children's development (with some exceptions) do not match the broader biological and cultural design. It is an unavoidable fact that, through no fault of their own, most deaf children have a late start at language acquisition." The link between this late language acquisition and the development of literacy—especially the kind of literacy taught and valued in schools—"has consequences for all areas of deaf children's lives, but it especially threatens their schooling . . . [since] schooling is organized on the assumption that children enter their years of formal education with native command of their first language." What is needed, Ramsey argues, is the "culturally designed support" of language learning for these young deaf children—the kind of support, she points out, that "rests on several centuries of problem-solving history undertaken by people who also could not make use of spoken language . . . only cultures of Deaf people provide this specific kind of support."

To support this argument further, Ramsey returns to the three times of cultural evolution and transmission in order to point out that almost all of the focus in centuries of deaf education thus far have centered on one kind of time—ontogenetic, the individual's developmental span. She comes hard and fast to a key point about the relationships between language, literacy, and deafness in a cultural frame: "Partial or ambiguous access to language does not fill the requirements for participating in culture, nor does receiving basic skills instruction second-hand through an interpreter." And on the question of culture—specifically deaf culture—Ramsey concludes with a manifesto that returns to the question in her title, reassuring us, for example, that "deaf culture does not isolate deaf children from the 'real' world, where the normal people live. It is more likely, in fact, to do the opposite" because, she maintains, "irrational rumors to the contrary, the culture of Deaf people does not want to trap deaf children—only to offer them strategies so they can learn, use, and improve upon the innovations of history to make living in the world possible." Much like Humphries in his opening essay, Ramsey also asserts that deaf people themselves should play a primary role in education and literacy learning for deaf children, since they do have a rich cultural history and strong habits that are full of "innovations to problems of learning and development, information about language structures, discourse patterns, teaching strategies, values about English, knowledge about hearing people and the larger culture."

Situating her study of the histories and habits surrounding deaf education before the development of the modern deaf self that begins, according to Tom Humphries, in the 1960s, Susan Burch offers another analytical angle on who has had a hand (and who has not) in educating American deaf people. The particularly potent merger of oralist philosophies, advocated primarily by powerful white hearing men at the turn of the last century, with the feminization of American teacher forces that also affected deaf education at this time is the subject of "Double Jeopardy: Women, Deafness, and Deaf Education." As Burch assures us, "the ramifications of oralism's popularity and the feminization of teaching were immense for the Deaf" and perhaps "the most obvious aspect was the direct assault on Deaf cultural values"—both by denying the use of sign language and by significantly removing the reliance on (primarily male) deaf educators within most deaf schools at the time.

In this situation, "Deaf men faced the double insult of watching opponents to their culture weaken the ties between the schools and the Deaf community, and to have women, viewed as the inferior sex, replace them at work." Yet, as Burch goes on to point out, it was actually "deaf women [who] experienced perhaps the greatest marginalization and disempowerment, both in terms of their educational-career opportunities and social choices." The dominoes that fell down upon deaf women went something like this:

> Hearing women struggled to attain an independent livelihood and higher social status for themselves [via employment in Deaf education, controlled primarily by hearing men]. Their efforts contributed—albeit not maliciously or even intentionally—to the disempowerment of Deaf men and women. Deaf men tried to defend their livelihood, status, and identity not only by battling oralism, but by enforcing sexist stereotypes of both hearing and Deaf women. Deaf women, having the most limited options of any of these groups, sought to defend deaf education, sign language, the Deaf community, and Deaf men from both oralism and displacement by hearing teachers. In so doing, they fell into even more subordinated roles. (62)

Burch goes on to illustrate how gender roles further complicated deaf education during this period in that, for example, "the face of oralist educators was a [hearing] female one, but so was the image of the ideal student [as a deaf young woman]." As teachers focused on the particular oral success of young deaf girls, they became role models of a sort as the "link between oralism, normalcy, and physical beauty." Burch exemplifies this link by pointing out how lipreading abilities often served as a marker of success for these students and the various ways that young deaf girls were especially educated to act and appear as "'hyper' American." She offers two developed illustrations of these hyper-American, orally successful deaf women who were educated in this system: Helen Heckman, a celebrated dancer of the 1920s, and Mary Williamson Erd, who performed for the National Association of the Deaf's commissioned sign language masters' films in 1938. Paradoxically, as Burch points out, celebrated and orally successful deaf women like Heckman and Erd were caught in a double bind: While they were celebrated by the deaf community (both appearing often in deaf newspapers, for example, with favorable articles surrounding them and titles such as "Beautiful, though Deaf!"), the measure of their success presented them as "normal" (i.e., not deaf, but effectively orally educated). Ironically, as Burch concludes, the American deaf community of the early half of the twentieth century placed their concept of normalcy squarely on the body "but often denied the deafness of the female body." The normalcy of their bodies was also directly linked to their presumed literate abilities. In this linkage, deaf women's bodies at this time could, in effect, present them as literate subjects, "normal" in the face of dominant standards for literacy.

The double jeopardy of performing literate normalcy also often appears as a master trope in deaf women's autobiography. The performance of literate normalcy while also developing or maintaining (or sometimes even denying) a deaf identity that comes through in an autobiographical account by a deaf woman is the subject of the last essay in this opening section. In "Deaf, She Wrote: Mapping Deaf Women's Autobiography," Brueggemann explores the "emergent personality of deaf women writers as they master the tribal speech (and sign too) of their particular region, nation, or era as well as the tribal speech of gender overlaid with the tribal speech of deafness, disability, 'normalcy,' and difference." In this exploratory essay, Brueggemann begins to map the ways that deaf women autobiographers compose themselves (in the dominant language's print system) as *deaf*, as *she*, and as *writer/author*. She illustrates by focusing on three sample autobiographical texts from three different eras, nations, literate abilities, and gendered perspectives: Teresa de Cartegena's companion texts from 1452 to 1454, *Groves of the Infirm* and *Wonder at the Works of God*; Emmanuelle Laborit's memoir at the age of twenty two, translated from the French, *Cry of the Gull*; and the recently removed from print "as told to" autobiography of Anne Bolander (with Adair Renning), *I Was Number 87*.

Using rhetorical theory that centers on the relationship between author, audience, and subject and also more current critical autobiographical scholarship that reads women's autobiography especially, Brueggemann outlines at least seven ways in which a deaf woman autobiographer, as "Other," operates in the space of dominant literacy: (1) She becomes what feminist ethics calls "the constructed knower" (following on the work of Belenky et al. in *Women's Ways of Knowing*); (2) she works to address her (imagined or real) audience, as classical rhetorical theory has always recommended; (3) she practices what Gilmore has called "autobiographics—a feminist theory of women's self-representation"; (4) she engages in the "mirror talk" that often confronts identity crisis (Egan); (5) she masters "whatever tribal speech happens to be [her] particular symbolic environment" (Burke); (6) she writes for herself but still feels guilty for it (as expressed by French feminist Helene Cixous); and (7) she encounters the power and paradox of writing in the styled absence of a known audience (Derrida).

Brueggemann concludes with a challenge to better understand the potential and real audience(s) for deaf women's autobiography. Such an understanding, she offers, might further illuminate how deaf people's literacy (as well as women's literacy) was imagined, received, responded to, and further shaped in any culture, era, or context—both by "insiders" and "outsiders" to their experience. A better understanding of the audience for deaf women's autobiography might also create a kind of rhetorical mirror that could also then reflect back much about dominant perspectives on literacy. This concluding idea is a reflection on how Margret Winzer has also suggested that the study of special education matters in the larger scheme of things: "This history [of special education] mirrors our progress toward appreciating the basic humanity of all people."

## MULTICULTURAL AND BILINGUAL PERSPECTIVES

The second section features five chapters that explore the contextual and cultural relationships between literacy and deaf people, yet these five articles turn to specific scenes and sites that involve either (or both) multicultural and bilingual literacy instruction when deaf children are involved. In the first chapter of this section, "The Relationship between Language Experience and Language Development," Elizabeth Engen and Trygg Engen offer the results of a Norwegian study. The research presented here is part of a larger project on "bilingualism and literacy in deaf children" that was developed in 1997 to gather data on the current linguistic status of 213 deaf children in Norway (representing 50 percent of the total population), prior to the implementation of a new curriculum that had a "goal of developing bilingualism, with Norwegian Sign Language as a first language and Norwegian as a second language to be used in print mode" for the education of Norway's deaf children. The major instrument of their study is a questionnaire given to mothers and teachers of deaf students in order "to examine the relationship between the degree of consistency of their linguistic experience [with their students/children] and results of assessments of literacy" that were also performed on these children. Significantly, the results of their study indicate that deaf students who had consistent experience with the Norwegian language (the dominant literacy) performed better on literacy tests than students whose experience involved Norwegian sign language or various forms of code mixing.

To contextualize their own study, Engen and Engen first offer a brief history of deaf education in Norway, beginning with the first school for the deaf in Trondheim in 1825. They bring this history up to the current context—"a national reorganization of special education programs in Norway in 1992 [and] a new curriculum for deaf children instituted in 1997 . . . [that] stated that Norwegian Sign Language (NSL) would be considered the first language and language of instruction for deaf children, and Norwegian developed as a second language through print forms, with the ultimate goal of bilingualism and literacy." As they discuss, many studies about deafness and literacy development and deafness and language acquisition "have noted the special problems that occur when there is a mismatch between the hearing status of parent and child, resulting in diminished parental interaction in the early years." Because "many studies of both hearing and hearing-impaired children have focused on language development or language experience, [and] thereby leav[e] the question of the relationship [between the two] undeveloped," Engen and Engen aimed to gather data "on the use of language at home and at school, in relation to the resulting language abilities of the students."

Two sets of data were used to explore the question of language experience and its relationship to these students' language development. First, the *language milieu* was explored by interviewing mothers and teachers of the children and asking them to judge the child's language competency and usage (mothers and teachers were interviewed separately and not informed of each other's judgments about the child). Second, the relationships between these mother/teacher judgments (the language milieu) and the child's actual performance on various measures of literacy (the language competency) were established. Teachers and mothers were questioned about: (a) the student's/child's "best language" (their highest language competency), (b) their own preferred or dominant language use with the student/child, and (c) their own self-rating of NSL ability.

The ratings of both teachers and mothers showed "striking differences regarding judgments of *language competence* and the *languages used* at school and at home." The authors offer several angles for interpretation and discussion of these striking differences and conclude that the results "seem to be a valid reflection of the variability in the students' experiences with communication, that is, that the language used with many students is not necessarily the one in which he/she is judged to be the most competent and the results of code mixing indicate that many students do not experience a clear linguistic model." As Humphries and Ramsey might nod, the gap between a student's language/literate abilities and the language/literate mode they are being asked to use to interact at home and school with (as led by their parents and teachers) do not often seem to coincide.

Indeed, Engen and Engen go on to explore the results of the second part of the study that "pertains to the problem of developing a level of literacy that will prepare children with hearing loss to become independent adults who can function successfully in two cultures; that is, to be bicultural." In this exploration, they find that the students who were deemed most competent in Norwegian (as opposed to having the highest competency in NSL or in "disparate" languages/modes between Norwegian and NSL) significantly scored above average on the literacy assessments. In offering general conclusions and implications to their study, the authors emphasize that their work demonstrates "the importance of understanding their [deaf children's] linguistic experience in analyzing information about their [deaf children's] language development and in planning appropriate educational programs for them" (brackets mine). Citing the seminal literacy research of such noted scholars as Halliday (1989) and Bruner (1990) and building upon the results of their own research here, Engen and Engen turn to a more complex meaning and goal for literacy than just reading and writing in the dominant language: "If the goal for students with hearing loss is to become literate, then the goals for an educational program have to go beyond development of face-to-face language and the skill of reading and writing to this higher level of using language cognitively in thinking and organizing mental events."

In sum, based on their research of language/literacy competencies and uses among Norwegian deaf children, they echo I. King Jordan, as quoted in an August 2000 *Boston Globe* article: "You can't teach to an ideal. You have to reach out and teach to the individual"—and they caution deaf educators everywhere against making "a priori judgments based on general group membership. . . . The school must know what a student brings to the educational situation so that it can take advantage of his/her strengths." In this caution then, Engen and Engen perhaps address the "alternative perspective" that Claire Ramsey has also called for (see epigraph above).

C. Tane Akamatsu and Ester Cole present another kind of multicultural, bilingual context for language milieu and competency among deaf children in their chapter "Deaf Immigrant and Refugee Children: Institutional and Cultural Clash." From the outset, they argue that in the case of immigrant and refugee children, "deafness acts as a complicating factor, rather than as an explanatory factor" for literacy instruction and that, further, "deafness complicates an already complex situation, and constrains how intervention is to be delivered." The focus of their study is on refugee and immigrant populations in the United States and Canada and, in particular, on the deaf children in these populations where, they argue, "the implications for [these] children from disadvantaged living conditions and disruptive schooling are staggering." Their goals for this chapter are perhaps no less staggering: "to sensitize professionals to issues when working with 'multicultural' deaf individuals and families, and to outline issues and questions to ask before considering a service delivery model." Literacy instruction often falls into such a service delivery model. Akamatsu and Cole do, in fact, specifically "examine issues of schooling, language, and cognitive development" for these children once they have first presented basic information that they believe is "pertinent to deaf children within the refugee and immigrant population, focusing on migration, adaptation and acculturation."

For example, Akamatsu and Cole discuss how "a family's perception on the needs of their deaf child is shaped by their culture's view of deafness, which can, in turn influence decisions about enrolling the children in school, finding housing and employment, and creating a new identity and attachment to the new society." Thus, the cultural context of beliefs that an immigrant or refugee family may have about deafness and deaf people can come to greatly impact the deaf child's literacy learning and linguistic abilities long before the child even sets foot in a school. In the case of immigrant and refugee deaf children, it may then become necessary for both teachers and school psychologists to counsel the entire family "through the process of understanding the psychoeducational implications of their child's deafness."

The authors discuss further how the U.S. model for determining school placement for deaf children is often "initially based on audiological information" and yet, especially in larger cultural contexts that immigrants and refugees may bring to the placement situation, "audiological needs, while appearing rather simple to address on the surface, are quite complicated." Again, the complications of a seemingly simple audiological assessment can increase considerably when the way that parents will react to the diagnosis and make decisions on behalf of their child is often influenced by their cultural interpretation of deafness. Additionally, the likelihood that the deaf immigrant/refugee child will have been exposed much to either a spoken/written or signed language before coming to the United States is not great. Thus, the authors go on to discuss the various complications that will further arise from attempting to immerse the deaf immigrant/refugee child in a language and literacy-learning rich environment once they are past the critical age of optimal language acquisition. Here even "ASL cannot be viewed as the language panacea for these children" since "ASL appears to have a critical period [for optimal first language acquisition] similar to that of English." On the basis of previous research (Mayer and Akamatsu 1999), these authors suggest that "natural sign systems—the naturally evolved systems that deaf people use to communicate with hearing people—may provide a bridge."

The authors also discuss the role of the family in supporting the deaf child's education (and how immigrant and refugee parents are not often well equipped or comfortable in offering school support at home) before they focus the rest of their chapter on issues of assessment for these children. Assessment, they note, is often seen as "the very process that causes marginalization and disenfranchisement" to begin with and thus, the "delay or exemption from participation in assessment" for deaf immigrant and refugee children is suggested as a "viable alternative." Along with this delay in assessment, Akamatsu and Cole explain the need for a multidisciplinary team that engages in "assessment that goes beyond standardized testing" and includes "thorough background testing" (see Engen and Engen, this volume) because, as Marschark (1993) has established, the long-standing "literature on deafness is fairly consistent about the disadvantage at which deaf students find themselves when faced with measures of ability which do not adequately differentiate between language-related difficulties and the actual level of knowledge or skill the students possess."

In sum, Akamatsu and Cole suggest assessing academic achievement and social adjustment of deaf immigrant and refugee children in at least four different contextually based ways in order to attain a complex and meaningful assessment: (1) how the individual student has done academically and socially since arrival; (2) how the student compares to others with similar immigrant or refugee backgrounds; (3) how the student compares to the general deaf population on any academic or social measure; and (4) how the student compares with "normally hearing peers." They also move to more specific strategies and suggestions for supporting the schooling success of these deaf immigrant and refugee children. For example, they suggest the use of cooperative learning and a peer helper "in dealing with both social and academic issues," and they also support encouraging self-initiative and demonstrations of responsibility taken for their own learning among these children.

Lillian Buffalo Tompkins grounds her chapter, "Cultural and Linguistic Voice in the Deaf Bilingual Experience" in a question: "What can we learn from the unique perspectives of deaf adults who recount their life experiences of becoming and being bilingual in American Sign Language and English?" Tompkins first explains that "the overarching theme of finding one's cultural and linguistic 'voice'" kept resurfacing in her research with six individuals who were Gallaudet University students, prelingually deaf with deaf signing parents, ASL users from their first language of memory, and competent users of both ASL and English. She recognizes resonance between this overarching theme and "the need for self-definition" that was "as strong for them as it has been for such minority voices as Frederick Douglass, bell hooks, and Gloria Anzaldúa" who also all shared "the common experience of having to virtually create their being out of nothingness." Like these minority voices, Tompkins argues, the DD (deaf children of deaf parents) participants in her study had to "create for themselves a meaningful definition of deaf bilingualism where none had previously existed."

Tompkins's essay patterns the various features of her six subjects' bilingualism and centers mostly on elements and experiences they largely seemed to have in common. For example, she illuminates how each of her subjects "emphasized their constant—differentiated from simultaneous—use of both ASL and English" and how they varied their language choice and use "according to situational and practical needs." Likewise, she offers, "Each of the six participants reported a strong and sustained inner motivation to learn the nuances of and to creatively use both of their languages."

She also outlines the growing sociolinguistic and cultural "groundswell of ideas" that contributed to the possibilities for her six subjects to even come to an understanding of themselves as "bilingual"—events like the publication of Stokoe, Casterline, and Croneberg's *A Dictionary of American Sign Language on Linguistic Principles* (1965); Johnson, Liddell, and Erting's famous document on *Unlocking the Curriculum: Principles for Achieving Access in Deaf Education* (1989); Padden and Humphries' groundbreaking *Deaf in America: Voices from a Culture* (1988) from the prestigious Harvard University Press; and, of course, the Deaf President Now protest on the campus of Gallaudet University in March 1988, followed by the first DEAF-WAY international conference in 1989. From these events, deaf education moved into "Total Communication" (TC) in the mid-to-late 1970s, which then evolved into simultaneous communication (SimCom) or signing with voice support (SSS, Sign Supported-Speech). And, as Tompkins outlines, each of these communication methods had more than its share of faults and detractors, but each, in its own way, also led to the "experimentation and rhetoric concerning conceptualizations of bilingual deaf education."

While all of this morphing over methods of communication and various forms of contact signing in deaf education (and increasingly in mainstreamed classrooms) was happening, Tompkins reports that for most of their school experiences, her six participants "experienced a virtual nullification of American Sign Language" that was contributed to, in part, by their teachers whose "literacy practices often exhibited degrading beliefs about their students' language(s), backgrounds, and abilities." Again then, context is everything. While great changes were stirring for ASL and the deaf community, it was also a hard time to be a deaf student in school. Although the awareness of ASL and the deaf world was growing in the culture at large, "between the deaf signing homes and deaf classrooms and programs, there was a dissonance of beliefs, conditions, and practices" that essentially led to primarily negative exchanges between hearing teachers and deaf students. For example, teachers began to distance themselves from students who were growing increasingly politically active and socially aware of the deaf community and culture. It is in this charged context—in this language and literacy-learning milieu—that Tompkins' six participants found themselves growing into adults, learning literacy, and becoming intent on finding and using their "voice." At this point in her own essay, Tompkins chooses to let their six voices come forward as she offers case excerpts for each of them (about 1–2 pages in length) in order to understand their own individual experiences with language use, literacy learning, and coming to identity/voice. Yet the voices swell into a chorus again in conclusion as they highlight how "the deaf experience of coming to know and coming to voice remains situated within a complex cultural, linguistic, and educational arena."

Sherman Wilcox's chapter, "Struggling for Voice: An Interactionist View of Language and Literacy in Deaf Education," strikes harmony with Tompkins' chapter in its title and more. Although Wilcox's contribution to this volume is a reprint from a 1994 volume *Sociocultural Approaches to Language and Literacy: An Interactionist Perspective*, a significant "coda"—a meaningful voice—has been added to it for this collection; the primary subject of Wilcox's 1994 version of this essay, BoMee, has now signed on herself to write a postscript. In "Struggling for a Voice," Wilcox effectively blends voices in order to explore the interaction of "the pathological versus the cultural view of deafness, and the conception of knowledge as actively created versus passively received" in order to conduct his "exploration of language and literacy." The voices he calls upon in this chapter include deaf poets, such as Ella Mae Lentz and Lex Lohman, writing on language and literacy experiences; key language and educational theorists such as Paulo Friere, John Dewey, Henry Giroux, Mikhail Bahktin, and Lev Vygotsky; and a young deaf Korean adoptee, BoMee, and her family.

Wilcox begins his analysis and argument of how language and literacy are viewed in the competing pathological and cultural views of deafness by foregrounding an understanding of the deaf experience. Using the "voices" of deaf poets and leaders such as the esteemed National Theatre of the deaf performer Bernard Bragg, to bring his audience to this experience first, Wilcox then moves into a case study with the young deaf girl BoMee as he chronicles some of her key milestones and moments in language acquisition and literacy learning. Raised in a rich multilingual, multicultural environment, BoMee's experience has, Wilcox argues, "provided her with an environment in which clear and easy communication can take place with family, adults, and peers; and, it has provided her with a secure sense of who she is and where she fits into the world." He goes on to offer warrants for these claims as he outlines several key communicative moments in BoMee's young life that might have been difficult, if not impossible, had she not had the bilingual and bicultural flexibility with both English and ASL. He further illustrates how BoMee performed some of the hallmarks of linguistic and literate success—carrying out the private problem-solving kind of "speech" (she would sign to herself to solve problems like finding her shoes) that Vygotsky claimed was the central social-cognitive purpose of language in children and also displaying metalinguistic awareness and knowledge of sociolinguistic variation among those whom she saw signing in her world.

From a pathological view of deafness, however, Wilcox also outlines at length how BoMee transferred her knowledge of the present progressive verb tense (the –ING form) between ASL and English. But her teachers only translated her language behavior in this regard as "lacking" when they concluded "that Deaf children always have difficulty with English present progressive. It is, they declared, a particular characteristic of the abnormal language development of deaf children." In a counter to the damage that teachers of deaf children can do when operating from pathological perspectives like this in their "language-mediated interactions with Deaf students," Wilcox offers at least five general suggestions to address how "teacher training programs [can] turn out Deaf educators who are capable of acting as transformative intellectuals" (in the way that educational theorist Henry Giroux imagines teachers as transformative intellectuals). Three of these suggestions are briefly and generally mentioned (though probably no less important), but the last two receive a little more development.

ASL, Wilcox claims, "must play a much more active role in Deaf education," and further, "students should be receiving formal classroom instruction not only *in* ASL but also *about* ASL." Here again, he relies not only on educational theorists to support his claim (Friere, Shor, Giroux, etc.) but also on deaf scholars and leaders such as Merv Garretson, Barbara Kannapell, and the venerable George Veditz, telling us in his 1913 film *Preservation of the Sign Language*, that "our beautiful sign language [is] the noblest gift God has given Deaf people."

The other weighted suggestion—and the one that Wilcox ends with—is that deaf people should create and learn "writing in our own words." By first outlining six of the major literacy functions that writing affords a culture and its individuals (beyond those provided by spoken or signed languages), Wilcox calls for a written version of signed languages. He argues that "written ASL does hold the potential for empowering Deaf people, and this is precisely what we need. Why should the only avenue to literacy for Deaf people be through English?"

Ten years later, almost in answer to that question, his primary subject in "Struggling for Voice," writes back and offers a postscript to this reprint. Now a student at Gallaudet University, BoMee reports how many people recognize her from the two articles in which she was featured. She guesses they are so interested because "at the time the article was written, it was unusual to talk about or think about raising a child bilingually and biculturally." However, almost on cue with Wilcox's closing claim, she also adds, "The most common question that I have been asked about my bilingual upbringing [is] related to my ability to read and write in English." She confesses that she thinks "this is looking at a very small part of who I am as a whole person" and goes on to assure us that she does "enjoy English" but that despite the "many terrific technological advancements made in the last fifteen to twenty years" that have supposedly made communication and life easier for deaf people, "none of these have come close to or have in anyway replaced the accessibility provided through American Sign Language." As she composes her postscript here—in the clever form of an end-of-film roll of the credits—she wishes "for every child to have as much language as possible" and admits that while she is competent and can indeed do it, "writing in English can still sometimes be a slow process for me."

Almost as if continuing BoMee's postscript, Kathleen M. Wood's chapter provides a sociolinguistic analysis of her own work as an English teacher recording the "literacy narratives" of deaf undergraduates at Gallaudet University who were majoring in English. "English Literacy in the Life Stories of Deaf College Undergraduates" offers a critical look at a subject not much explored in the substantial literature on deaf people's literacy—the literacy learning and strategies of postsecondary or adult deaf people. In this unexplored space, Wood's article aims to explore three connected questions:

> How is the social institution of literacy translated for a deaf individual's use? Or, more specifically, how do (deaf) tellers of life stories narrate their lives in relation to the surrounding social institution of literacy? And what is the relationship of sociocultural contexts (in this case, the Deaf Education English Literacy System, the DEELS) to the discursive production of a literate deaf individual? (193)

Wood first outlines the kind(s) of English literacy(ies) that are promoted in the DEELS, "a subset of the larger deaf education system." She does this by aligning its ideologies—as unearthed in many of its key public documents, such as the curricula it uses and produces, letters to the editor of a major newspaper from members inside the DEELS, official reports, program review summaries, and a student handbook—in relation to the National Council of Teachers of English (NCTE) Position Statement on

Teaching Composition. By coding the key statements made in these DEELS documents into the five areas on the NCTE Position Statement on Teaching Composition, Wood comes up with twenty-six "systems of logic" in the DEELS that carry out how that system views: (1) the acts of reading and writing; (2) the purposes for reading and writing; (3) the scenes for reading and writing and the means for instruction; (4) the teachers of reading and writing, and (5) the students who study reading and writing. Viewing these twenty-six systems of logic together, she then names the DEELS as "an essay-text, hierarchical, aural-oral based, deficit-focused, fatalistic conception."

Working from within and under—and even sometimes, *despite* this literacy system, as Wood illustrates—deaf students who are college English majors tell literacy life stories that access several key narrative frames. The second half of Wood's chapter offers excerpts from and brief analyses of several literacy life stories of these deaf undergraduates majoring in English in order to illustrate three significant and oft-repeated narrative frames these students rely on: (1) hearing people as a resource; (2) struggle-to-success; and (3) literacy as personal discovery. On the basis of her examination of the literacy systems promoted by the DEELS and the ways that deaf students tell their own literacy narratives within and against this system, Wood concludes her chapter with six reasons why deaf students should be encouraged to tell—or write—their literacy life stories.

❖

There are surely more stories to be told and much more work to be done in contextual and cultural approaches to literacy and deaf people. Where Wood's work leaves off suggests to me one important place to pick up, since we know really so little about deaf postsecondary or adult literacy learners. Deaf education, and more specifically, the study of how deaf people become literate, seems stuck in time. Literacy development seems to end before the age of twenty for deaf people although, oddly enough, we know that is not true for literacy learners at large. A good deal of significant and further literacy learning happens in postsecondary education of all kinds, on the job, in acquiring various life skills, raising a family, making a living, paying taxes, buying a house, following a recipe, writing a will, helping your kids with their homework, and so forth. We know almost nothing about the post-adolescent deaf literacy learner in these continued acts of acquiring further literacy; studies of deaf people and literacy all but disappear into adulthood. This disappearance parallels the documented deaf world phenomenon of deaf children often growing up not knowing what will become of them as adults or even, since they rarely see deaf adults, assuming that they will die or be killed before they become adults.

We need many more studies of literacy learning by deaf people in different cultures, communities, and contexts. Almost ten years ago, I had the pleasure of interviewing Yerker Andersson (then the chair of Gallaudet's new Deaf Studies Department), and he claimed too that he believed we needed more ethnographically oriented studies of various sites, scenes, and locations in the overall global deaf world. We need more culturally and contextually based research into questions like these:

- What is it like for a single deaf child coming to literacy in a mainstreamed school on the plains of Nebraska?
- How do literacy-learning practices for deaf people in X country affect deaf people in Y country?
- How do deaf college students learn the kind of "critical literacy" that is so often required in college-level reading and writing classes?
- What literacy learning takes place for a deaf adult who finds him or herself suddenly thrust into an e-mail-rich work environment (having not grown up with e-mail or other computer-based forms of interaction and written communication)?
- How could an effective adult literacy-learning program be built for deaf adults? What are the limitations and advantages for such a program?
- What literacy-learning challenges do children with cochlear implants now face?
- How do senior citizens with serious progressive hearing loss negotiate new or different literacy skills with their changing social interactions?
- How is the thumb-writing of pagers changing the deaf visual field (and thus, changing their own dominant literacies)?
- How do people—deaf, hard of hearing, hearing, young, or old—read and make meaning with captioning?
- How is captioning (closed, open, real-time) changing the profession of interpreting—and vice versa?

- How were the "little papers" and deaf newspapers in America (before television) read and how did they impact the lives of the specific American deaf communities they circulated in?
- How do deaf people "read" the Internet?
- How is the popularity of ASL in high schools and colleges across the United States impacting the study of English and other language learning?

Here, I have only begun to list some of the contextual and cultural questions that interest *me* for further exploring how literacy engages deaf people and how, too, deaf people engage literacy. Perhaps with less focus on what goes wrong between deaf people and literacy, and also with a little less concern over finding just the one right or best way to educate deaf children, we could also then begin to attend more to these less-conventional "alternative perspectives" (as Claire Ramsey has called for in one of the opening epigraphs)—aiming instead for perspectives that explore the endless and exciting potential "happenings" between literacy and deaf people in contextual and cultural frames.

## LITERATURE CITED

Ahlgren, I., and K. Hyltenstam, eds. 1994. *Bilingualism in deaf education*. Hamburg: Signum Verlag.
Batson, L. G. 1989. Language without sound: The orality of literacy of the deaf and ASL. *The Writing Instructor* 8 (2): 68–75.
Bednar, L. 1989. Letter to the readers: Literacy and the deaf. *The Writing Instructor* 8 (2): 53–56.
Belenky, M. F. et al. 1986. *Women's ways of knowing: The development of self, voice, and mind*. New York: Basic Books.
Bolander, A., and A. N. Renning. 2000. *I was number 87: A deaf woman's ordeal of misdiagnosis, institutionalization, and abuse*. Washington, D.C.: Gallaudet University Press.
Brueggemann, B. J. 1999. *Lend me your ear: Rhetorical constructions of deafness*. Washington, D.C.: Gallaudet University Press.
———. 2001. Deafness, literacy, rhetoric: Legacies of language and communication. In *Embodied rhetorics: disability in language and culture*, ed. J. C. Wilson and C. Leweicki-Wilson, 115–35. Carbondale: Southern Illinois University Press.

Bruner, J. 1990. *Acts of meaning*. Cambridge, Mass.: Harvard University Press.

Burke, K. 1966. *Language as symbolic action: Essays on life, literature, and method*. Berkeley: University of California Press.

Cixous, H. 2000. The laugh of the medusa. In *French feminism reader*, ed. K. Oliver, 257–76. Lanham, Md.: Rowman & Littlefield.

De Cartagena, T. 1998. *The writings of Teresa de Cartagena*. Translated by D. Seidenspinner-Núñez. Cambridge: D. S. Brewer.

Derrida, J. 2001. Signature event context. In *The rhetorical tradition: Readings from classical times to the present*, ed. P. Bizzell and B. Herzberg. Boston: Bedford/St. Martin's.

Egan, S. 1999. *Mirror talk: Genres of crisis in contemporary autobiography*. Chapel Hill: University of North Carolina Press.

Fletcher, L. 1987. *Ben's story: A deaf child's right to sign*. Washington, D.C.: Gallaudet University Press.

Gilmore, L. 1994. *Autobiographics: A feminist theory of women's self-representation*. Ithaca, N.Y.: Cornell University Press.

Goody, J., ed. 1968. Introduction to *Literacy in traditional societies*. New York: Cambridge University Press.

———. 1986. *The logic of writing and the organization of society*. New York: Cambridge University Press.

Goody, J., and I. Watt. 1988. The consequences of literacy. In *Perspectives on literacy*, ed. E. R. Kintgen, B. M. Kroll, and M. Rose, 3–27. Carbondale: Southern Illinois University Press.

Gregory, S., and G. M. Hartley, eds. 1991. *Constructing deafness*. London: Open University.

Halliday, M. A. K. 1989. *Spoken and written language*. Oxford University Press.

Higgins, P. C., and J. E. Nash, eds. 1996. *Understanding deafness socially: Continuities in research and theory*. Springfield, Ill.: Charles C. Thomas.

Humphries, T., and F. MacDougall. 2000. "Chaining" and other links: Making connections between American Sign Language and English in two types of school settings. *Visual Anthropology Review* 15 (2): 84–94.

Johnson, R., S. Liddell, and C. Erting. 1989. *Unlocking the curriculum: Principles for achieving access in deaf education*. Gallaudet Research Institute, Working Paper, 89–3. Washington, D.C.: Gallaudet University Press.

John-Steiner, V., C. P. Panofsky, and L. W. Smith, eds.1994. *Sociocultural approaches to language and literacy*. Cambridge: Cambridge University Press.

Kintgen, E. R., B. M. Kroll, and M. Rose, eds. 1988. *Perspectives on literacy.* Carbondale: Southern Illinois University Press.

Laborit, E. 1988. *The cry of the gull.* Trans. C. Mitchell and P. R. Côté. Washington, D.C.: Gallaudet University Press.

Lane, H. 1992. *The mask of benevolence: Disabling the deaf community.* New York: Knopf.

Lou, M. W. P. 1988. The history of language use in the education of the deaf in the United States. In *Language learning and deafness,* ed. M. Strong, 75–98. Cambridge: Cambridge University Press.

Marschark, M. 1993. *Psychological development of deaf children.* New York: Oxford University Press.

Martin, D. S., ed. 1991. *Advances in cognition, education, and deafness.* Washington, D.C.: Gallaudet University Press.

Mayer, C., and C. T. Akamatsu. 1999. Bilingual-bicultural models of literacy education for deaf students: Considering the claims. *Journal of Deaf Studies and Deaf Education* 4:37–49.

Mittelman, L. J., and L. K. Quinsland. 1991. A paradigm for teaching written English to deaf students: A cognitive fluency assessment model. In *Advances in cognition, education, and deafness,* ed. D. S. Martin, 152–61. Washington, D.C.: Gallaudet University Press.

Moores, D. F., and K. P. Meadow-Orlans, eds. 1990. *Educational and developmental aspects of deafness.* Washington, D.C.: Gallaudet University Press.

Ong, W. J. 1982. *Orality and literacy: The technologizing of the word.* New York: Methuen.

Padden, C. A. 1990. *Deaf children and literacy: Literacy lessons.* Geneva: International Bureau of Education.

Padden, C. A., and T. Humphries. 1988. *Deaf in America: Voices from a culture.* Cambridge, Mass.: Harvard University Press.

Paul, P. V. 1988. *Literacy and deafness: The development of reading, writing, and literate thought.* Boston: Allyn & Bacon.

Ramsey, C. L. 1997. *Deaf children in public schools: Placement, context, and consequences.* Washington, D.C.: Gallaudet University Press.

Ramsey, C. L., and C. A. Padden. 1988. Natives and newcomers: Gaining access to literacy in a classroom for deaf children. *Anthropology & Education Quarterly* 29:1–20.

Reagan, T. 1990. Cultural considerations in the education of deaf children. In *Educational and developmental aspects of deafness,* ed. D. F. Moores and K. P. Meadow-Orlans, 73–84. Washington, D.C.: Gallaudet University Press.

Sacks, O. 1988. The revolution of the deaf. *New York Review of Books* 35 (June 2): 23.
Stokoe, W., D. Casterline, and C. Croneberg. 1965. *A dictionary of American Sign Language on linguistic principles*. Washington, D.C.: Gallaudet College Press.
Strong, M., ed. 1988. *Language learning and deafness*. Cambridge: Cambridge University Press.
Webster, A. 1986. *Deafness, development, and literacy*. New York: Methuen.
Winzer, M. 1993. *The history of special education: From isolation to integration*. Washington, D.C.: Gallaudet University Press.

# PART I

## "MODERNIZING" DEAF SELVES AND DEAF EDUCATION: HISTORIES AND HABITS

# The Modern Deaf Self: Indigenous Practices and Educational Imperatives

## Tom Humphries

Traditionally, the cultural practices of Deaf people and their children have had a covert, unappreciated, and unfulfilled impact on methods of educating Deaf children. Whatever influence on education practice Deaf people may have had was from their limited presence as teachers and counselors in schools. In more recent times, as ideas and ideologies have changed about signed languages and the cultural lives of Deaf communities, new ways of thinking have emerged about development and how we educate Deaf children. An intriguing question in modern Deaf life is: What ways of raising Deaf children to become effective learners and schoolgoers do Deaf people hold within their own systems of knowledge and habits of life? How does this knowledge inform the educational practices that Deaf teachers bring to the classroom?

Deaf people have always believed that they knew how to educate Deaf children, but their understanding of how this could be done has been largely unexplored and undocumented. They have accepted a general explanation that sign language has the power to somehow allow Deaf children to learn and other "folk" notions of how to teach Deaf children. In their belief system, sign language made it possible for Deaf children to communicate, and communication itself made it possible for Deaf children to access the world of knowledge. Sign language was necessary in schools, and Deaf adults were necessary as role models in order for Deaf children to achieve. These ideas, as true as they might seem, were unexamined, often dismissed, or considered simplistic and, thus, benignly viewed by hearing educators.

And tragically, Deaf people themselves had little theory how to make their own beliefs about how to teach Deaf children "work" in schooling. Deaf education practices used by Deaf teachers were invariably derived from the set of Deaf education practices developed by hearing professional educators for Deaf children. Little in the way of hard and specific educational practice was derived from Deaf people's intuitive knowledge of what works for Deaf children. But that was to change. During the past forty years, significant calls from within the Deaf community in the United States and abroad have resounded in support of education informed by Deaf people. Specifically, we have seen calls for bilingual education, second language teaching, Deaf identity development among Deaf schoolchildren, and a greater and more controlling presence of Deaf people in schooling decisions and management.

To understand, therefore, how modern ideas of bilingual education and Deaf culture in the classroom have emerged out of this history requires an understanding of what transformations have taken place in *the modern Deaf self*. Collectively and individually, Deaf people have participated in several decades of self-reflection and re-definition. In this process of renegotiating ideas of self, the past has had to be reconciled with emergent theories about their sign language, now called American Sign Language (ASL), and a new discourse of culture about Deaf people. The result has been the demise of Deaf-mutism. As recently as the 1950s, Deaf people used the label *deaf-mute* to refer to themselves, and after the 1960s, hardly at all. The label fell into disfavor and was abandoned as a means of self-representation (Humphries 1996). And why? Because the set of beliefs about themselves that was represented by the label *deaf-mute* (i.e., handicapped, language-less, silent, and dependent) no longer aligned with the set of beliefs that Deaf people wanted to identify with as a group or individually. Instead, they wanted to be thought of as linguistic and cultural beings, normal and whole.

*Deaf-mutism* was a phenomenon of others, a label and mindset from the hearing world that Deaf people internalized and operationalized in their relationships with each other and with people who hear. So powerful were the ideas of others about Deaf people that these ideas, once internalized, competed with and sometimes dominated any other ideas Deaf people might have had about themselves. In a sense, Deaf people prior to the 1950s dealt with two sets of identities, a duality of self, so to speak, and they developed sophisticated ways of reconciling these two identities within themselves. Coexisting within the collective and the individual were two different views of self: on one hand, Deaf people's knowledge that within their own community they were unremarkable, normal, and complete, and, on the other hand, their internalization of hearing people's view of them as imperfect, lacking, and exotic in the sense of having surrogate means of communicating (signing instead of speaking). For hundreds of years, these two views of self were very much a part of Deaf people's self-knowledge.

One possible explanation for the sudden and dramatic distancing of these two views of the self from each other, both within Deaf people and in the public sphere, is that after World War II, the economic prosperity in the United States and the corresponding expansion of the middle class included Deaf people as well as hearing people (Padden 1990). As Deaf people moved from working-class to middle-class sensibilities, they desired to be thought of differently. It was no longer acceptable to be thought of in ways represented by the label *deaf-mute*. The growth of a Deaf middle class coincided and perhaps contributed to a closer and scientific scrutiny of signed languages. Deaf people's consciousness of themselves as a people of language and culture became so attractive to them that they ultimately could no longer accept the coexistence within themselves of older ideas that others had about them. The new discourse of ASL and Deaf culture was so close to Deaf people's idea of themselves that they began to create greater and greater distance between themselves and the ideas of others about them.

Adopting a modern sensibility of self as people of culture was not without consequences. In the new discourse of culture beginning in the late 1960s and continuing into the 1990s, a new set of problems and questions arose. How do we define ourselves now? What words do we use and what do we call ourselves? What do we do with those ideas we used to carry inside ourselves that belong to others? What is our relationship now with hearing people? Even ultimately, who is Deaf now? Who is "in" the Deaf culture and who is not? In this process, new ways of seeing the self and each other had to be worked out. New language and communication protocols emerged that tried to equate ASL among other languages and reposition it in relation to a heretofore dominant English. An entirely new voice had to be found with which Deaf people could identify and in which they could think and communicate. Deaf people's struggle to make sense of a new consciousness of self was internal but also external. What new relationship did they want with hearing people in modern life?

From the 1970s to today, joint activity between Deaf and hearing people is characterized by new themes. Perhaps inevitably, today, interactions with hearing people tend to operationalize the duality of self, which Deaf people have tried to put behind them. To the extent that ideas of who Deaf people believe they are now encounter hearing people's ideas of who Deaf people are, there is always the possibility of relationships between these two peoples becoming problematic. The discourse of hearing people is still filled with representations of a view of Deaf people that Deaf people cannot now see as their own. While the discourse of others sometimes converges with the discourse of Deaf people, it also often diverges.

That these discourses converge and diverge is understandable to some extent. Since both Deaf and hearing people are governed by the social constructions of the other, Deaf people's models of themselves and hearing people's models of Deaf people are different (Basso 1979). While Deaf people have a model of themselves (DEAF in ASL) and a concept of hearing people (HEARING in ASL), hearing people have a model of Deaf people ("deaf" in English) and a model of themselves (no name in English), and none of these four models are the same. It is no wonder that in public discourse between Deaf and hearing people, there is a constant convergence and divergence of these four models of self and other. This results in a complexity that rivals other famous differences of consciousness—men and women, east and west, young and old. As the saying might go, "If hearing people are from Ear-th, Deaf people are from Eye-th."

The modern Deaf self is motivated by dominant themes or imperatives. In other words, central to new ideas of the collective self are certain desires, wants, and needs that are motivated from private life into public discourse and serve to drive people towards fulfillment of these desires, wants, and needs. Deaf people want to project into the public world manifestations of their newfound cultural identity. Prominent among these imperatives are an ideal of completeness and a concept of wellness (Humphries 1996). In short, the concept of a malfunctioning or unwell body that formed the basis for all previous views of Deaf people has to be replaced by a concept of biological intactness and wholeness. This is often a difficult concept for others to grasp. Hearing people often start from a certain view of the body and deduce that Deaf people have different bodies from their own, and so all other ideas about Deaf people are colored by what they see as this physical or biological difference. Somewhat similar to the misogynist notion of a woman's biology being inferior to a man's, this concept of the body as having more value in some biological forms than in others is a difficult one for many hearing people to transcend when considering the state of Deaf people. For Deaf people, it is not difficult; it is self-knowledge, and projecting this concept of wholeness of their bodies into public consciousness is the task of every individual Deaf person in the modern world.

This is why, to a large extent, distance from rather than solidarity with hearing people is another important theme in modern Deaf life. To achieve that distance between their ideas of themselves and others' ideas of them, boundaries have to be defined and moved. And to create space in public consciousness for change to happen, Deaf people have had to establish from their own internality what are the differences and similarities between themselves and others. Sometimes this has resulted in greater distancing from people who hear. We see evidence of this distance in struggles and tension between Deaf and hearing people in the past few decades over issues of control. For example, the "self-determination" movement of the 1970s and 1980s in California at the Greater Los Angeles Council on Deafness and the Deafness Counseling, Advocacy, and Referral Agency saw the rise of new kinds of community service agencies run "of, by, and for the Deaf." The political activism and clout of these agencies was no fluke; they were committed institutions acting out Deaf people's new vision of themselves in ways that often ran counter to what hearing people envisioned for them. They organized, protested, and lobbied for everything from rights legislation to captioning access and demanded Deaf control of services and educational institutions. And then there was the most famous struggle for control of them all in 1988—the public protests, marches, and subsequent installation of a Deaf president at Gallaudet University for the first time in its 125-year history.

Control of their own institutions, destiny, and image, however, were not the only cultural imperatives that Deaf people began to project into public space. Economic imperatives were evident in their push for more participation in the professional world, the push into higher-paying and more white-collar occupations. Law, medicine, academia, finance, and technology became fields that Deaf people aspired to and gradually entered in ever-larger numbers. Issues of access and participation in the economic life of the United States were inherent in well-organized and strongly motivated drives for telephone relay systems in every state of the union, in legal mandates for interpreting services, and in nondiscrimination legislation. All of these advances were ultimately designed to level the playing field for Deaf people to compete in the economic activity of this country. From being able to use a telephone relay service to order a pizza (and Deaf people did this in droves) to establishing their own successful businesses, Deaf people have been fulfilling economic instincts that they once could hardly have envisioned.

Another cultural imperative of the past forty years, and the one that is the subject of this paper, is to reorganize and operationalize the education of Deaf children in ways that fit the new Deaf consciousness. The intuition that Deaf children learn best in signing environments and among Deaf adults had to be re-thought in the context of social change. To think of signing as language (ASL, as it came to be known) and to think of themselves as a linguistic community of people having culture and history required that models of educational practice be examined. Calls for bilingual education, or as it became popularly known, "bi-bi" education, became the focus of school reform among Deaf people. Pressure points all over the country led to the adoption of the bi-bi philosophy in many schools and offered an alternative to "total communication," which was viewed as inadequate because of its association with older traditions of education in which Deaf people felt that both their language and their Deaf teachers were excluded.

"Talking up" ASL and Deaf culture not only was a process of self-transformation but also was a discourse of destiny. This public discourse moved from intuitive talk to rational talk. What were once largely private and instinctive arguments within groups of Deaf people became rational (and scientific) arguments in public space where both Deaf and hearing people were involved in the shaping of new ideas about socialization, development, learning, and teaching. Thus, Deaf people's desire to design educational environments for Deaf children according to their own instinctive notions of what works became rational arguments for bilingual education for Deaf children.

As the private expression of self becomes public, as a new kind of voice emerges and mediates language and discourse in public space, new initiatives and new practices are proposed and politicized as worth fighting for and winning. In education, this is particularly visible to us. For example, it is possible to trace direct lines from initial discourses of Deaf people about ASL and "my language is me" to discourses on an educational philosophy such as the bi-bi approach. Much happened in public discourse along that path, and much continues to happen.

How did what began as an overt expression of ethnic identity among Deaf individuals in the 1970s become a powerful influence on practice in the classroom? At times, this reorganization of educational practice has been in direct contradiction of prevailing "science" and beliefs about schooling for Deaf children. The discourse of others has historically put forward a certain subset of ideas about the development stages, paths, and trajectories (i.e., "abnormal," delayed, differentiated according to hearing loss, English and speech focused, etc.) that, in turn, has led to certain designs for educational intervention. In other words, the universals of hearing child development that were so well documented have been applied in the construction of a science of development for Deaf children. With this subset of ideas about Deaf children in hand, educators historically designed learning environments for Deaf children that were teacher centered, highly structured, and made heavy use of hearing technology, and they stressed monolinguistic language strategies and monocultural life as well.

A different subset of ideas about a Deaf child's development put forward in a new discourse of culture and the continued projection of the private world of Deaf people into public space have resulted in significant changes in local practice in many places. This subset of ideas about development of Deaf children (strongly influenced by studies of Deaf children of Deaf parents in ASL homes) paints a different picture of the Deaf child. This subset of ideas suggests that in ASL environments, Deaf children acquire language and achieve cultural and cognitive development in the same patterns and stages as hearing children and that this should be the basis for the assumptions and designs of learning environments for Deaf children. The types of practices that result from this subset of ideas are increasingly student centered, promote rich social environments in the classroom, and focus on multilinguistic strategies and multicultural life. These kinds of practices are the basis for transformation in many schools.

Historically, we can trace specific ways that Deaf people began to talk in public to ideas that shape current practice. Analysis of interviews and dialogue among teachers, parents, and others, as well as direct observation, reveal how once closely held perceptions in the Deaf community, increasingly made public, have reorganized views of Deaf children's development, teacher training practice, and classroom practice. In my view, there have been several stages in this process of private to public expression: maintenance, telling the story (and having it told back), emergence of a self-conscious discourse of culture, and projection into public policy.

## MAINTENANCE

Into the 1960s, Deaf people maintained a contradictory type of discourse that accommodated others' beliefs but asserted the normalcy of being Deaf.

> We note, too, that there is frequent reference in the press, over the radio, and on TV about "normalizing the Deaf" by restoring them to society. All of this is well-meaning, of course, but it is getting rather monotonous, to say the least.
>
> In the first place, the Deaf are about as normal as the fellow next door. True, he may be able to enjoy life a bit more due to his hearing and his fluent speech, but we think the Deaf individual can give him a close race for all-around happiness in the enjoyment of life. (*Silent Worker* 1954, 11)

In the same breath, Deaf people often asserted their "normalcy" while accepting the notion that they might enjoy life less than hearing people. This type of talk sought to reconcile both Deaf people's knowledge of themselves as normal and others' view of them as less than normal. This discourse was especially strong in regard to sign language:

> . . . the sign language is in danger of becoming a lost art unless something is done by the Deaf to keep it at a standard where it can be considered the medium of conversation of a *cultured* people (emphasis added). . . . The tendency today is away from standard usage, in favor of improvised signs and "slang" signs. If the tendency continues, the time will come when the sign language will no longer be universal, and the Deaf in one state will be unable to converse freely with those of another state.
>
> There exists today a notable carelessness in the use of the sign language. The old-time masters of the sign language used a clear-cut, carefully chosen style of delivery, which was easy to understand and pleasing to see. Today too many Deaf are inclined to slur over their spelling and crowd their signs, and in order to understand them, one must strain both one's eyesight and one's mentality. (Burnes 1950)

And in this:

> There seems to be a feeling among many of our sign slingers that it makes little difference what sign one uses as long as it is understood. People are losing sight of the fact that there are correct

signs, and a correct form of delivery, just as there is a correct form of English grammar. (Romero 1950)

In both of these texts, we can sense the effort to maintain the integrity of sign language and the Deaf culture (as the Burnes text does not quite but comes close to saying). While not going so far as to pronounce ASL a language, these texts do make it clear Deaf people consider sign language to have a "standard usage" and "a correct form of delivery," which was as close as they could get to protecting its status at a time when science had rejected its worthiness.

## TELLING THE STORY (AND HAVING IT TOLD BACK)

In the 1960s and early 1970s, a convergence of the discourse of maintenance and the science of others resulted in a public re-construction (discovery?) of signed languages and the social worlds of Deaf people. In other words, hearing people began to tell back Deaf people's story to them.

> By 1900, forty one of the states had at least one state-supported school for the Deaf. . . . The sign language of these schools was by no means only a code used for instructional purposes. It possessed the tenacity, flexibility, and the expressiveness characteristic of any language that is used for the natural communication of the daily thoughts, feelings, and needs of a close-knit group of people. The Deaf students leaving a school for the Deaf continued their association with each other and with students who had graduated from schools for the Deaf in other states. And the means by which they carried on that easy interchange of thoughts that is necessary for full social interaction was and still is the language of signs. Thus, sign language, while undergoing growth and evolution, has become a socially vital part of the *culture* [emphasis added] of approximately one hundred thousand American and Canadian Deaf who are members of both local and regional communities of Deaf persons and larger, more formal, national groups. (Stokoe, Croneberg, and Casterline 1965)

As can be seen in this example, hearing people began to probe the lives of Deaf people and translate what they learned from Deaf people into scientific texts. By the mid-1970s, after this had become a widespread practice, there was quite a bit of conflict over who was and should be telling the story of ASL and Deaf culture. For example, early linguistic studies of ASL structure were marked by some bitterness over authorship, with Deaf people often questioning whether their role of "language informant" should be acknowledged alongside the hearing linguists who wrote these studies. It would be another decade before Deaf people began to tell their own story in scientific texts in larger numbers.

## EMERGENCE OF A SELF-CONSCIOUS DISCOURSE OF CULTURE

By the mid-1970s, a new kind of consciousness was coupled with a self-conscious discourse of culture. This discourse was often marked by a questioning of the new Deaf self. For example, questions like "Who are Deaf people?" and "What is Deaf culture?" were frequently debated. The question of who "belonged" to the "Deaf culture" raised issues of authenticity for individuals. A discourse of boundaries and margins was prevalent. "Hard of hearing" people became potentially problematic in the struggle to re-define the category of "Deaf" as did people who became deaf later in life. Were the "true" or authentic Deaf people only those who had Deaf parents or spent twelve years in a residential school for the Deaf? How fluent did a Deaf person have to be in ASL to be considered "Deaf"? And culture became an object in public discourse. Deaf people themselves now engaged in this discussion, as illustrated in the following three excerpts:

> Ethnocentric attitudes and behavior often present serious conflicts when an unaware individual seeks to interact with members of the Deaf community, as evidenced by the conflicts our subjects are experiencing. . . . More acceptable behavior must be understood as a reaction toward conflicts arising from two cultures in contact. (Padden and Markowicz 1975)
>
> Often linguistic scientists seem to study language from very specialized points of view, as if people did not exist. For me, the study of language must be understood in the context of the whole person, and of the person's relation to the group. This means language and culture are interrelated. (Kannapell 1977)
>
> The Deaf community comprises those Deaf and hard of hearing individuals who share a common language, common experience and values, and a common way of interacting with each other and

with hearing people. The most basic factor determining who is a member of the Deaf community seems to be what is called "attitudinal Deafness". This occurs when a person identifies him/herself as a member of the Deaf community and other members accept that person as part of the community. Contrary to some beliefs, a person's actual degree of hearing loss . . . does not seem to be important in determining that person's identification with and acceptance by the Deaf community. . . . Deaf people who do not know ASL are not part of the Deaf community. (Baker and Padden 1978)

## PROJECTION INTO PUBLIC POLICY

By the 1980s, a discourse of language and culture of Deaf people insisted on changes in social institutions and undermined the traditional values of these institutions. Discourses around education, in particular, took on a different character. Deaf people began to insist that education address newly imaged development patterns for Deaf children with increased emphasis on bilingualism and first and second language development. From a panel discussion of Deaf professionals:

**Marlon:** I now teach in the California School for the Deaf at Fremont, where I experiment with innovative approaches in my English classroom. I have come to the conclusion that efforts within the classroom, by themselves, are not enough. We need to look at the larger picture and change the system so that Deaf children can become successful learners of English. My personal belief is that ASL is the means of achieving that end.

**David:** It is true that many programs in Deaf education history have been unsuccessful because of mistaken ideas. For example, the total communication philosophy spawned a whole variety of invented sign systems. . . . The systems were based on misconceptions regarding how effective language learning for Deaf children takes place. . . . We've arrived at a point where we know the Deaf view will work in the educational system. We need to begin now. . . . And it will work, because we've never before had Deaf people actively involved in the Deaf education system.

**Marlon:** A person's first language must be a human language, a language that is already in use, already in circulation. . . . That is ASL. ASL is the match for the child's visually based world.

**Minnie:** One thing I have learned about language acquisition for anyone, hearing or Deaf, is that the first language is normally learned in a natural language situation. . . . I am very interested in the idea of parallel languages: children who are bilingual learning ASL and English at the same time in a natural approach.

**Marlon:** How can we measure "bicultural success" for a Deaf person? It does not mean being able to use speech. It does mean being able to manipulate English through reading and writing. It also means being able to deal successfully with the hearing world, both personally and professionally. That would be successful biculturalism. (From TED 1981)

This pattern of change over the last half of the twentieth century is also evident in how teachers talk about their students and their practice. The following were culled from interviews with classroom teachers:

**Connie:** I think Danny has internalized language (you know he's hard of hearing). He can always unscramble the sentences correctly, so I think he has a natural internal sense of language. He's always listening and talks well. But his mother speaks Spanish and doesn't know ASL, but I noticed that since he's been here, he's been picking up ASL. His expressive signing is beautiful and is correct ASL structure. Ruth, and even Stephanie, at the beginning of the year, had no ASL structure—her signing was way off. . . .

Well, I guess Bi-Bi means using purely ASL in the classroom, not using anything else. . . . Well, we write a lot, and reading is taught through print, not through the use of speech at all. So that's reading and writing. . . . Also Deaf awareness, being conscious of the fact that we are Deaf and that we sign—that the only way we communicate is through signing. Don't think like hearing people do (as many people still do), but be aware that we are Deaf.

Before, they would read a sentence and spit it out in English; but by the end of the year, they were relating the story in ASL. Once we finished reading a story, we'd close our books, and I'd have them tell the entire story in ASL and they could do it—all in ASL. That was my goal.

That's one *big* difference between us. Barbara (her hearing co-teacher) likes to sit at a table with the kids in a circle around her. I can *not* do that. I have to have a lot of room to move around in.

I don't focus much at all on reading from the textbook; I never make them read the science or social studies textbooks. I teach all the

material in ASL. One girl I have has absolutely no language at all, no way to communicate her ideas. . . . She needs to develop a language base first, then she'll be able to pick up the rest quickly later on.
**Lewis:** [Making a connection between his experience and how he teaches.] This happened to me when I was a child. First I'd be exposed to information, then read, and later, I'd be able to access the information I'd been given and incorporate it into my writing in a rudimentary way. When asked by the teacher what my writing meant, I could say simply the words that were there (*sheep, cloud*), not making much of a connection. Then the teacher would expand on it, drawing greater connections for me (*the clouds look like sheep*), laying a foundation on which I could build.

First, I ask them if they know the signs. Some will know, but I ask them not to blurt it out. Then I tell the class that they already have a sign for each of the words on the list. A Deaf child in fifth grade has an extensive sign vocabulary, but their written vocabulary is much smaller. My job is to tie ASL vocabulary to each of the written English vocabulary words.

This is the idea behind the bilingual approach. You've got ASL and you've got English, a bilingual situation in which the two languages are constantly encountering one another.
**Tammy:** I need more, well, I have some ASL aides now, but that really needs to be all the time. . . . I need more Deaf ones, too, to help bring in that ASL component of sign language. . . . Hannah needs it. She's a very expressive person in ASL. . . . She tends to want a Deaf person. We really need more ASL. It really helps to boost their confidence.

Embedded in this discourse is the impetus for the creation of a new set of educational practices that are commonly referred to as "bilingual" in nature and in which American Sign Language and "Deaf-ness" are valuable commodities. It was the force of discussions like these, amplified and widespread, that served to influence the resultant emergence of bilingual education for Deaf children.

But still the question remains: What indigenous practices find their way into schooling informed by Deaf people? Aside from the pedagogy of bilingual education (mostly English-Spanish in this country), which is well established and adaptable for application with Deaf children, what habits of mind and behavior actually appear in the classroom when Deaf teachers and ASL are there? Or to put it another way, what does it mean to find specific cultural practices where there is a Deaf presence in the school?

A study done at the Research Program in Language and Literacy at the University of California, San Diego, looked at language use in Deaf and hearing teachers during "teacher talk" in real instruction time (Humphries and MacDougall 2000). This study also looked at language use across two types of school settings, a residential school with a bi-bi philosophy and a public school day program with a total communication philosophy. It attempted to understand how teachers make connections between English and ASL in natural ways during instruction.

Seven ASL-fluent elementary and middle school teachers were videotaped during instruction. Samples from the many hours of taping were analyzed focusing on teacher talk. Among other things, this study looked at the frequency of possible connectors between English and ASL: fingerspelling use, initialized sign use, and use of a technique or language feature we called "chaining." The study found that Deaf and hearing teachers use initialized signs with roughly the same frequency. However, we observed that the type of initialized signs used were different for Deaf and hearing teachers. We observed a greater use among hearing teachers of "new" initialized signs similar to those found in signed English systems. But we were unable to pursue this to a conclusion because of the difficulty in determining what is distinguishable and countable as a lexicalized sign that has a handshape that looks like a fingerspelled letter and those derived from signed English systems. (Native signers agree that FAMILY in ASL is an ASL sign but could not agree that CURRICULUM is an ASL sign. Some suggested it was; others suggested it was a SEE sign.)

But this study found that Deaf teachers fingerspelled twice as often as hearing teachers. In the sample segments (six fifteen-minute segments per teacher), Deaf teachers fingerspelled an average of 176 times, hearing teachers an average of 75 times. When analyzed according to school setting, residential school bi-bi teachers fingerspelled an average of 152 times and public school Total Communication teachers an average of 74 times. It is clear in our samples that Deaf teachers make frequent use of fingerspelling in making connections between ASL and English. It is also evident that school setting (and presumably, program philosophy) had an effect on the frequency of fingerspelling by teachers since native signers and Deaf teachers where distributed across both types of settings.

An examination of teachers' use of a process that we had noted in an earlier study and called "chaining" yielded differences as well. Chaining is a procedure for connecting texts such as signed, printed, written, or fingerspelled words. In this procedure, a teacher might, for example, fingerspell a word, immediately point to the word printed on the blackboard next to her, and fingerspell the word again. Or, the teacher may sign a word and immediately fingerspell it as well. Often the chains have two or three parts, and sometimes, four or more parts. This procedure seems to be a process for emphasizing, highlighting, objectifying, and generally calling attention to equivalencies between languages. There are several possible combinations of links in chains of this type. The following are some examples of chaining:

(THEORY) (T-H-E-O-R-Y) (THEORY)
initialized sign + fingerspelling + initialized sign

(H-O-N-O-R) (HONOR) (H-O-N-O-R)
fingerspelling + initialized sign + fingerspelling

(duty) (point) (DUTY) (D-U-T-Y) (DUTY)
printed word + pointing to word + initialized sign + fingerspelling
 + initialized sign

(grubs) (G-R-U-B-S) (point)
printed word + fingerspelling + pointing to word

(poem) (P-O-E-M) (point) (P-O-E-M)
printed word + fingerspelling + pointing to word + fingerspelling

In our samples, Deaf teachers used chaining with great frequency, hearing teachers much less. Deaf teachers used chaining an average of 30 times, hearing teachers an average of 5.5 times. There was a noticeable difference across school setting as well, with those teachers in the bi-bi program using chaining an average of 21.5 times and Total Communication teachers using chaining an average of 8.7 times.

What does all this mean? Why does language use in instruction appear different for Deaf and hearing teachers? What is the relationship between language use and ideology of the school? How can we account for the differences in Deaf and hearing teachers' use of fingerspelling and chaining according to the school setting in which they teach?

The greater use of fingerspelling by Deaf teachers in this study suggests that these teachers are engaged in a practice that provides access to English that is indigenous to Deaf communities. Anecdotal evidence of conversational practices among Deaf people and of home practices between Deaf people and their Deaf children seem to mirror this finding. The use of fingerspelling, signs, print, pointing, and facial markings during chaining strongly suggests that Deaf teachers achieve juxtaposition of ASL and English in both daily life and in classrooms in natural ways. Artificial modifications of ASL are not needed to achieve this linkage.

The difference between Deaf and hearing teachers found in our analysis suggests that their life experiences shape their talk, help them determine what the children they teach know and do not know, and lead them to provide a rich and recursive corpus of language use in their classrooms. The *cultural* in a bilingual, bicultural approach to educating Deaf children rests in the details of the language interaction of teacher and student, not just in the enrichment of curriculum with Deaf history, Deaf literature, and ASL storytelling.

As for the effect of school setting, the differences may be that teachers who possess certain repertoires of signing behavior or beliefs about the relationship of signing and English select the type of school setting where they are encouraged to make use of them. Since this study did find that hearing teachers in the residential school setting had higher frequency of both fingerspelling and chaining use compared to hearing teachers in the public school setting, it may also be that when hearing teachers teach in school settings that have large numbers of Deaf teachers, such as the residential bi-bi school, there is an effect of increasing hearing teachers' awareness of the use of fingerspelling and chaining through daily interaction both in class and socially with Deaf students and Deaf teachers. This effect is likely a product of the kinds of language and cultural knowledge that hearing people gain by association with large numbers of Deaf people in the residential school environment.

And finally, the differences between teacher signing behavior in a residential school where ASL and English are used alongside each other but each remain intact and a public school district where signing is strongly influenced by English in various ways remind us how much schools are the product of ideologies about teaching, about how Deaf children learn, and about the relationship between ASL and English. In a setting where ideologies of Deaf people are more dominant or at least influential, certain sets of language, communicative, and instructional practices that reflect Deaf community knowledge and practices are more prevalent. There may be other indigenous practices that can be identified that will inform the way we teach and how we train new teachers. It falls to educators, therefore, to see the potential of this and other indigenous practices to provide access to English for Deaf students.

I have attempted here to put into context and explain changes in Deaf people's ideas of themselves and what that has meant in terms of their wishes and desires and their relationship with hearing people. I have also focused on the institution of the school and what it means to have a Deaf cultural presence in the school, ideologically and in practice. The lesson I have learned from all this is that schools are cultural places—constructed from what we believe, whether we are Deaf or hearing—that reflect our own images of development, learning, and teaching. For Deaf people, the need to be present, to have voice, and to affect classroom practice and the education of Deaf children is a stronger instinct than ever before in history.

## LITERATURE CITED

Baker, C., and C. Padden. 1978. *American Sign Language: A look at its history, structure, and community*. Silver Spring, Md.: TJ Publishers, Inc.

Basso, K. H. 1979. *Portraits of "The Whiteman": Linguistic play and cultural symbols among the western Apache*. Cambridge: Cambridge University Press.

Burnes, B. 1950. The editor's page. *Silent Worker* 2.

Humphries, T. 1996. Of deaf-mutes, the strange, and the modern deaf self. In *Culturally affirmative psychotherapy with deaf persons*, ed. N. S. Glickman and M. A. Harvey, 99–114. Mahwah, N.J.: Erlbaum.

Humphries, T., and F. MacDougall. 2000. "Chaining" and other links: Making connections between American Sign Language and English in two types of school settings. *Visual Anthropology Review*, 15(2): 84–94.

Kannapell, B. 1977. The Deaf person as a teacher of American Sign Language. In *Proceedings of the National Symposium on Sign Language Research and Teaching*. Silver Spring, Md.: National Association of the Deaf.

Padden, C. 1990. Folk explanation in language survival. In *Collective Remembering*, ed. D. Middleton, 190–202. Los Angeles: Sage.

Padden, C., and H. Markowicz. 1975. Learning to be Deaf: Conflicts between Hearing and Deaf cultures. In *Mind, culture and activity*, ed. M. Cole, Y. Engeström, and O. Vasquez, 418–431. New York: Cambridge University Press.

Romero, E. 1950. The open forum. *Silent Worker* 2: 31.

Stokoe, W., C. Croneberg, and D. Casterline. 1965. *A dictionary of American Sign Language on linguistic principles.* Washington, D.C.: Gallaudet College Press.

Walworth, M., ed. 1991. *Teaching English to Deaf and second-language students.* Silver Spring, Md.: TJ Publishers.

# What Does Culture Have to Do with the Education of Students Who Are Deaf or Hard of Hearing?

## Claire Ramsey

In everyday discourse, we expect *culture* to point to a particular group and its features (e.g., Mexican culture, Russian culture, clothing, cuisine, and kinship patterns). However, the narrowness of everyday definitions of culture has become especially apparent in education (Sleeter 2001; Kalyanpur and Harry 1999) since some children's "cultural" backgrounds are associated with their schooling outcomes, positive or negative. Ogbu's (1987) treatment of this topic, while almost two decades old, is not out of date. Yet learning about national holidays, special foods, manners of dress, and folklore does not provide a helpful account of culture as it might interact with schooling. Indeed, such well-intentioned approaches frequently trivialize culture.

Although definitions of culture are problematic, the potential impact of culture on general education is a well-grounded topic, bolstered by a body of strategic and practical knowledge (e.g., Banks 1996). Special education as a broad field has also received attention from scholars of culture (e.g., Harry 1992; Kalyanpur and Harry 1999). In the United States, deaf education presents a more elaborate set of cultural problems, in part, because at least two sources of culture exist for deaf children—the culture of their families and the culture of American Deaf people. Cultural transmission is unusual in the case of deaf children. In fact, although some would argue that I am misinformed, the cultural status of most deaf infants is unclear because most are raised in families with no access to Deaf people or their culture. Additionally, impaired hearing, even mild cases, can lead to early development that unfolds without adequate language exposure. As a result, transmission of the family's culture to a deaf child may be incomplete. Many deaf children become expert border dwellers as they grow up, with knowledge of their family's cultural ways, as well as those of Deaf people. Many will, at some moment in the future, find that they are comfortably and culturally Deaf and align themselves with the adult Deaf ASL-signing community as their primary cultural identity. Still, the facts about interactions of culture with deaf education do not help us understand exactly why culture should be of concern in deaf education. As a colleague once said to me, "It's a disability. There's nothing cultural about it. We just try to fix it." Educational questions about culture are unresolved, even though it is becoming apparent that Deaf cultural ways, especially ways of using language, contribute to learning, (e.g., Ramsey and Padden 1998; Humphries and MacDougall 2000). Claims about the role of Deaf culture in the education of deaf children have rarely been elaborate enough to move us away from trait-based visions of culture. My argument here is that seriously thinking about culture in deaf education requires starting at the beginning, with a generic understanding of ways that this impressive human achievement provides a context for learning.

I know from my life experience that developing and holding a rich definition of culture, one that might help me see culture in schooling, does not come easily. Indeed, my persistence on this topic is driven by my personal history and curiosity as well as the many views of culture I have examined and rejected. I am a baby boomer child of the 1960s. In my first year of college, I enrolled in a Chicano studies course, which had a powerful impact on me, in part, because I was a very romantic, idealistic girl. But in the course, people with lives strikingly different from my own told their stories. I learned about genuine injustices that I had not understood before from those who had first-hand knowledge. I met people who could lay claim to a cultural heritage, many with active links to an exotic "foreign" homeland. I tried to examine my own heritage within the framework of 1960s radicalism. Like many Anglo people, I did not think I had any culture. What I could fashion from sets of family facts was very unsatisfactory. I learned that I could look backwards to slave owners, scoundrels who claimed Cherokee blood in order to get land in Indian Country, and a diluted gene pool. (My isolated, rural Norwegian ancestors intermarried and regularly produced severely developmentally disabled people.) None of the above, including a living *mormor*, my

Norwegian grandmother, added up to anything that I would call culture. None of it was romantic enough to satisfy my need for an authentic culture. I concluded that I was just a slice of Wonder Bread with no culture. I did not belong to any group.

## LEAVING THE CHIMPANZEES AND BONOBOS: CULTURAL TRANSMISSION

Why would I claim that something like culture is an impressive achievement? How has culture made a difference for human beings? Simply, the evolution and transmission of culture is the reason for our cognitive and linguistic successes. The ability to create and transmit culture allows individuals in each generation to save time, energy, and risk by making use of the already existing knowledge and skills of the human beings who went before us (Tomasello 1999).

On the African continent, between six million and 250,000 years ago, our primate ancestors split off from the ancestors of chimpanzees and bonobos. All primates had the capacity for cultural transmission, but our forebears apparently developed the ability to take advantage of it in a new and specific way. The fact that even six million years did not provide sufficient time for the genetic changes that would have been necessary for us to become so symbolically and materially capable indicates that we created something to speed up our development as thinking, symbol-manipulating creatures who passed our innovations to subsequent generations. The simple passage of time, even millions of years, could not have created among human beings the adaptations that have made us so skilled at recognizing and solving the problems that come with living in the world. The only way to explain how we managed the needed changes is through the development of a special capacity. Tomasello (1999) argues that the key development was the rapid evolution of the ability to accumulate culture, to participate in its ongoing invention and then transmit it to others. No material object, social practice, or symbol system was invented once and for all by an individual or group of individuals at a single moment in time. Rather, over time, between generations, creations arose, were modified, and passed on.

Tomasello posits three critical features in the evolution of culture. First, cognitive resources were pooled. A primitive invention was learned and used by others. Then it was improved upon, adopted by others, and passed on to another generation, who improved upon it, used it, and passed it on.

Many heads were better than one. (There is no doubt that other primates are creative in the wild. Their creations do not get modified, however, and to our knowledge, they do not accumulate or get passed on to new generations.) Second, the accumulation of new resources was faithfully transmitted to others, who adopted it. This created a stabilizing or "ratchet" effect (Tomasello 1999, 5), which prevented innovations from getting lost due to "slippage," or through forgetting. (Some cultural innovations are lost or rejected because they are not useful or because a better innovation replaces them.)

Cultural transmission is possible because we have an advantage. Early in life (at about age of nine months), infants begin to see that other people are like themselves, that they are like other people, that all of us have intentions and mental lives, and that all of us are members of social networks of others like us. Babies demonstrate this when they begin trying to get other people to share attention. (Current theory of mind research examines this phenomenon. Indeed, the fluent conventional use of language depends on the knowledge that people share intentions and mental lives [Moeller 2002; De Villiers 2000]). Tomasello's (1999) hypothesis is that the ability to see the world through the perspective of others is what bolsters and makes possible the pooling of resources and the transmission of innovations.

In order to delineate the time course of cultural evolution and its transmission, three kinds of time come into play. First, during the long evolutionary time span of humans (6 million to 250,000 years ago), we developed the ability to exploit cultural transmission. During the historical time spans of social groups, we rapidly accumulated symbolic and material cultural artifacts (250,000 years ago to present time, into the future). Developmental time in individual children (or ontogenesis) allows for the development of agency and knowledge of others in a cultural world and is an ongoing achievement in each new generation. Tomasello summarizes the three kinds of time by noting, "Human beings have the cognitive skills that result from biological inheritance working in phylogenetic time; they use these skills to exploit cultural resources that have evolved over historic time; and they do this during ontogenetic time" (1999, 48).

## "FISH IN THE WATER OF CULTURE"

These are the simple evolutionary, historical, and developmental processes that have contributed to and continue to contribute to our special ability to think and learn as human beings. This is the way educators must view culture in order to avoid resorting to stereotypes and trait lists. In all cultures, adults actively and regularly instruct the young. To participate in learning, all human children learn to detect the adult's goal, the strategies being used to approach the goal, and how to make these goals and strategies their own. All of us depend on our "dual inheritance" (Boyd and Richerson 1985; Durham 1991) that makes us both biological and cultural creatures. Biologically, we are not that different from our primate relatives. Our big advantage is that during development, we notice and exploit the reality that others are intentional beings, just like we are. This realization allows for continuing processes of collaboration among people to create culture in the form of material objects, ideas, and practices with accumulated histories (Tomasello 1999). Additionally, because learning is embedded in culture (in both historical and ontogenetic time), developing children learn how to use the artifacts that forebears, past and present, have created. In individual developing children, cultural resources—our historical accumulation—engage with developing intellects to create a unique human being with a miraculous set of linguistic and cognitive abilities. If we are looking for a definition of culture in this foundational sense, we cannot do much better than Tomasello's metaphor—we are "fish in the water of culture."

## HOW DID DEAF PEOPLE GET TO BE CULTURAL?

In the early 1980s, I was a graduate student at Gallaudet University. By that time, I had grown out of my 60s cultural romanticism; but like a lot of people, I had only gotten as far as "exotic traits." I remember with great affection a group of classmates, Deaf and hearing, who stuck around after anthropology class because we had discussed ourselves into a corner. We were very confused about the troublesome idea of Deaf culture and kept talking in circles. We knew enough to acknowledge that ASL offered a helpful hint that there was culture in there somewhere; but beyond that, we made little progress. Not completely frivolously, one of the Deaf students said, "OK, if it's a culture, then where are the Deaf ethnic restaurants? What do Deaf native costumes look like? Is Gallaudet like the Deaf homeland?" My Deaf classmates were all from hearing families, and all learned ASL well beyond infancy. They felt Deaf but, like I did in my Chicano studies class, longed for a list of traits that would document their authentic cultural connection to other Deaf people. Like me, they needed a richer way of thinking about culture, especially how groups of Deaf people might have become cultural.

Here the three kinds of time are illuminating. Like all of us who have received the benefits of a long span of evolutionary time, Deaf people have the full human linguistic and cognitive inheritance that comes with our biology. Additionally, culture comes into being "wherever people engage in joint activity over time" (Cole 1996, 301). Like all groups, Deaf people have a social history during which they created and improved upon innovations that took account of their lack of hearing and pooled their cognitive resources. Passing these innovations on ensured that individuals in following generations would not have to individually figure out the world into which they were born. No individual deaf infant has to invent a language that does not depend on hearing. No modern deaf infant has to devise technology to use the telecommunications system. Rather, each generation can use the cultural artifacts of the group; understand that others are intentional agents; and share a world full of objects, symbols, and social practices that previous members created for their use. Last, like all of us during our developmental time, deaf babies have the capacity to recognize the agency and mental lives of others and to acquire the symbol systems developed by their ancestors.

## DEAF CHILDREN IN THE CULTURAL WORLD

Typically, children grow up "in the midst of the very best tools and symbols their forebears have invented for negotiating the rigors of their physical and social worlds" (Tomasello 1999, 199). To use the artifacts as they were meant to be used and to participate in the social practices in the ways they were meant to be participated in, the child needs to place herself in the position of adults who use those artifacts and participate in social practices. She needs to comprehend how "we" (that is, the people like her) use those artifacts and practices. The gift of cultural inheritance prepares us to engage in certain types of social interactions, but it is participating in the interactions themselves that does the work. Just being prepared to interact is not enough. Participation is often, although not always, mediated through language. So, our biological and cultural histories ensure that children acquire and master most of their native human language early and quickly, within five or six years. But the circumstances of deaf children's development (with some exceptions) do not match the broader biological and cultural design. It is an unavoidable fact that, through no fault of their own, most deaf children have a late start at language acquisition. Acquisition of language is designed to begin at birth; indeed, late first-language acquisition is so atypical that is it virtually impossible to find (Mayberry 1993). This has consequences for all areas of deaf children's lives, but especially threatens their schooling. In our industrialized, information-steeped society, schooling is organized on the assumption that children enter their years of formal education with native command of their first language (i.e., "ready to learn").

It is unfortunate that the notion of culture has become clouded in deaf education. Discussions of culture sometimes disintegrate into pointless arguments about whether or not there IS a Deaf culture, whether ASL is a real language or not, who owns deaf children, what is the relative value of residential schools, and what is the "best" medium of instruction. This is not the way to think about either culture or Deaf culture if the goal is to determine how culture can be helpful to deaf children. Cole's garden metaphor offers a concrete way to think about culture and its role in human development generally as well as an objective way to consider the culturally rooted developmental difficulties that underscore deaf children's struggles in school. Cole describes a familiar kindergarten project, planting a seed in damp soil, keeping it in the dark until it sprouts, then placing it in the light to grow. If you leave the sprouting seed in the dark, the seed will stop developing and die; it cannot grow without sunlight. "Like a seed in soil, the human child must be provided with sufficient support to maintain life; it must be kept warm enough and fed, or it will die" (1996, 200).

While nasturtiums come prespecified to sprout leaves, human babies come with the need to live in a cultural world and the ability to acquire language. Babies born deaf also have this inborn capacity, but in most deaf babies, language does not take root. Because they cannot hear spoken language, the cultural medium that nourishes spoken language, which works perfectly for hearing babies, is not completely helpful for deaf babies. Babies who cannot hear spoken language require a somewhat different growing medium to acquire human language. (We also know that babies who have their sense of hearing boosted with technological devices will also need a growing medium that is fine-tuned to their needs, since they cannot take complete advantage of the medium that is designed for those with perfectly intact hearing.) In a "signed language growing medium," culturally designed support rests on several centuries of problem-solving undertaken by people who also could not make use of spoken language. To our knowledge, only cultures of Deaf people provide this specific kind of support. Indeed, this is the truly unique feature of Deaf culture, and the one most worth educational consideration.

It is a mistake to think that deaf babies do not get culturally designed support in the "spoken language" medium. Of course, they do. But they simply cannot take advantage of it to use their inborn language capacity. The deaf child is included in numerous social interactions culturally mediated by spoken language—families eat together, babies go with others on errands or to church, they are toilet trained. As Cole notes, "They live in a world that is suffused with meaning, although they lack access to the specifically linguistic behavior that fills the gaps between actions" (1996, 202). Even so, like all children, deaf children have active minds that develop ways to represent the world. This is enough to allow a kind of participation with others in many activities; it is a myth that deaf children begin their educations with no communication ability and no knowledge of the world. But communication is not always language, and partial knowledge and access are not enough for typical language acquisition to occur. Language acquisition requires full access and participation. Unfortunately, children who do not have full access to their family's language used in culturally organized contexts will not develop it, even if they can communicate and participate in some of the actions that occur in these contexts.

## CULTURE, DEAF CULTURE, AND EDUCATION

In evolutionary time, we got lucky. Over historical time, social groups made inventions and innovations and passed them on. This is what has made us who we are intellectually and made us very different from our closest primate relatives. But evolutionary and historical time are not right in front of us. Like geological time, these very long spans are difficult to imagine. What is in front of us are deaf children in their immediate time frame—their developmental time. Like all children, they should be able to depend on the pooled resources of others; and for most of their needs, they can. They enjoy the invention of devices that keep houses warm or cool, provide warm bath water and bubbles, cook food, produce entertainment, and print picture books. And they participate more or less willingly in social practices that keep them loved and adored, cared for, immunized against a variety of diseases, and treated for crooked teeth. Many even have access to devices that amplify sound or send pulses of electrical energy into their nervous systems. As cultural beings, deaf children are not completely unique. But there is one area where the resources accumulated over the history of the hearing cultural world are not as effective for deaf children as they are for hearing children. Obviously that is spoken language. And in most societies, the shared spoken language(s) is the key to gaining access to other highly valued social innovations, like learning in formal schooling.

We can hypothesize about whether or not a lack of ability to hear has ever been in the evolutionary, historical, or developmental plan. But it does not matter. The fact is that there are people who cannot hear, there always have been, and they have invented a variety of cultural solutions and transmitted them to others. We can state unconditionally that late, random, or degraded access to language is not in the plan. Partial or ambiguous access to language does not fill the requirements for participating in culture, nor does receiving basic skills instruction second-hand through an interpreter (Ramsey 2001). And living without the accumulated cultural inventions that boosted the intellects of previous generations is simply not in the plan either.

## DEFINITIONS OF CULTURE

Recently, I had a chance to consider a new millennium definition of culture that was conveyed to me by hearing undergraduates at a midwestern university. The university offers a four-course series of ASL classes. About half of the eighty students per semester who enroll in the courses do so to satisfy their "foreign language" requirement. In these courses, readings about Deaf culture are included on the assumption that learning a language entails learning about its culture. In the case of a minority language like ASL, sensitivity to the culture of Deaf people is required. The same is required for students of Spanish, Lakota, and all the other modern language courses at the university. To my surprise, and, I think, to the Deaf instructors' surprise, a large group of ASL students took an oppositional stance to the Deaf culture readings. They doubted the authenticity of a culture of Deaf people. Why, they asked, wasn't it good enough for Deaf people to just be deaf? Why did they have to come up with this idea of culture? Don't they like hearing people? Why can't they be like us, just "normal people"? Why go around inventing a culture to set themselves apart? It was as if even talking about the culture and lives of Deaf people took something away from the hearing students and threatened their own cultural connections. We managed to resolve this situation, but the fact that it arose taught me again that narrow definitions of culture are not only overly romantic and useless, but dangerous and intolerant. The cost of narrow, trait-based, ethnic identity definitions of culture may be quite high for those of us who are not just "normal people."

The garden metaphor definition of culture as a growing medium, calibrated over time to meet the needs of people in social groups, offers a more useful way to think about culture as it interacts with schooling. To acknowledge that culture, in the foundational definition that I have offered here, is to acknowledge that deaf children have the same inheritance that the rest of us are born with, and that they are born ready to develop according to the human program. They only need full access to the material and symbolic culture and the social practices that will support the specific developmental plan that comes with not hearing. This definition frees us from the overly romantic notion of culture, from confusing lists of traits and learning styles, and from discussions of culture as contests over which culture produces "normal people." In addition, the foundational definition of culture as an evolutionary, historical, and individual accomplishment and tool tells us what culture is not. Culture does not exist in a vacuum, does not have claws to snatch people, or snares to trap them. Culture emerges when people engage in joint activities, and all cultures take on life and adapt to changes in the world because people need and use them. And, like fish in water, most of the time we are unaware of our own culture until we are suddenly without it. I never thought of myself as a *gringa* until I started to spend time in Mexico. To my surprise, it turns out that I am one. And I never thought of myself as a hearing person until I learned ASL and started hanging out with Deaf people. Again, I learned that I am a hearing person, even though for half of my life, I did not know that category even existed.

Since teaching and learning occur through the medium of language, in activities created over time in the cultural setting of schools, the cultural solutions of Deaf people have a role in education. Hearing teachers and parents are not destined to be foreigners to Deaf culture. The language socialization, language use, and instructional discourse patterns of Deaf people are critical places to look for ways to make contact with deaf students and help them learn. Many of these patterns rest on knowledge of ASL. But good teaching practices that reach deaf children and serve their learning needs can be adopted by ASL-signing hearing people (see Ramsey and Padden 1998; Humphries and MacDougall 2000). Deaf culture does not isolate deaf children from the "real" world, where the normal people live. It will more likely, in fact, do the opposite. All people who are truly bilingual, even those who are forced by circumstances to be bilingual, know a great deal about both of their languages and how to use them. Bilingual Deaf people know more about English, even spoken English, than we think they do. Many Deaf adults continue to learn English after they leave high school (Ramsey 2000). A strength of American Deaf culture is its rich content about hearing people, English, reading, and how to approach and cross the porous boundary that separates Deaf from hearing people. The hearing undergraduates who took issue with Deaf culture were wrong in their assumption that culture creates separations. For marginalized groups, culture offers the information they need to comprehend and participate in the range of worlds they must enter, including their own and that of the powerful "others." Rather than assume that deaf children must be molded into hearing children, it is much more helpful to seek Deaf cultural knowledge about how the world is and how to make sense of it. Stripping culture down to its foundations is the best way to help all of us—the romantics, the trait-list makers, the doubters, and the teachers—understand why we cannot ignore its powerful presence in schools.

What does culture have to do with the education of students who are deaf or hard of hearing? Watch a skilled Deaf teacher teach English idiomatic expressions to another Deaf person, child or adult. Ask Deaf adults about their favorite teachers, and you will hear about at least one Deaf teacher who explained something about English in a clear way, who taught strategies for reading comprehension, or who explained how to use a library. Irrational rumors to the contrary, the culture of Deaf people does not want to trap deaf children—only to offer them strategies so they can learn, use, and improve upon the innovations of history to make living in the world possible. Look for Deaf innovations to the problems of learning and development as well as information on language structures, discourse patterns, teaching strategies, the values about English, and hearing people and the larger culture, and that is where you will find Deaf culture's role in education.

## LITERATURE CITED

Banks, J. 1996. *Multicultural education, transformative knowledge, and action.* New York: Teachers College Press.

Boyd, R., and P. Richerson. 1985. *Culture and the evolutionary process.* Chicago: University of Chicago Press.

Cole, M. 1996. *Cultural psychology: A once and future discipline.* Cambridge, Mass.: Harvard University Press.

De Villiers, P. 2000. Reference to protagonists' mental states in the written narratives of deaf children: The contribution of English syntax and ASL skills. In *Proceedings of the 24th annual Boston University conference on language development,* ed. S. Howell, S. Fish, and T. Keith-Lucas, 265–75. Somerville, Mass.: Cascadilla Press.

Durham, W. 1991. *Coevolution: Genes, culture, and human diversity.* Palo Alto, Calif.: Stanford University Press.

Harry, B. 1992. *Cultural diversity, families and the special education system.* New York: Teachers College Press.

Humphries, T., and F. MacDougall. 2000. "Chaining" and other links: Making connections between American Sign Language and English in two types of school settings. *Visual Anthropology Review* 15 (2): 84–94.

Kalyanpur, M., and B. Harry. 1999. *Culture in special education: Building reciprocal family-professional relationships.* Baltimore: Brookes.

Mayberry, R. 1993. First-language acquisition after childhood differs from second-language acquisition: The case of American Sign Language. *Journal of Speech and Hearing Research* 36:1258–270.

Moeller, M. 2002. Mothers' mental state input and theory of mind understanding in deaf and hearing children. Ph.D. diss., University of Nebraska, Lincoln.

Ogbu, J. 1987. *Minority education and caste: The American system in cross-cultural perspective.* San Francisco: Academic Press.

Ramsey, C. 2001. Below the surface: Theoretical frameworks shed light on educational interpreting. *Odyssey* 2:19–24.

———. 1997. *Deaf children in public schools.* Washington D.C.: Gallaudet University Press.

———. 2000. "I just gave up on it for awhile": Becoming a Deaf reader. Manuscript. Department of Special Education and Communication Disorders, University of Nebraska, Lincoln.

Ramsey, C., and C. Padden. 1998. Natives and newcomers: Gaining access to literacy in a classroom for deaf children. *Anthropology & Education Quarterly* 29:1–20.

Sleeter, C. 2001. *Culture, difference and power.* New York: Teachers College Press.

Tomasello, M. 1999. *The cultural origins of human cognition.* Cambridge, Mass.: Harvard University Press.

# Double Jeopardy: Women, Deafness and Deaf Education

*Susan Burch*

Scholars of Deaf culture locate the birth of this linguistic minority group in schools; the schools are also where intense battles over identity and autonomy developed. Founding the American School for the Deaf (ASD) in Hartford, Connecticut, in 1817, initiated the campaign for permanent, state-sponsored residential schools for the deaf. ASD co-founder Laurent Clerc, a French deaf man, provided the linguistic and pedagogical model of sign language-based education for the deaf. While schools did not generally provide sign language classes, this primary mode of communication and instruction dominated residential schools until the latter part of the century. Deaf residential schools offered Deaf people a "place of their own," a separate world where deafness was the norm; of equal importance, these schools provided Deaf people with a common sign language. Graduates of these schools sought to create new cultural "places," including alumni associations, Deaf newspapers, and churches. In the 1850s, some Deaf advocates argued for a state in the western territories inhabited only by Deaf people. And in 1864, Congress began to sponsor advanced education specifically for deaf students with the creation of Gallaudet College. Within decades of the founding of ASD, a distinct, American Deaf culture began to strengthen and spread. In part

---

Portions of this work were originally published in *Signs of Resistance: American Deaf Cultural History from 1900 to World War II* (New York: New York University Press, 2002).

because of its successful growth, educational reformers sought to introduce another methodology—oralism—into American schools that challenged cultural Deafness.

Oralists emphasized speech- and lipreading for communication by and among deaf people; strict adherents sought the exclusive use of speech over any signed communication. As a group, oral advocates generally agreed that their method best facilitated deaf people's assimilation into mainstream society. Formal oral education in residential deaf schools began at the New York Institution, which opened in 1818. Oralism's appeal increased over the next few decades, but advocates were unable to overcome the network and influence of signing educators. Yet by the 1900s, the strong position of manual communication had waned, giving way to more classes in and about the oral system. Prominent advocates, like Alexander Graham Bell, helped promote oralism. Endowed with sizable monetary funds and buttressed with savvy propaganda campaigns, oralists further empowered their community by forging strong ties to those with influence: parents and politicians. Oralist promises that deaf children could speak pulled at the heartstrings of parents who wanted to hear their children's voices, who wanted their children to be "normal" like them. Oralism also appealed to those involved with the growing Progressive spirit of the nation in the 1890s to the 1900s. Political and social reformers sought to integrate America's marginalized communities and create cultural cohesion, particularly after the recent Civil War and in the midst of a massive influx of immigrants, by creating a common spoken language—English. Oralists often included the rhetoric of Americanization in their campaigns, contending that speech training would make deaf people both less pitiable and more a part of normal society. For example, N. F. Walker, a longtime superintendent of deaf schools, argued, "The deaf who make English their medium of thought are less peculiar and less suspicious than those who do not" ("Use of English in Schools for the Deaf" 1920, 34–37). By the early twentieth century, most schools for the deaf had implemented strong oral programs into their curricula.

At the same time, women in general infiltrated the teaching profession in America, including special education. By the end of the First World War, women represented 85 percent of the teaching force; by the 1930s, they represented around 80 percent. This occurred, in part, because women often earned half of what men did and had to resign after getting married, allowing newer (and cheaper) women to fill positions (Moreg

1996, 7; "Salaries and Contracts" 1920, 253).[1] Changing student demographics, however, also helped produce the preponderance of female teachers. Oral programs encouraged younger students to enter schools. Believing that speech education should begin as early as possible, oral administrators encouraged parents with children as young as three or four to enter schools (although prestigious schools like the Clarke School for the Deaf in Massachusetts generally admitted children aged five to ten years old). The argument followed that women—as natural mothers—were innately fitted to teach little children. The belief that women instilled appropriate behavior and habits further legitimated their place within the school walls.

Oralism's popularity and the feminization of teaching strongly affected Deaf people's lives. One of the most obvious ramifications of these trends was the direct assault on Deaf cultural values: the use of sign language and the reliance on deaf educators within the schools. As hearing women increasingly dominated deaf education, a more spirited competition arose among Deaf people for the remaining teaching positions. In this struggle, Deaf men faced the double insult of watching opponents to their culture weaken the ties between the schools and the Deaf community and watching women, viewed as the inferior sex, replace them at work. While Deaf men lashed out at this trend, Deaf women experienced perhaps the greatest marginalization and disempowerment, both in terms of their educational-career opportunities and their social choices.

One of the leading oral schools for the deaf, the Clarke School, particularly illustrates the link between gender and deaf education. Led by Caroline Yale, the Clarke School promoted a strong oral program while describing their school in terms of an idyllic Christian family. School publications characterized teachers as surrogate mothers and the school as a family-like environment. The maternal overtones of the school soothed parents' concerns about the welfare of their children but also reflected broader trends in education.[2]

Clarke added their own teacher-training program in 1892 with the support of the AAPTSD (American Association for the Promotion and Teaching of Speech for the Deaf) and was closely aligned to public schools (Fay 1914, 468). The program promoted even greater numbers of female teachers. One National Association of the Deaf (NAD) report noted that out of seventy-seven teachers trained at its facility, only two were men. As one person quipped, "Almost to a woman they are women" ("Female Teachers" 1907, 27).

The network of Clarke-trained teachers in this case bears a striking resemblance to the settlement house movement led by Jane Addams at the turn of the century. Both vocations, oralist teaching and aiding poor immigrant communities, enabled educated women to enter a secure, respected profession in a virtually all-female environment. Caroline Yale stocked her teaching pool with graduates from Smith College, located right across the street, and from other prestigious women's colleges. This sort of recruitment established an additional dominion of female reform and employment.[3]

In creating more teaching opportunities for hearing women, oralists can be seen as having exploited—implicitly, if not deliberately—these women to achieve their agenda. Hearing women struggled to attain an independent livelihood and higher social status for themselves. Their efforts contributed—albeit not maliciously or even intentionally—to the disempowerment of Deaf men and women. Deaf men tried to defend their livelihood, status, and identity not only by battling oralism, but also by enforcing sexist stereotypes of both hearing and Deaf women. Deaf women, having the most limited options of any of these groups, sought to defend deaf education, sign language, the Deaf community, and Deaf men from both oralism and displacement by hearing teachers. In so doing, they fell into even more subordinated roles.

Open only to hearing graduate students, Gallaudet College actively sought to balance out the threat of staunch oralism and counter the feminization of the teaching profession by initiating a Normal (teaching) Department one year prior to Clarke. Gallaudet's first president, Edward Miner Gallaudet, argued that the rise of female teachers "is to be regretted upon very high grounds. . . . Women are naturally fitted by talent, tact and patience to teach little children; but when they are older they need sterner attributes of men, more logical faculties and stricter sense of justice that are masculine traits. The Normal department at Gallaudet has done something to start this improvement. Of their graduates more than 82% have been men."[4]

In running schools, these men often became administrators while women remained as teaching faculty. Continuing the metaphor of traditional "families," the men generally managed the schools, while the women/mothers did the primary rearing of the students. The language used to describe teachers during this period reveals an understanding of this employment model. All but two superintendents of state deaf schools were men, often described as "strong," "honest," "intelligent," and occasionally "stubborn." Ideal teachers demonstrated particularly feminine traits, such as charity, attention to moral behavior, kindness, sensitivity, and a strong nurturing nature. Many authors in both Deaf publications and oralist journals put a finer point on the matter, describing all teachers as "she" ("Tomorrow's Teacher of the Deaf" 1935, 470).

Historic documents by and about oralism strongly suggest that the face of oralist educators was a female one, but so was the image of the ideal student. Female teachers' interaction with students especially enforced common expectations for the female Deaf population. As the majority of the teaching and social workforce, educated hearing ladies practiced what they preached; recognized for their charity, patience, sweet disposition, in short their maternalism, these specialists set an example for their female pupils. As noted frequently in Deaf newspaper articles and speeches at Deaf conferences, they also gained praise from adult Deaf men.[5] Unlike teachers in mainstream schools, female educators and social workers for the deaf presented a behavioral model and not a career archetype for young Deaf girls. As hearing women who promoted oralism, they literally spoke to (and embodied for) young girls the social expectations of the broader community. While seeking to indoctrinate specific hearing values into girls, which included appropriate laughter, speech, breathing sounds, and other social etiquette, these professionals ultimately narrowed their abilities for self-sufficiency. Not only did oralism demand more time for one-on-one speech work, reducing the academic hours in school, but the feminization of these professions ultimately displaced educated Deaf women as well. Oralism's increasing demands for inexpensive hearing teachers who could work with younger populations dictated the rapid influx of hearing women into schools, and Deaf men could no longer afford to compete with single Deaf women for the rare and valued remaining positions. Thus, while mainstream society opened more opportunities for women in general, it closed doors for Deaf women, and the Deaf community further encouraged them to remain at home and allow men to demonstrate their abilities as workers instead.

For girls who excelled in school in spite of these and other limitations, becoming a member of the educated elite proved difficult. President Gallaudet clearly disapproved of females entering his school. After the first group of Gallaudet coeds had left the school, he closed admission to women. Several women took the lead in opposing their exclusion. After a decade of rejections, the college relented, opening their doors to women again in 1887. Even after coeducation resumed, however, Gallaudet, like other colleges, produced more male graduates than female.[6] Deaf women who continued to study at the Deaf college faced limited access to many clubs. Teachers also frequently placed them on a less-rigorous academic track. Outside the classroom, Deaf and oral advocates perceived women's bodies as central to their ideological expressions.

Print media coverage of Deaf women further illustrates the link between oralism, normalcy, and physical beauty. Oralism's presence in the Deaf community manifested in a particular view of Deaf women's bodies. The desire for Deaf women to "pass" as hearing was encouraged by both oralists and Deaf leaders. For example, contributors to the *Volta Review*, the preeminent oral journal, linked beauty and "passing" with hearing. Various articles explained to ladies how lipreading in front of mirrors helped cultivate beauty, including one entitled "How to be beautiful, though deaf." The author goes on to call oralism a miraculous art for ladies. Another article in the same issue continued, claiming that "Love May be Blind, but not Deaf" (De Young 1924, 205; Ferrall 1924, 258–61). Especially pervasive was the suggestion that sexual appeal demanded greater "normality" from Deaf women. Many parents particularly encouraged their deaf daughters to practice their oral skills in hopes of attracting hearing suitors. Although many still married Deaf partners, their training in speech informed their sense of self and often won them praise from Deaf leaders. The intention to present Deaf women as normal was, in fact, a conscious decision by Deaf male leaders. Like many other minority groups in early twentieth century America, Deaf leaders felt compelled to prove their value to society and thereby earn a place of equality rather than demand civil rights or government intervention on their behalf. This particular approach demanded that the community minimize their difference with mainstream society, often promoting an image of themselves as "hyper" American, and very specifically, not disabled, not different, not dependent, and not as "Other."

Such praise of Deaf women who "passed" these criteria often appeared in the popular and powerful Deaf press. As a visual culture, images held particular rhetorical and cultural power. With limited access to mainstream media, and before the invention of closed captioning and the TTY, the pictures "read" by the community in Deaf publications and films communicated expectations and ideals, often far more convincingly than the written word.[7] Several nationally recognized Deaf newspapers, including the *Silent Worker*, *Deaf Digest*, and *American Deaf Citizen*, frequently produced articles on and pictures of successful Deaf female dancers, beautiful women who resembled normal Hollywood starlets. By specifically praising professional dancers, they subtly attempted to pass Deaf women off as hearing. While Deaf people understood that music could be appreciated through vibration, mainstream society viewed music and dance as exclusively hearing entertainment.

Helen Heckman's success as a dancer exemplified this convergence of ideals. Heckman, who became deaf as an infant, received speech training in Switzerland. By the 1920s, she was a successful dancer, performing for the Congressional Club in Washington D.C., as well as various European nightclubs. In 1928, she authored *My Life Transformed*, describing how her education to be normal opened doors into the exotic world of travel and dance. The Deaf community applauded her success, emphasizing her abilities to woo crowds over her marginal use of sign language and absence of Deaf activism. The Oklahoma starlet received the greatest exposure of all Deaf dancers in the community press. Deaf readers appreciated that she was liberated from the common image of dependent, while maintaining the necessary virtues of talent and sexual appeal. In one interview, Heckman described her Cinderella story:

> When I think of myself at the age of twelve, a fat, lazy ignorant girl, using signs in lieu of words, deficient in the sense of balance, unable to eat without smacking or to exert myself without making unnatural sounds, feeling nothing in common with those of the hearing worlds.... After training in speech, reading lips, and playing piano, [I could] move about in the hearing world as a normal, happy being without the finger of pity being pointed toward me. ("Dreams That Come True" 1928, 267–68)

Her popularity in the Deaf press belies the conflicted perceptions of cultural identity within the community, because Heckman, as well as other female performers, promoted oralism and mainstreaming and only mentioned her physical condition as a marker of her ability to overcome. Heckman's consistent praise of her upbringing, while appearing to support the goals of Deaf females, actually challenged the traditional values of Deafness expressed for and by male leaders. As a professional who depended on her body rather than her "voice," she maintained the normal expectations of women in general, and showed, albeit in ironic ways, the possibilities of Deaf women in particular.

Other Deaf female dancers earned high praise from male leaders and newspaper editors. What is striking about their appearances in the press—

not only the frequency but the presentation—is how these women are seen literally (and figuratively in this sense) by readers. They are not "seen" in a deaf sense—to be seen is to be heard in their world. Heckman is never pictured speaking. Body language here is literally her body. At the same time, the written articles about Heckman and these other women always emphasized their abilities to speak and their purported "success" in oral programs. This has added meaning because the issue of oral "failures" plagued the community—then as it does even now.

An example from the NAD enforces this contradiction between women's bodies, traditional Deaf values, and oralism versus sign language use. In the early 1900s, the NAD collected $5,000 to produce films featuring sign language masters in an effort to counter oralism's deleterious effect on their cultural language. The series boasted roughly twenty films, but included only one woman signing a monologue. And her recitation represented a significant departure from the norm. Dressed in Indian costume, Mary Williamson Erd performed, in 1938, Henry Wadsworth Longfellow's poem "Death of Minnehaha." While elegant in its flowing execution, the work is less formal than the other NAD films. The visual framing of the scene often belies the intention of capturing master signers. Unlike the films featuring male orators, this work captures Erd from a distance, so the audience can take in her whole body and the woods surrounding her. Presenting herself as Minnehaha, Erd appears more as an adroit actress than an elite signer. Henri Gaillard, a French Deaf man who visited America in 1917, saw part of this film and praised Erd's "inspired fervor and perfect sense of the poetry," as well as her ability to show the subtlety and complexity of sign language. However, his critique of Erd also emphasized her physical beauty and the performance nature of the piece, contrasting it with the powerful, filmed speeches given on behalf of sign language by male teachers of the Deaf. Gaillard made no reference to the physicality of the male orators (Buchanan 2002, 35).

Erd physically and dramatically resembles Heckman in more than a superficial way. Perhaps she resembled her too much here. Members of the organization thought that her contribution did not invoke the rich heritage or moral rectitude that infused all the other performances. In a letter to a colleague, George Veditz (the president of the NAD who founded this series) wrote, "The Minnehaha film I regard as a failure. Mrs. Erd has not a 'film face' and the declamation as filmed lacks in great measure the charm of her living personality. Besides it was not the sign language. Too much gyration for our purpose" (29 March 1915, n.p.).

The images of Deaf women in the Little Paper Family (LPF) and in staged, filmed performances resonate with their actual position within the community. The NAD, for example, had a few female officers in the 1920s, but they and other female members had no voting rights in the organization until 1964. The National Fraternal Society for the Deaf (NFSD) denied women membership altogether, claiming that women should stay at home.[8] Indeed, female participation in the NFSD remained one of the more acrimonious bones of contention in the early decades of the association's development; they had no voice in management until 1951 when thirty-nine auxiliaries and a membership of nearly 1,500 women persuaded officers to include them as insured participants (Sullivan 1987, 224–27; Schowe n.d., 51). While many state and local organizations allowed female members, few had positions of power. Some, like the New Jersey Association of the Deaf rejected female membership until the Second World War ("The Gleaner Says" January 1939, 2). Thus, while allowed to express themselves in select discussions and social activities, few women had any political or social authority in the efforts to preserve and promote sign language or to publicly preserve and promote general Deaf culture. In this way, Deaf women had a physical presence in Deaf "places"—the organizations—but not a political (and it appears much of a signed) "voice."

State and local community leaders covertly and overtly defined Deaf women's place through their bodies in more tangible ways. Beauty contests for single women were exceptionally popular forms of entertainment and fundraising at schools and local organizations.[9] In 1926, for example, Pennsylvania Society for the Advancement of the Deaf members elected Anna Joy Bauerle queen over thirty other women at a well-attended dance and competition. Bauerle went on to compete against women from across the country in a "Miss Deaf America Pageant." Combining looks with social attributes (like high moral standards, modesty, and charity), the winner of the event was slated to play a leading part in a Deaf film. By the 1930s, bathing suit contests also began to flourish, and major cities boasted Deaf beauties who, like mainstream contestants, embodied both movie star glamour and feminine virtues, such as domestic skills and strong religious training ("Miss Deaf Philadelphia" 1936, 10; "Chicago's Queen Challenges KC" 1935, 1; "The Biggest Hit During the Convention" 1940). It must be noted that women also played an active role in this social creation. While similar in mindset to hearing contestants, most Deaf beauty contestants truly appreciated the contests for added reasons. Because many girls had vocational training in the art of beauty—cosmetology, hairdressing, and dressmaking—the competitions allowed them to demonstrate their own handiwork as well as their figures. Moreover, unable to gain entrance into mainstream film and theater because of communication issues, aspiring actresses and models found their greatest opportunities for fame at Deaf social events like the contests. Also, as the highlight of social interaction, conventions and club galas provided the most exciting and meaningful possibilities to meet eligible suitors. To this day, Deaf beauty contests remain a popular form of entertainment and profit for clubs across America.

Broad social and legal changes encouraged the attempts of Deaf people to pass as normal. The rise of eugenics exacerbated the marginal place of all disabled people and many racial and ethnic groups in America. In its most extreme form, eugenics encouraged invasive measures like sterilization. Clearly, Deaf people and other populations hoped to avoid this or other demeaning acts. Leaders feared that affiliation with groups considered dangerous and inferior would harm the community's image and status. Already marginalized by hearing educators and policy makers, Deaf people resisted the possibility of further emasculation by outsiders—or insiders—in their community. In the end, this meant that Deaf elites—mostly men, but also women—fought to uplift only their own people. But "own people" had different meanings in different contexts. In the process, they overlooked or dismissed the potential of solidarity with other struggling communities, including subcommunities of Deaf people. Most Deaf leaders equated citizenship with normalcy. Deaf activists protected aspects of their cultural identity that did not fully conform to the mainstream, but tried to minimize all other differences between them and mainstream society.

Oralism continued to be defined by its pedagogical meaning, but its application had subtle and obvious gender connotations. While Deaf boys entered oral programs as well, girls especially were targeted by oral advocates and educators. Parents appear to have contributed strongly to this tendency, presumably because they believed that their daughters could attract hearing suitors if they spoke well. It seems that most educators and parents did not believe that Deaf boys could attract hearing women, and thus they focused more on boys' abilities to support themselves financially, to be, simply, good—albeit handicapped—men. For Deaf women, however, this reality had several implications. Deaf men would marry, presumably and in reality, Deaf women. Yet mainstream society strongly encouraged the same women to marry hearing men, to be "normalized" through these marriages. Explicitly and implicitly, it was believed that these "mixed" marriages were more likely to produce hearing offspring than those of deaf-deaf marriages. Once again, women, at once the embodiment of deafness and at the same time its displaced opponent, were expected—by both Deaf and hearing leaders—to produce hearing children.

This latter aspect shows the confluence of oralism with broader trends like the rise of eugenics and the Deaf community's general strategy for achieving equal status in society. However, the presence of oralism and the feminization of the teaching profession exacerbated the tensions between the sexes by emasculating Deaf men, weakening their education by focusing attention on lipreading skills rather than regular academic subjects and ultimately by physically replacing them in the classroom. Thus oralism posed multiple threats—to the positive cultural identity of Deaf men and to their sense of masculinity. While often fighting against hearing women as the symbol of oralist influence, Deaf men expected their female peers to embody oralist skills and ideas. This may have occurred, in part, as a gesture of their own masculine power to woo Deaf women who could have chosen hearing suitors, but it seems more complicated than this. That many Deaf women had the approval of oralists and appeared normal in ways that more Deaf men could not—meaning they could speak and replicate other hearing behavior—seems to have empowered Deaf spouses. That these same women tended to reflect society's other expectations—to be good mothers, wives, and helpmates—could not have hurt matters.

As the population who stood behind Deaf culture more often than for it, Deaf women remain difficult to assess. Most did not join mainstream associations because of communication and other barriers, and Deaf clubs, schools, and the press often neglected their opinions and contributions. What is more apparent is that American Deaf women strove to be "normal" and that the Deaf community encouraged an interpretation of "normalcy" that ran counter to the group's carefully crafted definition of itself. Their concept of normalcy played out primarily on the body, but often denied the deafness of the female body. How Deaf women responded to these pressures and interpretations remains a neglected area of study, but it assuredly offers important insights into the Deaf community and presents valuable lessons in the formation of identity.

## NOTES

1. In one essay entitled "Tomorrow's Teacher of the Deaf," S. S. Slaughten, director of the division of exceptional children in Milwaukee, referred to all teachers as "she." See *Volta Review* 37 (August 1935): 470. New attendance mandates and improved hearing tests resulted in greater numbers of children going to school. This exacerbated the need for less-expensive support staff and faculty.

2. Margret Winzer noted that, in contrast, manual schools—at least in the nineteenth century—were masculine in tone—strictly regimented and institutionalized. See Margret Winzer, *History of Special Education: From Isolation to Integration*. (Washington, D.C.: Gallaudet University Press, 1993), 129.

3. The Seven Sister schools appreciated Yale as well. She was awarded honoree degrees from Wesleyan in 1896 and from Mt. Holyoke in 1927. The Clarke School also enjoyed the patronage of President and Mrs. Calvin Coolidge. Mrs. Coolidge taught at Clarke for two years, and the first couple spearheaded the Coolidge Endowment Fund, which reached $2 million by 1929 and was used for research, new construction, and teacher support. See Winzer, *History of Special Education*, 243; Mary E. Numbers, *My Words Fell on Deaf Ears* (Washington, D.C.: Alexander Graham Bell Association for the Deaf, 1974), 59–60; and H. Willia Brelje and Virginia Tibbs, *The Washington State School for the Deaf: The First One Hundred Years, 1886–1986* (Vancouver: Washington State School for the Deaf, 1986), 94, 116. This financial boom helped buttress the school as the Depression began and allowed Clarke to increase support for research with Smith College and other medical programs. See also Robin Muncy, *Creating a Female Dominion of Reform, 1890–1935* (New York: Oxford University, 1991).

4. In a 1921 article in the *American Annals of the Deaf*, the author explained how economic upheavals, wars, and so forth had driven men from the profession. The author tellingly tied the hopeful return to normalcy in society to the return of normalcy—meaning having male teachers—in deaf schools. See "Is the Male Teacher Becoming an Extinct Species?" *American Annals of the Deaf* 66 (1921): 29–31. Many of the Gallaudet Normal School graduates became administrators at the deaf schools.

5. For example, see "Carrie Hess," Pennsylvania Society News (June 1931): 37; "Miss Lula Edgar Wharton," Mississippi Institute Bulletin 1

Dec. 1915: 8–9; "In Memory of Mrs. S.T. Walker," (Kansas School for the Deaf Marra Museum: Superintendent File).

6. The double-discrimination of being African American and female barred this minority group from graduating anyone from Gallaudet until 1957. See Mabs Holcomb and Sharon Wood, *Deaf Women: A Parade Through the Decades* (Berkeley: DawnSign Press, 1989), 48.

7. The Little Paper Family (or LPF) were Deaf-produced newspapers, originally created in schools as vocational training projects, which served as another form of cultural "glue." Like hometown papers, the LPFs focused on local members and events over national, mainstream politics. Although many LPFs included national news, they maintained a folksy and intimate "tone." It appears that many deaf school and Gallaudet graduates subscribed to LPFs during their lifetime.

8. See debates on the Frat in "Admission of Women," The Frat (May, 1929): 5; "Woman Question Again," The Frat (June 1929): 2.

9. For example, see J. N. Funk "Manhattan," *The Frat* (April 1931): 20.

## LITERATURE CITED

Admission of women. 1929. *The Frat* (May): 5.
The biggest hit during the convention. 1940. *Silent Broadcaster* (September): n.p.
Brelje, H. W., and V. M. Tibbs. 1986. *The Washington State School for the Deaf: The first one hundred years, 1886–1986*. Vancouver: Washington State School for the Deaf.
Buchanan, B., ed. 2002. *Gaillard in deaf America: A portrait of the deaf community, 1917*. Gallaudet Classics in Deaf Studies series, vol. 3. Washington, D.C.: Gallaudet University Press.
Hess, C. 1931. *Pennsylvania Society News* (June): 37.
Chicago's queen challenges KC. 1935. *American Deaf Citizen* (21 June): 1.
De Young, D. 1924. Love may be blind but not deaf. *Volta Review* 26 (June): 205.
Fay, E. A. 1914. *Progress in the education of the deaf*. Washington, D.C.: Bureau of Education.
Female teachers. 1907. *Proceedings of the Eighth Convention of the National Association of the Deaf*, 27.
Ferrall, J. A. 1924. How to be beautiful, though deaf. *Volta Review* 26 (June): 258–61.

Funk, J. N. 1931. Manhattan. *The Frat* (April): 20.
The Gleaner says. 1939. *Jersey Booster* (January): 2.
Heckman, H. 1928. Dreams that come true. *Silent Worker* (April): 267–68.
———. 1928. *My Life Transformed.* New York: Macmillan.
Hudson-Makuen, G. 1911. The medico-education problem in the deaf child. *Volta Review* 13 (4) (September): 211–14.
In memory of Mrs. S. T. Walker. n.d. Kansas School for the Deaf Marra Museum: Superintendent File.
Is the male teacher becoming an extinct species? 1921. *American Annals of the Deaf* 66: 29–31.
Miss deaf Philadelphia. 1936. *Pennsylvania Society News* (June): 10.
Miss Lula Edgar Wharton. 1915. *Mississippi Institute Bulletin* (1 December): 8–9.
Moreg, D. W. 1996. *Schools in the Great Depression.* New York: Garland Publishing.
Numbers, M. E. 1974. *My words fell on deaf ears.* Washington, D.C.: Alexander Graham Bell Association for the Deaf.
Salaries and contracts. 1920. *American Annals of the Deaf* 65: 250–70.
Schowe, B. n.d. *The NFSD story: A brief account of the perilous first years.* National Fraternal Society of the Deaf Archives. Unpublished manuscript.
Sullivan, F. B. 1987. National Fraternal Society of the Deaf. In *Gallaudet Encyclopedia of Deaf People and Deafness*, ed. J. V. Van Cleve. 224–27. New York: McGraw-Hill.
Tomorrow's teacher of the deaf. 1935. *Volta Review* 37 (August): 470.
Veditz, G. 1915. Letter to R. Stewart, 29 March. R. E. Stewart Papers, Gallaudet University Archives.
Walker, N. F. 1920. Use of English in schools for the deaf. *Proceedings of the Twenty-Second Convention of American Instructors of the Deaf*, 34–37.
Winzer, M. 1993. *The history of special education: From isolation to integration.* Washington, D.C.: Gallaudet University Press.
Woman question again. 1929. *The Frat* (June): 2.

# Deaf She Wrote: Mapping
Deaf Women's Autobiography

*Brenda Jo Brueggemann*

> This book is one of life's gifts. It will let me say to both deaf and hearing people what I've always held back.
> Emmanuelle Laborit, *The Cry of the Gull*

I became interested in deaf women's autobiography as a literacy site for several reasons. From one angle, my interest came from seeing a fair amount of it as the editor for the new Deaf Lives series from Gallaudet University Press, which was initiated in 2003 and which will focus on deaf autobiographies, memoirs, personal essays. Four out of the first six authors in this series are women. From a second angle, I also became interested in deaf women's autobiography because I write some of it (as a self-labeled "hard of hearing" woman) in scattered essays I farm out to whatever collection or press will let them pass as academic essays. From a third angle, I am also interested in the life stories that deaf women have written (and are writing now) because I have long been researching all the women who "write" deafness—the astonishing percentages of women that occupy most of the ancillary fields surrounding that ever-so-potent noun-state of "deafness": audiologists, speech/language pathologists, deaf educators, sign language interpreters (Brueggemann 1999). And, oh yes, mothers too. These are the people, I argue, who most often authorize deafness. That is, these women play a major role—willfully, deliberately, or not—in constructing our culture's ideas about, and responses to, deafness and deaf people.

With these three angles combined, I approach the topic of deaf women's autobiography from a triangulated perspective—at least for now. Later, who knows, my geometry may change. But my method of critical analysis will remain largely the same. My analytical handle is *rhetoric*—a body of knowledge that employs both theory and practice in producing and analyzing various kinds of discourses that persuade, motivate, change, argue for or against, empower, enlighten, manipulate, oppress. In using rhetoric as my critical lens, I am most interested then in the power that comes from within *language*—and that which also evolves out of it—and how the words we use and choose, and the ways we use and choose them, come, in a sense, to define who *we* are, who *they* are, and who *you* are.

I believe, as did one of the greatest rhetorical scholars of the twentieth century (or probably any century), Kenneth Burke (1966) that: "The human animal, as we know it, *emerges into personality* by first mastering whatever tribal speech happens to be its particular symbolic environment" (1340). Applying Burke's idea, I am interested in mapping the emergent personality of deaf women writers as they master the tribal speech (and sign too) of their particular region, nation, or era as well as the tribal speech of gender overlaid with the tribal speech of deafness, disability, "normalcy," and difference.

I am suggesting at the outset of this initial mapmaking—for no one has yet studied deaf women's writing, and this project too is preliminary—that there is typically more than one "tribe" for deaf women to master, more than one path and personality to emerge into and from, more than one symbolic environment for them to enter and exist in. Each one of the seemingly simple single-syllable words in my title stands potent with figurative possibilities for these authors (and their audiences):

- Deaf. At the very least, we (and she) will no doubt seek an understanding about who is (and is not) deaf, how she can be deaf, why she is deaf, and in what ways she can enact, experience, construct, and perform "deaf."
- She. We (and again, she) will likely work to understand her experience as opposed to, and yet always in relation to, *he*; we will also want to consider the she who is one (individual, unique) as well as the she who might be many (common, representative).

- Wrote. We will ask her (and ourselves) just as she will ask herself (and us): Why did she write? How did she write? What literate practices and processes are available to her—and then used by her? (What remains unavailable and unused?) What writing will (most likely) be read—and how will it be read? Should she (and how can she then?) "write" in sign? Or, should she write in print English (or another dominant discourse)? And too, what happens in the path and process from *writing* to *wrote*—from doing to having done?

In approaching the literate construction of identity in deaf women's autobiography with these three terms marking some of my boundaries, there are also some angles I will not use. My exploration of deaf women's autobiography is not, for example, a comparison/contrast with non-deaf (i.e., hearing) women's autobiography, nor is it a comparison/contrast with non-women's (i.e, men's) deaf autobiography.

I could not care less, really, about how it "stacks up" against those others. I have been compared and contrasted, stacked up and down enough by audiologists, speech pathologists, and school counselors in my earlier years, with regards to what, comparatively, I could/should/would *not* be able to do, to know the straightjacket of that kind of analysis. Typically, they make a chart—and then you go somewhere on the grid. I am more interested in the constructed knowing and rhetorical acts that arise from the thing itself. Let her write, I say. Then we will read and follow from what, deaf, she wrote.

## WRITING: THEORY TIME

I find feminist critical studies of women's autobiography to be quite rhetorical; before I come to the three autobiographies I will center the rest of my discussion on, I will illustrate some of that overlap between these two discourses since that shaded area is primarily where I will locate my own map of deaf women's autobiography. At the dawn of contemporary feminist theory—time when Belenky and her coauthors published *Women's Ways of Knowing* in 1986—and I was, coincidentally, just starting graduate school after having given up five very exhausting years of teaching high school English and stirring nacho cheese in the basketball games' concession stand along with abandoning a deeply boring marriage to my old high school sweetheart—they framed the female intellectual as a "constructed knower." It is within this frame that I would like to begin mapping deaf women's autobiographical acts—as acts and arts of constructing knowledge for, in, around, and out of their own experiences while also attending to (her) audience.

The autobiographer as a "constructed knower" is not necessarily a new or novel idea. But it *is* a rhetorical idea in the way that it foregrounds the construction of a persuasive exchange between a speaker/writer/performer and her audience over the subject of "a life." And the kind of persuasive exchange that might be conveyed in deaf women's autobiography can best be attended to by at least starting with, if not exactly following, what Leigh Gilmore (1994) terms as "autobiographics—a feminist theory of women's self-representation." Autobiographics, Gilmore explains,

> Mark a location in a text where self-invention, self-discovery, and self-representation emerge within the technologies of autobiography—namely those legalistic, literary, social and ecclesiastical discourses of truth and identity through which the subject of autobiography is produced . . . [It] is concerned with interruptions and eruptions, with resistance and contradiction as strategies of self-representation . . . an emphasis on writing itself as constitutive of autobiographical identity . . . and the effects of the gendered connection of word and body. (42)

Each one of these four elements of autobiographics could be used as a rhetorical location for mapping deaf women's autobiography (and I will employ them so in a moment). Just as helpful to me are the rhetorical handles that Susanna Egan offers in her book *Mirror Talk: Genres of Crisis in Contemporary Autobiography* when she theorizes that much contemporary autobiography is about how:

> Making one's self visible or mapping identity are not only figures of speech but also tropes for recovery of understanding, which is always elusive. Because these genres [self-visibility and identity mapping] foreground the plurality and process of identity and of autobiography, they are also transformative; neither the person nor the text can reveal any single or final truth, but both can provide activities of interpretation, in which the reader is compelled to join. . . . We become part of the map of interpretation. (226).

Here in what Egan calls the "mirror talk" of "crisis" autobiography, we enter into the rhetorical triangle—the contract and construction that occur in the space at the center of speaker/writer/performer, audience, and subject. In ourselves (as readers), becoming part of the map of the autobiographer's interpretation of her life, in being compelled to join in the transformative possibilities of both plurality and individuality in her experience, we enact a rhetorical exchange.

## TELLING TEXTS

Let us read then how a twenty-two-year-old French award-winning actress, Emmanuelle Laborit, builds this rhetorical triangle. In her 1998 memoir, *Cry of the Gull*, published by Gallaudet University Press, Laborit explains her reasons for *writing* her life story so far (she is only twenty-two at this time). Deaf, she wrote:

> I need other people, dialog, a community. I couldn't live without the hearing and I couldn't live without the deaf, either. Communicating is a passion of mine. . . .
>
> A while back, when I began the difficult task of writing this book, it made me tremble with apprehension. But I wanted to do it because writing is important to me. It's a form of communication that I hadn't attempted with any degree of seriousness yet.
>
> Hearing people write books about the deaf. . . . I don't know of any books written by deaf people in France, or Europe for that matter. Some people told me I wouldn't be able to do it. But I wanted to make it happen with all my heart, as much to speak to myself as to deaf and hearing people. I wanted to give the most candid account possible of my life so far.
>
> I especially wanted to do it in your native language. The language of my parents. My adopted language.
>
> The seagull has grown up and flies with her own wings.
> I see just as I might hear.
> My eyes are my ears.
> I can write as well as sign.
> My hands speak two languages.
> I offer my difference to you.
> My heart is deaf to nothing in this double world.
> It's very hard for me to leave you. (146–147)

Of course, in writing her memoir—in your/our language, not in her own, and further, in writing it at the unconventional autobiographical age of twenty-two, Emmanuelle has done anything but leave us. She has

**FIGURE 1** Cover illustration of *The Cry of the Gull*.

etched herself pretty strongly in my own memory at least. Employing "apprehension" over using "your native language" and "the language of my parents" (written French)—a language that is shot through with the contradictions that it is not her own, but rather her "adopted language"—Laborit manages to emerge, as Gilmore (1994) theorizes, "within the technologies of autobiography" (using printed words in both prose and poetry forms) and to make "writing itself as constitutive" of her identity: "because writing is important to me" and "I can write as well as sign," she assures us. She dwells (and writes) in resistance—"some people told me I wouldn't be able to do it"—and also in contradictions—"My hands speak two languages./ I offer my difference to you" (147).

Laborit also connects "word to body," as Gilmore claims is common for autobiographics, when she ends (and also begins) her book by recounting the name given to her as a young deaf child whose shrill cries startled everyone. In her second chapter, she writes, "They called me their little seagull. But the French words for 'seagull' and 'mute' look and sound practically the same: *mouette/muette*. So which was I?" (5). And she returns to that self-invented word/body representation of herself in her closing lines: "The seagull has grown up and flies with her own wings" (147). With embodied words, she also writes, "My hands speak two languages" and "my eyes are my ears."

In the "mirror talk" function of identity crisis that is expressed in much contemporary autobiography (Egan 1999), Laborit makes herself most visible when she steps forward, almost right off the page, to sign/write a poem for us in the end. Just at the point of her almost-absence, she makes herself powerfully present: "It's very hard for me to leave you" (Laborit, 147). Appropriately enough, the cover image for the book (see Figure 1), also positions Laborit looking into/through a window frame, positioned so that we, the readers, see only her profile—while her own reflection is mirrored back to us as a full face. In a frame that also invites us to look in on her experience (and self-invention) in several different ways, Laborit also "foregrounds the plurality and process of identity" in this closing passage (and elsewhere throughout the memoir) and "provide[s] activities of interpretation, in which the reader is compelled to join" (Egan, 226). "I need other people, dialog, a community," Laborit writes with rhetorical sensitivity, as she compels both deaf and hearing readers to join her in her own "recovery of understanding" (Egan, 226): "I couldn't live without the hearing and I couldn't live without the deaf, either . . . as much to speak to myself as to deaf and hearing people" (Laborit, 146). Uncannily, it is almost as if Laborit is in dialogue (trialogue?) with Egan and Gilmore, autobiographical critics on the other side of the Atlantic Ocean who are writing about feminist theories of self-representation almost at the same time that Laborit herself is writing within them.

She has also uncannily enough answered the direct charge of another French writer eighteen years before her time. Emmanuelle Laborit would have been four at the time that Helene Cixous wrote her feminist text, *The Laugh of the Medusa*, and spurred us with:

> And why don't you write? Write! Writing is for you, you are for you; your body is yours, take it. I know why you haven't written. . . . Because writing is at once too high, too great for you, it's reserved for the great—that is, for "great men"; and it's "silly." Besides, you've written a little, but in secret. And it wasn't good, because it was in secret, and because you punished yourself for writing, because you didn't go all the way; or because you wrote, irresistibly, as when you would masturbate in secret, not to go further, but to attenuate the tension a bit, just enough to take the edge off. And then as soon as we come, we go and make ourselves feel guilty. (1525)

Even in the way the young author, Laborit, must explain, rationalize, justify, prove, and reprove herself for writing what she has just capably written for 146 pages, "trembl[ing] with apprehension," you can almost hear the whisper of Cixous in Laborit's ears. *We go and make ourselves feel guilty . . . and why don't you write?*

This guilty whisper is also heard in another "cry of the gull" kind of text that I take as my pivot point for a rhetorical mapping of deaf women's autobiography. Teresa de Cartagena was a Castilian conversa nun who wrote a remarkable "consolatory treatise" (as it has been figured) around the year 1452. In this text, *Groves of the Infirm*, Teresa sought to console herself over her deafness. She was also seeking, I am convinced, to use her deafness to "cloak" her gender—to call attention to her disability in order to be able to "pass" as an author at a time when no woman of the church could author-ize. She is writing, as Cixous suggests women often do, in secret. This is important. Not her deafness so much (although it is clearly the consolatory impetus) but the act of authorizing herself through and with her deafness. Teresa's text stands near many other candidates for "first autobiography"—Margery Kempe and Julian of Norwich chief among them. Even the critical introduction claims that "its theme is the spiritual benefits of illness, and Teresa's own deafness serves as autobiographical exemplum" and further that it "is the only extant *consolatio* written from a woman's position" (1–2).

**FIGURE 2** Cover illustration of *The Writings of Teresa de Cartagena.*

In the words of contemporary autobiography scholars Sidonie Smith and Julia Watson, Teresa was "getting a life" (1996); in becoming an author, Teresa was setting herself (and us then too) down in her "groves of the infirm." In the words of Susanna Egan, Teresa was "making [herself] visible" as she sought consolation, a "recovery of understanding, which is always elusive" and provided us (and herself) with "activities of interpretation, in which the reader is compelled to join"—interpretation aimed mostly at finding her fit with God in a hearing world and a men's world (226). In authoring her (deaf) consolation, Teresa also engaged in self-invention that, as Gilmore claims, "emerge[d] within the technologies of autobiography—namely those legalistic, literary, social and ecclesiastical discourses of truth and identity through which the subject of autobiography is produced" (42). Bound by legal, literary, social, and ecclesiastical discourses that dictate her inability to author, or to "hear" the word of God, or to interpret text, Teresa's text is a triumph of resistance and contradiction, a tale of interruption and eruption. Within her *Groves of the Infirm*, Teresa stands quite firm as "writing itself [becomes] constitutive of [her] autobiographical identity" (Gilmore; my brackets, 42).

Ironically, however, even while she was carving out a firm disability identity in this text, she was also trying to downplay her gendered identity. In this fifty-page treatise and the one that followed it, *Wonder at the Works of God* (another text she wrote as a defense two to three years later, apparently in answer to the detractors and doubters who read *Groves of the Infirm* and either scorned her as an author or did not even believe that she did, or could, author such a text), we read Teresa de Cartegena doing what both Leigh Gilmore and Susannah Egan explain in scholarship on contemporary autobiography. For example, Teresa engages in self-invention through the "technology" of ecclesiastical discourses of truth and identity, and she also composes herself (twice over) with and through interruptions and eruptions as her first text is received with what she calls "malicious wonder" (see below). Teresa must also use resistance and contradiction as strategies of self-representation when she negotiates what she knows is an audience that doubts her ability to author in the first place (and here she is more "infirm" in her gender than she is in her deafness). Part of the original intent (the rhetorical thrust) of *Groves of the Infirm* emphasizes writing itself as constitutive of her autobiographical identity (see below) as she explores the connection of word and body when she writes, for example, that "since my suffering is of such a treacherous nature that it prevents me from hearing good as well as bad counsel. . . . I must recur to my books, which have wonderful graftings from healthful groves" (23–24).

Through these texts, of course, Teresa makes herself visible—so much so that she had to write again and come out of her *Groves of the Infirm* in order to address her critics with *Wonder at the Works of God*. In both treatises, she reaches for recovery and understanding, not only of her place in a hearing world (from within "a convent of the suffering") but also within ecclesiastical discourses at large, as she claims, for example, that "language by itself is only valuable in two ways: one is to praise and bless God, the other is to preach to the people, for these two things one can do without any reply" (27). Through her recovery of understanding, she foregrounds her plurality as well as her process of self-identity as she writes her treatise in part to "the sick with whom I have signed a pledge of sisterhood" (45): "If by glorying in our sufferings we can bring to our soul such a good guest as the virtue of Christ, no invalid should be sad. . . . We who have been professed in the convent of afflictions should rejoice" (42).

But "autobiographics" is also about the mirror talk that Egan claims connects us to others; autobiography is as much about audience as it is about self. In this way, in *Wonder at the Works of God*, Teresa compels us to join her in her own map of interpretation, especially as she cleverly defends her first text (*Groves of the Infirm*) from the "malicious wonder" over her authorship:

> People marvel at what I wrote in the treatise and I marvel at what, in fact, I kept quiet, but I do not marvel doubting nor do I insist on my wonder. For my experience makes me sure, and God of truth knows that I had no other master nor consulted with any other learned authority nor translated from other books, as some people with malicious wonder are wont to say. . . . (1023)

And oh yes, Teresa is feeling guilty about writing it all down too. Deaf, she wrote:

> [F]or according to the nature of my suffering, if you look closely, you will see me more alone in the company of many than when I retreat to my cell all by myself.
> This is the reason why: when I am alone, I am accompanied by myself and by this poor sense I have, but when I find myself in the company of others, I am completely forsaken, for I cannot profit from the joy of companionship nor from the speech of those around me nor from myself. . . . And where hearing fails, what good is

speech? One is left dead and completely isolated. Thus, for these reasons, and because my experience lends them credence, you can well believe how very lonely I am; and since I cannot rid myself of this unsparing and lasting loneliness, I want to combat my idleness by busying myself with this little treatise, which one might well say is neither good nor even ordinary, but rather completely bad. (25)

Here you can almost imagine Teresa as a modern-day scholar: "It's only a draft . . . I know it's not very good." The problem seems to have been, however, that it was very good. And her readers were not fooled by the ruse of her deafness as a mask for her *real* disability at the time—her gender. Much like Helen Keller was accused of plagiarism at age eleven, there was apparently some "wondering" about Teresa's own "wonder" and her ability to write such a text. So, she had to go back and defend her authorship—and do so as a woman this time—in *Wonder at the Works of God*. She hardly mentions her deafness in the second text except—and this is important—to continue to cite it as the source of her seeking consolation in the first place and turning, as it were, to the wonder in the works of God.

"Autobiography," writes Leigh Gilmore, "provokes fantasies of the real" (16). Teresa's own wonder, her coming to the groves of the infirm and finding consolation there, as well as the wonder with which her audience receives her "little treatise," proves the provocative and real fantasy of writing (as) *deaf*, writing (as) *she*. Moreover, both author-wonder and audience-wonder in Teresa's case are paradoxically wondrous. First, they are constructively wondrous, since they draw her toward what Egan calls "mirror talk," bringing her into being as Belenky's "constructed knower"—making meaning, mapping identity, becoming visible, recovering understanding of herself in the world. Yet the wonder is also, as Teresa herself calls it, "malicious" for "although it is said that their wonder is flattering, to me it seems offensive and clear that they offer me scathing insults and not empty praise . . . This can ruin the substance of my writing and undermines greatly the benefit and grace that God wrought for me" (88).

In this passage, as she encounters the inherent oppression in her reader's "wonder," Teresa is beginning to understand the power—and paradox—of writing. Plato himself worried a great deal about this power and paradox. As Jacques Derrida describes the Platonic distrust of writing in *Signature Event Context*: "A written sign is proffered in the absence of the receiver. How to style this absence?" (1478).

How to style the absence of an audience for a deaf woman autobiographer? This is a problem with which Teresa was most certainly grappling. And as she pondered this in 1452, perhaps we can authorize an understanding of that absence by simply chalking it up to "the times." But 550 years later, another deaf woman autobiographer is—or rather was—still wrestling with much the same problem as she writes what I would also call a "consolatory treatise." Anne Bolander's "as-told-to" autobiography, *I Was Number 87*, was published by Gallaudet University Press in 2000. (And Bolander's authoring this book through the hand of another, Adair Renning, is surely an interruption and eruption worth noting.) *I Was Number 87* is a story, as the subtitle declares, of "a deaf woman's ordeal of misdiagnosis, institutionalization, and abuse" multiple times over. It begins with her early placement into a startlingly abusive institution for determined mental retardation (she is, in fact, deaf)—the Stoutamyre "School of Special Education."

Cixous was apparently buzzing in Bolander's ear as well: *why don't you write?* Near the end of the book, Bolander (as written through/with Adair Renning) confesses from her own groves of the infirm:

> As I began to share the story of my life with the doctors, I also started to reconstruct the journal I had kept in high school, which Linda had destroyed. The doctors provided me with loose-leaf paper and a ballpoint pen, and I began by writing my earliest memories. The medications I was taking helped to keep me calm during the writing but I often had flashbacks at night. Now, instead of banging my head against the wall, I wrote. I wrote about Margie, Warren, Pat, St. Mary's, Ruth, Glenn, and Anna. I wrote about my mother—how angry I was that she had left me with no mother, that it was her fault that nobody taught me all the things that she was supposed to have taught me as a child. And as I filled the pages, I could see the book that I had used to threaten Nora Stoutamyre. . . .
>
> Later I wrote a letter to each of my brothers telling them that our father had raped me. I put each letter in an envelope, and addressed and stamped them. Then I put them in my safe deposit box, waiting for the right time. I told myself that the next time I got mad at my father I'd mail them. But I could never bring myself to do it; something inside me told me to let go of those feelings. Eventually I cleaned the box out and threw the letters away. (168, 171)

Yet in telling the untold, in rewriting, as it were, the absent letters, Bolander's book has now also been cleaned out and thrown away. Anne Bolander's book is currently absent; thus, styling the absence of the receiver is an even bigger problem here. This text, erupted, has now been interrupted: *I Was Number 87* has been pulled from print because of questions and allegations regarding the "truth" of some of Bolander's experiences, particularly her claim of being raped by her father. Her brothers, who had money and lawyers, demanded that. (This act of deliberately styled absence—of censure even—is perhaps even more remarkable when placed against the enormous popularity and considerable critical attention to Lauren Slater's "metaphorical memoir," *Lying*, published just as Bolander's text perished.)

I do not know all of the story surrounding Anne Bolander's autobiographical appearance and then disappearance—so I will not even pretend to tell it here. But I do know that indeed, it seems that "autobiographies [can] provoke fantasies of the real" (16). For regardless of whether her accused father can tell the truth (which is, I might emphasize, only *his* truth) through the sons seeking to protect his name, and regardless of whether Anne's story is "true"—and there are some troubling confessions she also makes in her book about her own tendencies to seek attention in various ways—the censorship and styled absence of her text is very real at this point. Five hundred and fifty years earlier, Teresa at least had a chance to answer her detractors, to come at the story another way, to counter wonder for wonder. Teresa's absent receiver becomes actually quite present for her, so she rises to the rhetorical occasion and writes again. Perhaps Anne Bolander will rise and write again too—this time in a book titled with a name, not a number. I, for one, will be present to receive that.

For in attending to deaf women's autobiography rhetorically, the audience matters. If deaf, she wrote . . . who then (and how then) will read? Who will answer back? And how? Will they censor, or assure, her textual performance? When she offers her difference, what will come back? In order to understand, read, receive, and critically map deaf women's autobiography, we will need as well to understand her audiences—those she imagined and aimed to write for, those who read it anyway, and those who wondered, in both affirming and malicious ways, at her ability to master the tribal speech and "get a life" in the literate act of autobiography.

**LITERATURE CITED**

Belenky, M. F. et al. 1986. *Women's ways of knowing: The development of self, voice, and mind.* New York: Basic Books.

Bolander, A. and A. N. Renning. 2000. *I was number 87: A deaf woman's ordeal of misdiagnosis, institutionalization, and abuse.* Washington, D.C.: Gallaudet University Press.

Brueggemann, B. J. 1999. *Lend me your ear: Rhetorical constructions of deafness.* Washington, D.C.: Gallaudet University Press.

Burke, K. 2001. From language as symbolic action. In *The rhetorical tradition: Readings from classical times to the present*, eds. P. Bizzell and B. Herzberg, 1340–1347. Boston: Bedford/St. Martin's.

Cixous, H. 2001. The laugh of the Medusa. In *The rhetorical tradition: Readings from classical times to the present*, eds. P. Bizzell and B. Herzberg, 1524–1536. Boston: Bedford/St. Martin's.

de Cartagena, T. 1998. *The writings of Teresa de Cartagena.* Trans. D. Seidenspinner-Núñez. Cambridge: D. S. Brewer.

Derrida, J. 2001. Signature event context. In *The rhetorical tradition; Readings from classical times to the present*, eds. P. Bizzell and B. Herzberg, 1475–1490. Boston: Bedford/St. Martin's.

Egan, S. 1999. *Mirror talk: Genres of crisis in contemporary autobiography.* Chapel Hill: University of North Carolina Press.

Gilmore, L. 1994. *Autobiographics: A feminist theory of women's self-representation.* Ithaca: Cornell University Press.

Laborit, E. 1988. *The cry of the gull.* Trans. C. Mitchell and P. R. Côté. Washington, D.C.: Gallaudet University Press.

Slater, L. 2001. *Lying: A metaphorical memoir.* New York: Penguin Books.

Smith, S., and J. Watson, eds. 1996. *Getting a life: Everyday uses of autobiography.* Minneapolis: University of Minnesota Press.

# PART II

# MULTICULTURAL AND BILINGUAL PERSPECTIVES

# The Relationship between Language Experience and Language Development: A Report from Norway

*Elizabeth Engen and Trygg Engen*

This study is part of a larger project titled "Bilingualism and Literacy in Deaf Children," which was developed to gather data on the linguistic status of deaf children in Norway in 1997. Norway has a long history of "education for all" as a basic precept. The Ministry of Education, Research and Church Affairs established, by law, the right of all citizens to be educated in their first language, including the Sami, Norway's indigenous population; the Kvens, Finnish-speaking Norwegians; other language minorities, and students with special needs. Students in regular education can decide which of the two forms of the Norwegian language they will use, both orally and in print. The ministry published a report in 2001 stating that pupils who have sign language as their first language have the right to use and be educated through the medium of sign language in primary and lower secondary schools.

Education for deaf children in Norway began with a school for the deaf in Trondheim in 1825. The main qualification required of teachers was knowledge of sign language. In 1848 a private school was founded in Oslo that introduced the oral method in the country. An article in 1875 by Sigvald Skavlan, principal of the school in Trondheim, opposed oralism, stating that sign language had a grammatical structure that was fully capable of expressing complex and intimate thoughts and ideas. In 1881 a law was passed that stipulated that the schools for the deaf were to use only one known method, either oral or manual, but not a mixture of methods. Although oralism gradually became the method used by all schools, by the 1970s Total Communication had come into favor, and most teachers used a combination of both sign and speech (Arnesen 1999).

As a result of a national reorganization of special education programs in Norway in 1992, a new curriculum for deaf children was instituted in 1997. This curriculum stated that Norwegian Sign Language (NSL) would be considered the first language and the language of instruction for deaf children and that Norwegian would be developed as a second language through print forms, with the ultimate goal of bilingualism and literacy.

A program was also developed for the parents and siblings of deaf children that provides forty weeks of education in NSL spread over their child's first sixteen years. This program is fully funded, including funding for transportation to centers where the courses are held and housing for family members who also receive their normal salary while attending the courses.

"Bilingualism and Literacy in Deaf Children" was developed, in part, to study questions raised by the new curriculum. Two hundred and thirteen children with moderate to profound hearing loss from the entire country were identified, representing 50 percent of that population. These students ranged in age from eight to fifteen, with 80 percent placed in schools for the deaf and 20 percent in mainstreamed settings. A detailed questionnaire using a variety of item types, including rating scales, was designed to collect a wide range of background data on the students, including their linguistic experience. Among other topics, parents and teachers were asked to describe various aspects of the child's language competence and usage by using a list that classified the possibilities by language and mode, including various forms of code mixing. Complete data were collected from 182 parents. All data were obtained from parents and teachers by trained interviewers from Norsk (Norwegian) Gallup.

The focus of this chapter is the effect of *consistency* of the students' linguistic experience at home and in school on the development of language and literacy as reported by their mothers and teachers. It is based on data from a subset of sixty-eight students who were given language and literacy tests and the questionnaire data from their mothers and teachers. The students were from the fourth, eighth, and tenth grade classes and approximately of ages nine, twelve, and fifteen.

One of the essential and unresolved questions in deaf education today is how to provide an environment in which children with hearing loss can experience and develop both the natural sign language of the deaf community and the majority language of the hearing community, that is, to become bilingual. This question involves some basic aspects of the necessary conditions for language acquisition. There has been extensive research on this topic, and agreement now exists on at least three prerequisites:

1. **Access to language.** Language experience plays an essential role in language development (i.e., what is experienced is what will be acquired).
2. **Interaction with speakers of the language.** Development of language requires active participation not simply passive observation.
3. **Access and participation at the right time.** Language acquisition must occur during the period in which language can be acquired naturally and without explicit instruction.

Research has shown that by four to five years of age, children who have access to language have acquired the basic core grammatical structures (Bloom 1991; Pinker 1994; Radford 1997). It is also known that delayed acquisition of a first language has serious consequences (Snow 1987; Mayberry 1993; Newport 1990; Johnson and Newport 1991) and that both the quantity and quality of early linguistic experiences are vital to language development. Correlations between language experience and language development provide important clinical data and address theoretical issues regarding the nature of language acquisition.

There are, of course, unique factors involved in the interaction of children with hearing loss and their hearing parents. A number of studies have noted the special problems that occur when there is a mismatch between the hearing status of parent and child, resulting in diminished parental interaction in the early years. In the past, however, many studies of both hearing and hearing impaired children have focused either on language development or language experience, thereby leaving the question of the relationship unanswered (Hoff-Ginsberg 1998). Spencer (1993) concluded that studies that purport to assess the effectiveness of communication should begin by documenting the extent to which children are actually exposed to language.

That was the aim of the present study; *that is, to obtain data on the use of language at home and at school, in relation to the resulting language abilities of the students.* It differs in many respects from similar studies in the United States. Items from the questionnaire that addressed mothers' and teachers' responses to questions about the children's language competence and usage were used to assess the similarities and differences in the information elicited from them. Rating scales were developed to reflect the relative consistency of experience for each student, and the results were then correlated with the literacy assessment data.

There were two main parts to the question of experience. Part A concerned the language milieu; that is, the language competence and language usage as judged by mothers and teachers. Two types of measures were used: (1) a list of possible linguistic categories and (2) rating-point scales of various abilities to be used by the respondents. The obtained data resulted in a characterization of each child's language milieu in both home and school based on these judgments. An important aspect of the study was to examine the results in terms of the agreement between the judgments of mothers and teachers regarding language competence and language use with a particular child. *Note that parents and teachers were interviewed independently and were not informed about each others' responses. All interviews were with a single teacher, at school, while parents were interviewed together in the home.*

Part B concerned the relationship between these judgments and measures of literacy as assessed by various tests of reading comprehension and decoding ability (matching words and pictures), plus a test of comprehension of syntactic structure.

## PART A. THE LANGUAGE MILIEU

We first present *group* results from the responses of mothers and teachers overall, and secondly *individual* results, that is, the judgments (ratings) made by each mother and teacher on competence and use with their particular child at home and in school. Table 1 presents the linguistic categories used for these judgments.

### Group Results

*Students' language competence.* We first tallied the responses from mothers and teachers regarding their judgments of language competence. Mothers and teachers, interviewed separately, were presented with the list of language categories and asked to select one of them in response to the question "Which language does the child/student command best"?

## TABLE 1
### List of Language Categories

*Sign Without Speech*

1. Norwegian sign language (NSL), the natural language of the deaf community
2. Norwegian-influenced NSL (sign without speech, but not completely adhering to the grammar of NSL)
3. Signed Norwegian without voice (sign without speech, but adhering to the grammar of Norwegian)

*Speech Without Sign*

4. Norwegian (the oral language of the hearing community)
5. NSL-influenced speech (speech without sign, but not completely adhering to the grammar of Norwegian)

*Both Sign and Speech*

6. Sign with speech support
7. Simultaneous speech and sign (signs partly following the grammar of NSL, speech partly following the grammar of Norwegian)
8. Signed Norwegian with voice (simultaneous sign and speech, both signs and speech following Norwegian grammar)
9. Speech with sign support
10. Another language, which?
11. Gestural communication
12. Don't know

From the results, we noted whether the mothers and teachers, using the list of language categories, made the same choices for their judgments of each student's "best language." Mothers' responses were mainly spoken Norwegian (no. 4) and NSL (no. 1), over 40 percent for each. Teachers also selected spoken Norwegian and NSL, but chose nearly 50 percent for Norwegian, only 33 percent for NSL, and a bit more than 10 percent for categories from the language list that involve mixing languages and modes (nos. 6, 7, and 9). Their responses differed in these proportions and in that teachers were more likely to choose Norwegian plus code mixing as one of their choices. In general, there was a tendency to base judgment of the students' language competence on language rather than mode, that is, selecting categories 1 and 4 from table 1.

*Language Use.* Results were tallied using the following questions—for mothers: "Which language is used most in communication with the child?"—and for teachers: "Which language do you usually use when you are teaching the whole class?" The responses to these questions were more varied. There were no outstanding categories, such as in the previous question regarding language competence.

For language use, the problem of code mixing is evident. Most of the mothers (37 percent) stated that they used mainly oral Norwegian, 21 percent chose NSL, and others responded with categories of code mixing (nos. 6, 7, and 9 from table 1). However, teachers said they used a wider variety of forms involving NSL and Norwegian-influenced sign language as well as oral Norwegian, all of them from 20 to more than 25 percent, the highest being "speech with sign support" (no. 9).

In general, there were differences regarding the judgments about the students' best language and the languages actually used by both mother and teacher. Variability in the languages used at home and at school is apparently an inherent problem, as is code mixing. This is considered further below. We next address the related problem of how mothers and teachers rated their own ability in Norwegian sign language.

*Self-Rating of NSL Ability by Mothers and Teachers.* Norwegian was the primary language of both mothers and teachers, but it is important to know how they judged their ability in NSL. For this, they were asked to use a ten-point rating scale. The question to both groups was: "To what degree do you think that you command Norwegian sign language all in all? Choose a number on a scale from 0 to 9 where 0 represents 'does not command' and 9 represents 'commands very well.'"

The average ratings (means) are very similar and relatively low for both mothers and teachers: 4.4 and 4.5, respectively. In other words, both teachers and mothers rated themselves in the middle of the scale. However, the individual differences in ratings are large (as indicated by standard deviations of 2.4 and 2.5). Clearly, neither group tended to estimate their abilities very highly. In general, these results document another important, though expected, source of variability in the children's language milieu, namely the nature of their experience with NSL at home and in school. The same question was asked regarding their ability in speech with sign support (no.6), and both rated themselves significantly higher, nearly two steps higher on this than on NSL. The average ratings by teachers and parents are the same.

To summarize, the group results show a difference in the judgment of competence and language use. For judgment of competence, both mothers and teachers tended to base their judgment on language (Norwegian or NSL) rather than mode. The judgment of language use, however, includes categories that mix speech and sign in varying degrees (e.g., categories 5, 6, 7, and 9). The higher rating for speech with sign support implies a consistent use of Norwegian, but an incomplete and possibly random use of sign. Since this study was conducted at the beginning of the NSL courses for parents, it was expected that in the future, parents will be more consistent in their use of sign and improve their understanding of the difference between "sign" and NSL.

**Individual Results**

The group results described above show group differences. The next step examined *student-centered results*, that is, what a mother and teacher reported independently about both competence and use with their common subject, that is, their child or student. The purpose was to describe his or her language experience and how consistent it was from one situation to another. Finally, agreement in these judgments by mothers and teachers was analyzed across the categories. The question was: Did they concur regarding both the individual student's best language and the language used with that student at home and in school? The most consistent linguistic milieu would be one in which the mother and teacher made the same judgment regarding a student's best language and both actually used that language with the student.

A total of twelve items from the questionnaire (translated from Norwegian), six from each informant, were used to rate concurrence for the fifty-seven students for whom there were judgments from both mother and teacher.

**Questions Regarding Language Competence**

"If a first language is the language a person used first in life, what is the child's first language?"

"If primary language is the language a person uses most in the course of a week, what is the child's primary language? The question applies regardless of whether the child is at school or at home."

"What is your impression regarding which language the child commands best?"

**Questions Regarding Language Use**

"Which language is used most in communication with the child?"

"Which language is used most in the family (or in the class)?"

"Which language is most effective, contributes most to mutual understanding?"

In analyzing these ratings, the judgments from the language list (table 1) were reorganized into three categories based on language (Norwegian and NSL), mode (speech and sign), and mixtures of language and mode, as shown in table 2. The purpose was to focus more specifically on *languages per se*.

### The Concurrence Rating Scale

A rating scale was developed by which the authors compared the concurrence between mothers' and teachers' judgments regarding both primary versus best language and language versus code mixing. It was a nine-point rating scale where 0 meant totally disparate judgments, the middle of the scale represented judgments based on best and/or primary languages, and 9 meant that teacher and mother agreed, both on the child's best language and the language actually used with the child.

*Results.* The fact that the respondents, both parents and teachers, used most of the categories from the language list is positive, revealing that the categories were meaningful and relevant. However, the ratings show striking differences regarding judgments of language competence and the languages used at school and at home. The correlations between them are low (Pearson product moment r of 0.27) which indicates that the language used with a child does not match very well with what he or she knows best. These judgments of competence and use are similar to the

**TABLE 2**
**Language Categories Organized by Language, Mode, and Mixtures of Language and Mode**

*Category 1. The two languages as used in their natural mode*

a. NSL, Norwegian sign language, (visual/manual mode)
b. Norwegian-influenced NSL (visual/manual mode, but not completely adhering to the grammar of NSL)
c. Norwegian (oral mode)

*Category 2. The various ways in which Norwegian can be combined with signs*

d. Oral Norwegian with sign on some words
e. Signed Norwegian with voice
f. Signed Norwegian without voice

*Category 3. Code mixing in which languages and/or modes may be mixed*

g. Sign language-influenced speech
h. Sign with speech support
i. Simultaneous speech and sign, speech following rules for Norwegian and sign following rules for NSL

group results above and raise the question of how this inconsistent linguistic milieu may affect their potential for both language and learning.

To appreciate these results, it is important to note that there were considerable differences in the results obtained for *use* of the two languages, Norwegian and NSL. The finding to be emphasized here is the difference in the number of students who were judged to have a compatible milieu (complete agreement in the judgments regarding both competence and use). For NSL, there were only *five* students in this category, and the inevitable conclusion in this case is that even when there is agreement on competence in NSL, it does not necessarily result in the student having the advantage of the use of that language.

The results for Norwegian are noticeably different in that concurrence on language use is even larger than concurrence on competence, with a much higher number of concurring judgments (*more than nineteen*) for both categories. Clearly these students had a linguistic advantage of a compatible milieu at home and in school.

For a third group, for whom teachers and mothers made disparate judgments regarding language competence and use, the lack of concurrence tends to involve combinations of NSL, various forms of Norwegian (different modes), and very frequently, code mixing. The concern here is that not only did the judgments of mother and teacher not concur, but also that the possibility of such code mixing results in the student not experiencing a clear model of either Norwegian or NSL. This lack of consistent experience with language may have serious consequences for development of both language and literacy.

**Discussion**

It is important to understand a child's access to and experience with language as a basis for interpreting information about development. Although some previous studies have attempted to gather this type of data, the questionnaire data from the present study provided a detailed source of information with which to pursue these questions. The results seem to be a valid reflection of the variability in the students' experiences with communication, that is, that the language used with many students is not necessarily the one in which he or she is judged to be most competent, and the results of code mixing indicate that many students do not experience a clear linguistic model.

Another important observation is that the results showed a tendency to describe students' *competence* in terms of language rather than mode, while for language *use*, there were more judgments involving mode and coding mixing. The *unique milieu* of children with hearing loss, which involves language and mode in various combinations, may complicate the ability to judge language use in particular.

It should be noted that the specific effects of code mixing are unknown. It may be more serious for children with hearing loss than for hearing children in a bilingual situation (e.g., in learning to distinguish between languages). Because sign languages and the various systems for signing an oral language share a lexicon, but have different grammars, code mixing and unclear models may result.

## PART B. LITERACY ASSESSMENTS

The second aspect of the study pertains to the problem of developing a level of literacy that will prepare children with hearing loss to become independent adults who can function successfully in two cultures, that is, to be bicultural. In the present study, this question involves the relationship between the consistency of the judgments by mother and teacher and the results from literacy assessments. These assessments included a test of comprehension of syntactic structure, reading comprehension (decoding and text), and an elicited written narrative.

### Results

*The syntax test* is a Norwegian version of the Rhode Island Test of Language Structure (Engen and Engen 1983), which assesses comprehension of syntactic structures in a picture verification task. In this study, the sentences (unlike the original version of the test) were presented in print and therefore involved the ability to read the test items. The results show a distinct ceiling effect, that is, generally high scores which would tend to diminish correlations with other measures. Of the fifty-one students who took the test, 53 percent made either no errors or less than ten, while 47 percent of the students made between ten and thirty-eight errors, which were focused on a small set of syntactic structures.

Some interesting comparisons can be made with results from several studies involving a large number of students with hearing loss acquiring American English: the standardization study (Engen and Engen 1983), a longitudinal study (Engen 1985), and a study of the relationship between language and literacy (Engen 1996). Even though the English and Norwegian tests differ in some respects and are administered differently (manually coded English versus Norwegian in print), the results are remarkably

The Relationship between Language Experience and Development  101

similar. In both cases, the syntactic processes found to be most difficult are those which:

1. violate word order (passives and clefts):
 "The boy is being washed by the man."
 "It is the cat that the dog is chasing."
2. interrupt a main clause (medial relative clauses):
 "The girl who is washing the boy is drinking soda."
3. delete a constituent (conjoined sentences with "gapping"):
 "The girl is kissing the man and loses the hat."

These structures have also been found to be late acquisitions by hearing children, although they usually are understood by those ages six or seven (Engen and Engen 1983). What is important is that students with hearing loss acquire understanding of these particular structures much later than hearing children. This prolonged period of language development, combined with the fact that such structures are very important to language in print and to text understanding, makes it essential to give special attention to these results.

The decoding (picture to word) and reading comprehension tests were developed for hearing children by the Center for Research on Reading in Stavanger, Norway. Each of the three classes was tested on the two subtests. In order to make the scores comparable for the three classes, involving resolving basic differences in the number of questions for each class, the scores for each class were converted to so-called T-scores with a mean of 50 and a standard deviation of 10. This is a common measure of individual differences on many national tests.

*Decoding.* For this test, the student was shown a picture of a pair of skis planted in the snow with a mountain sketched in the background with four (Norwegian) words—*sik, skip, si,* and *ski*—and asked to choose the word that matched the picture.

*Reading Comprehension.* The texts presented were examples of culturally appropriate narratives and expository texts, varying in difficulty over the three class levels. The students read the selection and responded to multiple choice questions about the content.

**Results from the Three Classes**

The reading scores used here were the sum of the correct answers on the various subtests with different stories (also converted to T-scores). There is a good range of scores; they tend to be high but show individual differences. Regarding the level of performance by the students, the results on reading are similar to those for decoding. Because decoding is an important predictor of reading, it is important to observe the correlation between these subtests. The Pearson product moment correlation coefficient ($r = 0.70$) clearly supports the value of testing for ability in decoding. The results from each of the three classes for decoding and reading text also show similarly high positive intercorrelation on the three tasks: syntax, decoding, and reading.

## RELATIONSHIPS BETWEEN LITERACY ASSESSMENTS AND LANGUAGE MILIEU

The following discussion describes the performance of the students grouped according to the concurrence versus disparity of their language experience and how that relates to performance on the literacy tests. Inspection of the results for individual students indicated that there was clear evidence of a relationship between these tests and the concurrence on judgment of competency by teacher and mother. The ratings of *competence* were used rather than those for *use* because the former were less variable and more constant and stable, as discussed above. The results are shown in table 3.

TABLE 3
Average Results on Literacy Tests for Three Language Groups

|  | Reading | Decoding | Syntax |
|---|---|---|---|
| Norwegian |  |  |  |
| N | 21 | 22 | 18 |
| Mean | 56 | 55 | 91 |
| SD | 6 | 6 | 3 |
| Norwegian Sign Language (NSL) |  |  |  |
| N | 14 | 13 | 16 |
| Mean | 48 | 46 | 82 |
| SD | 11 | 10 | 12 |
| Disparate |  |  |  |
| N | 15 | 15 | 14 |
| Mean | 47 | 47 | 86 |
| SD | 12 | 12 | 9 |

The students were thus divided into two groups, those judged to be competent in Norwegian and those in NSL. A third group consisted of those about whom the judgment of competence was disparate, that is, mother and teacher did not concur in their judgments. Table 3 shows the average (mean) performance of these three groups and individual differences on the three literacy tests. The differences in results for the three groups are not unexpected because the tests depend on knowledge of the Norwegian language.

However, what is important is that the table shows clearly that the performance of the disparate group and the NSL group are quite different from the Norwegian group. (Recall that the mean of these standard scores is 50, the standard deviation, 10.) The members of the Norwegian group scored above average, and the other two, NSL and disparate, below average. For coding and text, their scores are approximately one standard deviation below that for the Norwegian group. (A one-way ANOVA for the three groups also reveals a significant difference between them with $p = 0.002$).

It should also be noted that the individual differences between the students in the Norwegian group are much smaller (with a standard deviation nearly half of that for the other groups). In other words, it is also a more homogeneous group, presumably related to consistency of language experience in various situations, in contrast to the heterogeneous disparate group on the other end of this continuum. Such a difference in variance could affect the statistical evaluation, which is an important point with potential practical educational significance in dealing with individual students, a point referred to below.

*The writing task* involved eliciting narratives from the subjects after they viewed a videotape entitled *The Pear Story*, which was developed by Chafe (1982) and has been frequently used in many such studies. Written narratives were elicited from forty-five students in classes 8 and 10. (Students in class 4 were not given the task, as it was considered too difficult for them.) The results are considered separately here because the analysis of these samples was qualitative rather than quantitative, which makes comparing the results from the reading test less direct.

It has been shown repeatedly that particular syntactic structures serve special functions in written text and are essential to creating cohesive and coherent written discourse (Engen 1996). A well-organized and understandable text is dependent on the use of subordinated structures, such as relative and adverbial clauses, complement structures, and passives for creating extended written text. For this study, the narratives were analyzed for the use of these four structures.

## THE RESULTS OF THIS ANALYSIS

### Group 1

About half of the students (23 students or 51 percent) produced texts which contained examples of both relative and adverbial clauses and complements. However, there was a wide range in their ability to use these structures to create a cohesive text.

### Group 2

Thirteen (29 percent) of the students produced texts that were characterized by the use of syntactically simple and coordinated structures, with some run-on sentences unmarked by punctuation and therefore difficult to analyze.

### Group 3

The remainder (9 or 20 percent) of the texts was predominantly at a simple sentence level, with many incomplete sentences and random marking of sentence boundaries. Often there was not a clear sense of text, as the sentences were organized as a list.

It should be noted that although the task of creating a text in print is considerably more challenging than demonstrating text understanding in a multiple choice task, the results distinguished three groups of students not on only in terms of "writing" but also in their ability to use complex syntax to create text. The ratings of linguistic milieu showed that the students with a consistent Norwegian milieu (table 2) were also consistent in their ability to produce subordinated structures, whereas the other two groups (NSL and disparate) were more variable. The results therefore are similar to results from the literacy tests in terms of demonstrating the crucial link between language and literacy.

It is also important to consider the variability and individual differences in this group of students. As an example, two of the students competent in NSL were in Group 1 (those who used subordinated structures) and among the thirteen who produced exceptionally well-organized tests. These students also had high scores on the syntax and reading tests.

Conversely, two of the students in Group 3 (at a simple sentence level) had a consistent Norwegian milieu.

The purpose here was to attempt to describe the various languages and modes a child with hearing loss might encounter in school and home and to assess the effect of such experience on literacy. The results indicate clearly that language experience is a fundamental factor of critical importance to a child's literacy. The focus on the language milieu of the project makes a special contribution and also raises questions and hypotheses that must be pursued further experimentally with the variables assessed here.

There are, of course, other factors such as etiology, age of onset of hearing loss, and socioeconomic factors, which might affect literacy. The degree of hearing loss is perhaps the one universally considered crucial factor. The common categories used in Norway are, "deaf" (> 96-dB loss) and "severe hearing loss" (71- to 95-dB loss) and were of main interest in planning the project. It turned out, however, that 17 (8 percent) of the students included in the study had hearing losses of less than 71 dB.

Comparison of the two first groups (deaf and severe hearing loss) showed that they had very similar scores with nearly identical means and standard deviations on syntax, coding, and reading. Those students who were classified as hard of hearing had, on average, scores of about one standard deviation higher on all the tests.

In order to perform another quantitative analysis of the effect of hearing level, the students were compared on the basis of the traditional measure of hearing loss, the dB hearing threshold in the best ear, based on an average score of 500, 1,000, and 2,000 Hz. (See Powers [2003] for a related discussion of this measure.) For the present subjects, these scores range from 30 to 113 dB and form a smooth distribution without any gaps corresponding to the above categorizations of hearing loss. The scores tended to cluster at the high end, which reflect the initial aim to obtain students categorized as "deaf" and with "severe hearing loss."

The correlations between the dB threshold measure and syntax, decoding, and reading are only about 0.30. Although this indicates that the greater the hearing loss, the poorer the performance on the tests, this association is of questionable practical usefulness in predicting performance on tests of literacy.

Moreover, a multiple regression analysis showed that the correlation between scores on reading and decoding are not confounded by the students' hearing loss as measured by the dB thresholds. Scores on decoding and reading are more useful in understanding differences in literacy.

## GENERAL CONCLUSIONS AND IMPLICATIONS

The results from the study of the students' milieu provide additional and new information about students with hearing loss and demonstrate the importance of understanding their linguistic experience in analyzing information about their language development and planning appropriate educational programs for them. One of the key topics of this unique Norwegian study is the emphasis on questions regarding the access students have to various languages at home and in school.

In regard to literacy, these results document that if one is to be competent in reading, it is necessary to be competent in the language of the text, in this case, Norwegian. That decoding was also significant is important. It adds weight to other studies which have shown that competent deaf readers can and do utilize decoding in the reading process.

The title of the Norwegian main project was "Bilingualism and Literacy in Deaf Children," and it is important to consider the larger picture of what it means to be literate. *Literacy* means more than the skills of reading and writing and has been conceptualized in different ways. Researchers in this field have characterized the differences between spoken and written language as "different ways of learning because they are different ways of knowing (Halliday 1989), the "sustained meaning-making that is characteristic of written language" (Wells 1981), and the "ultimate tool for thinking which requires grasping not simply what is written but what is meant" (Bruner 1990).

If the goal for students with hearing loss is to become literate, then the goals for an educational program have to go beyond the development of face-to-face language and the skills of reading and writing to this higher level of using language cognitively in thinking and organizing mental events.

However, goals for educational programs cannot be determined by an all-encompassing "policy" that decrees the same approach for every student. As I. King Jordan, president of Gallaudet University, put it, "You can't teach to an ideal. You have to reach out and teach to the individual" (as quoted in the *Boston Globe*, August 30, 2000). Individual differences, as we have seen in the data presented above, are primary facts of life.

There are many examples in deaf education of stereotyping hearing impaired children. Thus if a new child appears in school and comes with a label of some sort, one is likely to think in terms of what is typical for a group with that label. It would be defined by the average (as for example, the mean of a group listed in table 3 above). However, taking into account the individual differences in the group (as represented by the SD in that table) is critical to making a sound judgment about this new child. For example, it was noted above that while there is a tendency for certain aspects of literacy to be affected by hearing loss, the variability of the literacy test scores around any one value of hearing loss (e.g., 100-dB threshold) is so large as to make that average measure almost useless for practical prediction of literacy.

Three groups with different environmental language experiences emerged from the results in the present study, and they were characterized as Norwegian, NSL and Disparate. The average scores for these three groups are the best general description for them in syntax, decoding, and reading comprehension. However, the extent of individual differences (SDs) vary for the group, and thus averages (Ms) have different degrees of precision as descriptions of any child categorized as belonging to one of the groups. The best prediction of the child before being tested is that he or she would be average, typical for the group. Because the individual differences are large, with scores overlapping for the three groups, a child categorized as NSL, for example, may score as well as those in the Norwegian group.

The fact is one cannot make a priori judgments based on general group membership. Each individual must be assessed. The purpose of grouping the students in this study was not to contribute to stereotyping. The average scores for the groups describe the facts of environmental influences on the children's performance on literacy tests, and that is information that should be taken into consideration in planning curricula and other programs. In general, it should be born in mind that an essential purpose of statistical analysis of results is to elucidate individual differences in the search for their causes.

There is another reason for observing individual differences. The fact that standard deviations were smaller for the Norwegian group means that the average for the test is more reliable for a member of that group with that linguistic experience than for a member of the two other groups. One could hypothesize that this may stem from the fact that both parents and teachers are native speakers of Norwegian and therefore more consistent in their use of language. One caveat that must be observed here is that one cannot view the lower scores from students in the NSL and Disparate groups as similar in nature or in their implications. The acquisition of natural sign language is important linguistically and culturally for this population. However, students who have experienced code mixing and who may not have a well-established primary language are disadvantaged both regarding language and literacy, and this is clearly not a positive result.

The school must know what a student brings to the educational situation so that it can take advantage of his or her strengths. For bilingual programs, this implies assessment in two languages as well as individual goals for acquisition of these languages. For literacy, it means that the differences between face-to-face language and language in print have to be understood and taught so that students can attain that epistemic level and all that it includes.

## NOTES

1. This project is entitled in Norwegian "Tospråklighet og lesing/skriving hos døve barn." The investigators were Knut Arnesen, Regi Theodor Enerstvedt, Elizabeth A. Engen, Trygg Engen, Grete Høie, and Arnfinn Muruvik Vonen. The present study would not have been possible without these coworkers but the authors are responsible for the interpretations and opinions expressed in the present study.

2. The data were analyzed with a Systat program. Differences described as significant are based on appropriate statistical tests. Statistical details were omitted at the request of the editor to make the paper suitable for a wider audience.

## LITERATURE CITED

Arnesen, K. 1999. Education of the deaf in Norway. In *Global perspectives on the education of the deaf in selected countries*, ed. H. Brelje. Hillsboro, Ore.: Butte Publications.

Bloom, L. 1991. *Language development from two to three*. Cambridge: Cambridge University Press.

Bruner, J. 1990. *Acts of meaning*. Cambridge, Mass.: Harvard University Press.

Chafe, W. 1980. *The Pear stories: Cognitive, cultural and linguistic aspects of narrative production*. Norwood, N.J.: Ablex.

Engen, E., and T. Engen. 1983. *The Rhode Island test of language structure*. Austin: Pro-Ed.

Engen, E. 1985. A longitudinal study of the development of comprehension of language structure. Paper presented at the International Conference for Educators of the Deaf, Manchester, England.

Engen, E. 1996. English language acquisition in deaf children in programs using manually-coded English. In *Bilingualism and literacy concerning deafness and deaf-blindness*, ed. A. M. Vonen, K. Arnesen, T. Enerstvedt, and A. V. Nafstad. Proceedings of an International Workshop, November 1994. Oslo: Skådalen Resource Centre.

Halliday, M. A. K. 1989. *Spoken and written language*. Oxford: Oxford University Press.

Hoff-Ginsberg, E. 1998. The relation of birth order and socioeconomic status to children's language experience and language development. *Journal of Applied Psycholinguistics* 19: 603–29.

Johnson, J. S., and E. L. Newport. 1991. Critical period effects in second-language learning: The influence of maturational state on the acquisition of English as a second language. *Cognitive Psychology* 21: 215–58.

Mayberry, R. I. 1993. First-language acquisition after childhood differs from second-language acquisition: The case of Amcrican Sign Language. *Journal of Speech and Hearing Research* 36 (6): 1258–270.

Newport, E. I. 1990. Maturational constraints on language learning. *Cognitive Science* 14: 147–72.

Pinker, S. 1994. *The language instinct*. New York: Morrow.

Powers, S. 2003. Influences of student and family factors on academic outcomes of mainstream secondary school deaf students. *Journal of Deaf Studies and Deaf Education* 8 (1): 57–78.

Radford, A. 1997. *Syntax: A minimalist introduction*. Cambridge: Cambridge University Press.

Report from the Ministry of Education, Research and Church Affairs. Norway, Ministry of Education, Research, and Church Affairs. 9 August 2001.

Snow, C. 1987. Relevance of the notion of a critical period to language acquisition. In *Sensitive periods in development: Interdisciplinary perspectives*, ed. M. Bornstein. Hillsdale, N.J.: Erlbaum.

Spencer, P. E. 1993. The expressive communication of hearing mothers and deaf children, *American Annals of the Deaf* 138 (3): 275–83.

Wells, G. 1981. *Learning through interaction; The study of language development*. Cambridge: Cambridge University Press.

# Deaf Immigrant and Refugee Children: Institutional and Cultural Clash

## C. Tane Akamatsu and Ester Cole

This chapter focuses on immigrant and refugee children who are deaf. In this sense, deafness acts as a complicating, rather than an explanatory, factor in how these children are to be taught. It is essential that the professionals serving these children and their families be sensitive to and account for the cultural interpretations concerning deafness, disability, and special education services. It is necessary to acknowledge that within the realm of special education services, deafness (and more specifically Deaf culture) can no longer be viewed as the central driving force informing how services are to be provided. Rather, deafness complicates an already complex situation and constrains how intervention is to be delivered.

### INTRODUCTION

Both Canada and the United States are countries of immigrants, and the rate of immigration to both has increased over the past decade. Moreover, nearly three-quarters of immigrant children are of school age (Coelho 1994; Cole 1998; U.S. Census Bureau 2000). Among these are children

---

An earlier version of this paper was published as C. T. Akamatsu and E. Cole. 2002. Deaf immigrant and refugee children: A different kind of multicultrualism? In *Effective consultation in school psychology*, ed. E. Cole and J. Siegel. Toronto: Hogrefe.

from war-torn countries, developing nations, and cultures where services for the disabled are minimal or nonexistent. According to the U.S. Committee for Refugees, a *refugee* is defined as "a person with a well-founded fear of persecution on account of race, religion, nationality, membership in a particular social group, or political opinion, who is outside the country of his or her nationality and is unable or unwilling to return" (U.S. Committee for Refugees 2002). The increase and decline of refugees from various world regions can be traced from recent news events through to the immigration services of various countries, and finally into the resettlement patterns across the country.

Tables 1 and 2 summarize information on countries from which people frequently sought asylum and the approval rates by nationality from 1998 to 2001 for the United States and Canada.

In the United States, asylum seekers most frequently come from Mexico and other Latin American countries (most notably Cuba, El Salvador, and

TABLE 1
Leading Source Countries for Refugee Claims to the United States and Canada, 1998–2001 (United States Committee on Refugees)

| Source Country to United States | 1998 | 1999 | 2000 | 2001 |
| --- | --- | --- | --- | --- |
| Mexico | 6,677 | 2,542 | 3,936 | 9,178 |
| Guatemala | 5,821 | 2,716 | 2,084 | 1,990 |
| El Salvador | 5,918 | 2,783 | 2,686 | 2,063 |
| China | 5,795 | 5,218 | 6,476 | 8,760 |
| Haiti | 3,375 | 2,977 | 4,683 | 5,068 |
| India | 2,664 | Not available | Not available | 2,125 |
| Somalia | 2,324 | 3,147 | 2,415 | 1,853 |
| Colombia |  | 399 | 2,747 | 7,280 |

| Source Country to Canada | 1998 | 1999 | 2000 | 2001[b] |
| --- | --- | --- | --- | --- |
| Sri Lanka | 2,526 | 2,915 | 2,906 | 3,000 |
| Czech Republic | Not available |  | Not available |  |
| India | Not available | 1,346 | Not available |  |
| Iran | Not available |  | Not available |  |
| China | 2,048 | 2,436 | Not available | 2,400 |
| Pakistan | 1,757 | 2,335 | 3,111 | 3,200 |
| Hungary | 1,383 | 1,581 | 2,304 | 3,800 |
| Chile, Argentina, Mexico, Colombia | Not available | Not available | 1,000–2,000[a] | 1,000–2,000[a] |
| Zimbabwe | Not available | Not available | Not available | 2,300 |

a. Figures for China, Argentina, Mexico, and Colombia were given as estimates.
b. Approximate numbers are given here.

TABLE 2
Source Countries with the Highest Approval Rates for United States and Canada, 2001

| Source Country to United States | Approval Rate | Source Country to Canada | Approval Rate |
|---|---|---|---|
| Afghanistan | 89.5% | Afghanistan | 97% |
| Ethiopia | 72–76% | Somalia | 92% |
| Sudan | 72–76% | Sri Lanka | 76% |
| Somalia | 81% | Congo-Kinshasa | 76% |
| Burma | 89% | Colombia | 85% |
| Iraq | 82% | | |

Source: U.S. Committee on Refugees, 2002.

Guatemala). However, the rate of approval of refugee status for these countries is very low, under 10 percent. Until recently, Canada typically had not had as many asylum seekers from these countries, but had numbers of people who entered Canada from other countries via the United States. According to the U.S. Committee for Refugees, countries or ethnic groups that currently generate the most refugees worldwide are the Palestinians, Afghanis, Sudanese, Iraqis, and Burmese. As can be seen in Table 2, countries with high approval rates for both the United States and Canada have suffered from war and internal political upheaval. As well, the countries that are most affected change across time. Therefore, the kinds of services that are needed will also change from time to time as new groups make their way into North America.

Approximately one-half of the world's children are refugees (U.N. High Commissioner for Refugees 1994), and over half of these children come from single-parent, low-income families (Burke 1992). Canada, which like the United States is a nation of immigrants, experienced a doubling of immigration during the late 1980s and early 1990s (Coelho 1994), with three-quarters of immigrant children being of school age. This rise in immigration has presented Canadian schools with the tremendous challenge of meeting the educational needs of a rapidly changing population (Cole 1996a, 1998). The implications for deaf children from disadvantaged living conditions and disruptive schooling are staggering (Hafner and Ulanoff 1994; Thomas 1992).

Issues of migration and resettlement are complicated, and deaf and hard of hearing children within the immigrant and refugee population often experience stresses that can have a negative impact on their educational experience. A typical case history might include birth and early experiences in a refugee camp, living in more than one country en route to Canada, lack of access to educational opportunities for deaf children in these countries, family separation (sometimes including the deaf child's separation from his or her own family), the family's lack of ability to cope with the child's deafness, exposure to multiple languages during the migration period, and the deaf child's lack of access to spoken language, with its cognitive and linguistic implications.

The goals of this chapter are to sensitize professionals to issues when working with "multicultural" deaf individuals and families and to outline issues and questions to ask before considering a service delivery model. We begin by presenting information pertinent to deaf children within the refugee and immigrant population, focusing on migration, adaptation, and acculturation. Next, we examine issues of schooling, language, and cognitive development. We then conclude by discussing the implications for school psychology consultation concerning the needs of deaf and hard of hearing children.

## MIGRATION, ADAPTATION, AND ACCULTURATION: IMPLICATIONS FOR DEAF CHILDREN AND THEIR FAMILIES

Immigrant children have the advantage of having had a planned migration. A new country is specifically targeted by a family as the ultimate destination for a new, and possibly improved, life. Yet, some families may come with unrealistic expectations of what the new country can offer in terms of educational and/or medical interventions for their deaf children. A family's immigration may have been planned around the deafness, with the (unrealistic, yet understandable) hope that the new country will provide medical interventions that will "cure" the deafness. Cochlear implants, in particular, have this allure. Yet, the therapeutic intervention itself is expensive and requires other commitments (e.g., appointments and therapy) that the family may not be in a position to make. This is not to say that immigrant and refugee children should not receive cochlear implants. While there is not much one can do prior to a family actually arriving in a new country, schools need to work with hospital programs in counseling parents prior to their making a decision as irrevocable as an implant.

In contrast, refugee migration is an unplanned move, when people are forced from their homes with little notice. There is often no target country. Families may have to travel to several different countries before one will allow them to stay on a permanent basis. It is not uncommon for education to be interrupted and languages incompletely learned. This has serious implications for both deaf and normally hearing children.

Both immigrant and refugee children undergo similar adaptation and acculturation stresses. Their histories may include information about disrupted lives; inadequate health care resulting in disease and malnutrition; social, emotional, and physical deprivation; significant personal losses; and educational gaps (Cole 1998). Consequently, the children are likely to experience cognitive and emotional difficulties (Ajduković and Ajduković 1993; Motta 1995).

## CULTURAL VIEWS OF DEAFNESS

A family's perception of the needs of their deaf child is shaped by their culture's view of deafness, which can, in turn, influence decisions about enrolling the children in school, finding housing and employment, and creating a new identity and attachment to the new society (Christensen and Delgado 1993). For example, if the child's deafness is perceived as a source of shame, then building the child's self-esteem will be a challenge. On the other hand, if deafness is believed to be the result of the parents' or the child's actions in a past life, then an attitude of helplessness may prevent proactive change from occurring. Similarly, if deafness is perceived as an unavoidable but unfortunate event, the family may react with helplessness, or conversely, may try to maximize the child's potential. Differences between a family's view and that of the medical or educational establishments can lead to challenges in service delivery. The new technology available through cochlear implants, for example, may mislead some people into believing that deafness can be "fixed" with the device, without a full understanding of the long-term educational commitment and prognoses of children with implants (Spencer and Marschark 2003).

One common misperception is that a deaf child is incapable of much learning. While academic learning is predicated on a solid language base, many families continue to confuse the inability to speak with lack of knowledge of a language, and to infer the inability to learn on the basis of the inability to speak. This is understandable, particularly in countries where special education services are unavailable. However, this common confusion may also lead parents to deny their deaf children the opportunity to learn through sign language until after they learn to speak, thus furthering language delay and postponing understanding and acceptance of deaf children and their needs. It is well documented that specific family responses to deafness can affect an immigrant or refugee deaf child's educational process and mental health (Christensen 2000; Christensen and Delgado 1993). Counselling a family through the process of understanding the psychoeducational implications of their child's deafness is a crucial role for both teachers and school psychologists (Montanini Manfredi 1993).

## ISSUES FOR CONSIDERATION BY SCHOOL PERSONNEL

Schools are the most significant change agents at the societal and the individual level. They are becoming sites not only for academic learning and remediation, but also for mental health services to aid in acculturation and adaptation. Therefore, effective interventions with immigrant and refugee children and their families must be founded upon knowledge and awareness of the issues and challenges that face them.

The effects of the migration experience at both the individual and familial level should not be ignored. Beiser and his colleagues conclude that the combination of supportive traditional cultural elements and new cultural norms allow for the maintenance of ethnic pride and contribute to good mental health (Beiser et al. 1995; Edwards and Beiser 1994). The immigrant or refugee deaf child's eventual acculturation to both North American society and North American Deaf culture depends on the interaction among general migration factors, personal and familial factors, and ethno-cultural views of deafness.

Many newly arrived deaf students lack not only English, but also any form of language (spoken or signed) or appropriate study skills for North American schools. Their families may lack basic information about deafness, the importance of language and communication, the partnership role that families and schools can play, special education opportunities, and information about their own as well as their children's rights and responsibilities as members of a new society (Branson and Miller 1998; Turner 1996). Yet deaf children, like others their age, must come to feel socially and academically competent if they are to become productive members of society (Benard 1993).

### Issue 1: Educational Placements for Deaf Children

Once a child has been identified as having a hearing loss that impacts significantly on his or her ability to learn in the regular classroom, the question of placement arises. Based on the several (U.S.) federal regulations,

Marschark noted that placement decisions should be made on the basis of "1) linguistic needs, 2) severity of hearing loss and potential for using residual hearing with or without amplification devices, 3) academic level, 4) social, emotional, and cultural needs, including opportunities for interaction and communication with peers, and 5) communication needs, including the child's and family's preferred mode of communication" (1997, 113).

Since eligibility for placement into programs for deaf and hard of hearing children is initially based on audiological information, it would appear that assessing a child's degree of deafness is a rather simple matter. However, audiological needs, while appearing rather simple to address on the surface, are quite complicated. Indeed, most parents, regardless of their point of origin, have difficulty grasping the full implications of a diagnosis of deafness. On the one hand, most parents know that their child is deaf prior to entering the new country. On the other hand, how they react to the diagnosis and make decisions on behalf of their child will be influenced by their cultural interpretation of deafness.

The expectations of each kind of program interact with the specific abilities and resources that a child brings to that program. Therefore, the kinds of interventions that school psychologists can provide or suggest will vary by program. For example, a profoundly deaf immigrant child who is unable to lipread English may find that an oral program is extremely frustrating. In such a case, counseling parents about the child's needs and about the role that sign language can play for this child is an important service. A severely traumatized but mildly hard of hearing child may benefit from being in a segregated class to allow him or her to receive more teacher attention.

## Issue 2: The Language Challenge for Deaf Immigrant and Refugee Children

One key factor in the deaf child's development is schooling and language development, which provides an avenue for further education, socialization, and the acquisition of life skills. Hearing students who are learning English as a second language may already possess a range of communication skills in their native language when they first arrive at school. Some may have had little or no schooling, whereas others may have come from communities with strong literate traditions and high educational standards. Thus, they often come equipped to build a second language on the base of their first. Students who are already literate in their first language may bring an additional foundation on which to build their English skills.

Research studies have documented that there is great variability in the length of time it takes normally hearing children to learn English as a second language and the kinds of instructional interventions necessary to promote this process (Cole 1996a; Corson 1993). It is widely accepted that it takes second-language learners five to seven years to become academically fluent in a language, a process that is facilitated through the acquisition of literacy (Cole 1998; Cole and Siegel 1990; Cummins et al. 1984). Cummins's Linguistic Interdependence theory (1991) suggests that students who can use both their newly acquired oral skills and established literacy skills from their first language are best positioned to acquire literacy in their second language. Moreover, the nature of the writing system of the child's first language may impact on how well first-language literacy supports second-language literacy (Cummins et al. 1984).

There is little reason to expect the case for immigrant or refugee deaf children to be different or easier. Because schooling is inextricably linked to English proficiency, communicating in English is a prime goal for all immigrant and refugee children. Difficulties with language acquisition tend to hamper education, social integration, and employment opportunities. For most deaf immigrant and refugee students, attendance at school provides their first accessible exposure to any language. Depending on the age of the student at the time they enter school in North America, first-language acquisition may be delayed to the point where complete acquisition is impossible, even under the best of conditions. This can have devastating consequences for subsequent cognitive and literacy development (Akamatsu 1998; Bonkowski, Gavelek, and Akamatsu 1991).

For deaf immigrant and refugee children who arrive at school past the optimal age of language acquisition, it is paramount to expose, indeed immerse, these children in a comprehensible, language-rich environment. Because language development underlies cognitive, social, and emotional development, the lack of language logically predicts generally atypical development.

American Sign Language (ASL) is probably the language that is most accessible for deaf students who begin to learn their first language at a late age.[1] Because ASL uses the visual modality, it can take advantage of visual iconicity and natural gestures (Mylander and Goldin-Meadow 1991; Newport 1996). Skills developed even in home sign can be brought to

---

1. What holds true to English and ASL in English-speaking Canada likely holds true for French and Langue Signes des Quebecoise (LSQ) in French-speaking Canada.

bear on learning ASL and other natural sign systems (Fischer 1998; Lucas and Valli 1992; Mayer and Akamatsu 1999).

However, ASL cannot be viewed as the language panacea for these children. ASL appears to have a critical period similar to that of English (Fischer 1998; Mayberry and Eichen 1991), and therefore, we might expect that immigrant and refugee deaf children who arrive without a first (signed) language will be disadvantaged in ways similar to hearing children who have not acquired a solid first language. That is, although they will be able to communicate adequately in a face-to-face situation, they will have difficulty acquiring complex syntactic structures with native-like fluency.

ASL, while useful for interpersonal and instructional purposes, is but one language to learn in the acculturation process. English, at least in written form, must also be mastered. Given how difficult literacy acquisition is for native-born deaf children whose parents already speak, read, and write English, it requires little to imagine the daunting task facing refugee and immigrant children. To further complicate matters, Mayer and Wells (1996) pointed out that deaf children who are fluent only in ASL are doubly disadvantaged when trying to learn to read and write in English. Not only do deaf students have severely restricted access to English (and therefore to the phonological component), they also cannot transfer any literacy skills from ASL. Whereas ASL may give the children the ability to conceptualize and communicate ideas in face-to-face conversation, Mayer argues that "there is some minimum threshold level of [English] proficiency required" before a deaf student can productively read and write (1999, 39).

Mayer and Akamatsu (1999) questioned the exclusive use of ASL as the instructional language of choice and suggested that natural sign systems (i.e., "the naturally evolved systems that deaf people use to communicate with hearing people" [Fischer 1998, 17]) may provide a bridge between a native sign language and English because of their linear mapping with (English) and their use of lexical and certain grammatical constructions from ASL. They further suggested that natural sign systems could be used effectively to establish an English language base and to support engagement in literacy activities at the morphosystactic level. Indeed, Engen (this volume) and Nielsen and Luetke-Stahlman (2003) found that the closer the signing system is to the target language of literacy, the higher students scored on various measures of literacy, including vocabulary knowledge and command of syntactic structures.

In the best-case scenario, refugee and immigrant deaf students may have been exposed to other languages or dialects and may not have had time to consolidate even face-to-face communication skills. Upon arrival in Canada, even students who appear to learn to sign rapidly within the first two years may be unreasonably expected to perform academically like their same-age peers who have had many years of signing. For example, Mayer and Akamatsu (2000) reported on a student who used Czech Sign Language at home and ASL and English-based signing at school. Although this student was quite capable of communicating face to face with his peers, his command of written English remained rudimentary many years after his arrival in Canada.

**Issue 3: The Role of the Family in North American Schooling**

Many immigrant students lack the appropriate study skills for North American schooling. Their parents may not understand what these "appropriate skills" are, and therefore may not be able to reinforce these skills at home. Secondary effects of deafness, such as language delay, lowered parental expectations and perceptions, experiential deficits, lack of appropriate educational experiences, and increased stress have been documented in the literature (see e.g., Calderon and Greenberg 1993; Gregory 1998; Lederburg 1993 for relevant reviews). In general, this literature has suggested that deafness disrupts normal parent–child relationships by changing the nature of how deaf children experience the world and making communication difficult so that parents cannot adequately mediate these experiences. As a result, parents become psychologically unavailable and more physically controlling with their deaf children than with their hearing children. In extreme cases, interactions between deaf children and their parents can appear to be either neglectful or abusive.

School personnel must remember that immigrant and refugee parents may not view themselves as equal partners in their children's learning. Contact with a counselor who is knowledgeable about a students's cultural background and sensitive to immigration may prove beneficial. It is likely that regularly scheduled appointments (e.g., daily, weekly) would be most effective. Families will continue to require ongoing information and support in order to collaborate with the school and revalidate the value of the home language as well as sign language.

Misconceptions about sign language may inhibit parents from interacting with their children in sign, perhaps because their culture frowns upon overly expressive body language, or because they feel that signing is not a valid form of language. The parents may also recognize that their deaf child has a greater command of sign than they do and feel powerless to interact with the child because they have no common language. Many students respond well to role-playing techniques that enhance low self-esteem, improve social skills, increase sensitivity to the thoughts and feelings of others, and decrease aggressive behavior (Cole and Siegel 1990). These can be used in the context of the classroom, as part of an arts/drama curriculum, or in collaboration with a counselor or school psychologist.

Although studies have concluded that parental involvement in school has a positive impact on children's academic achievement (Alter 1992; Grace 1993), parents may not feel empowered to work as partners with the school. As a result of linguistic barriers, cultural differences, and adjustment difficulties, immigrant parents may feel misinformed or ill-informed about the school system and yet be reluctant or unable to approach the school system for help (Cole 1996b).

In certain cultures, the schools are charged with the responsibility for educating as well as socializing children. Parents, having provided for the basic needs of the child, may feel that it is now solely the school's mandate to teach the child to become a functioning member of society. Because of their own limited education or inability to function in English or sign, parents may be unable to help their children with homework. They may find it difficult to participate in sign language classes because these classes are taught in English and/or because of their working conditions.

Home-school communication is often a new concept for parents. In many other countries, the school is expected to deal not only with learning, but any other behavior that the student exhibits. For students whose cultural adaptation has been difficult, maladaptive behaviors can develop and interfere with learning. Parents may respond to the school's request for cooperation as an indication that the school (or the teacher) is incompetent and thereby lose confidence in the school. Other parents may resist involvement as a way of preserving their cultural integrity (Gerner de Garcia 2000). This is not to suggest that home-school communication be abandoned, but rather that expectations for communication–and guidance for doing so–be set up as part of the placement and registration process.

For some parents, communicating with the school is intimidating. Particularly for refugee parents, the school represents a government institution, and a healthy distrust of any government institution may already exist. Add to this the difficulty of communicating in English, and the stage is set for communication breakdowns. Teachers could reassure parents that even simple drawings and a few words may go a long way in developing the kind of trust that is needed for home and school to work together. For parents who have some command of English, notes could be sent between home and school when an incident is known to have set a student off, so that both are aware of what might be upsetting that student. The parents can also call the school if, for example, there is an incident at home or related to the bus that morning.

Spoken language interpreters are crucial in providing the link between the family and the school. Because finding interpreters can be difficult, particularly for languages with few local speakers, interpreters might be community social service providers, friends of the family, or family members of all ages who speak some English.

Using interpreters can be a complex process. Given the variety of English language skills to be found among users of this service, it is particularly important that the interpreter also be a cultural broker, able to interpret not only the verbal information of both parties, but also to interpret the intent of the message. Furthermore, because persons functioning in this role might be family members or close friends and therefore have a personal or vested interest in the target family, they should receive clear information about their role when functioning as interpreters.

Obviously, if there is no shared language, interpreters and their services are crucial to enhanced communication. Most schools and programs for deaf children are familiar with using signed language interpreters; but even so, difficulties tend to emerge. Relay interpreters (two or more intermediary interpreters) are needed if a teacher is deaf. That is, the deaf teacher needs an interpreter to translate from signed ASL to spoken English so that the spoken language interpreter can translate between English and the home language for the parents. Key concepts related to education systems (e.g., the difference between a special program and a specific school placement, curriculum vs. teaching strategies) might not be clear to the interpreters involved.

## IMPLICATIONS FOR ASSESSMENT AND INSTRUCTION

Currently, assessment (particularly in the form of standardized testing) acts as a lightning rod for those who feel marginalized and disenfranchised (Cole 1996a), including deaf and hard of hearing children. Assessment may be viewed as the very process that causes marginalization and disenfranchisement. In the interest of preventing further discrimination and limitations in opportunities based on their performance on various assessments, delay or exemption from participation in assessment is tabled as a viable alternative. However, indefinitely delaying or exempting these individuals from any kind of assessment puts them outside the system of accountability and can have serious implications for the provision of appropriate programs and services and the preparation of students who are self-sufficient and able to exercise the rights and responsibilities of citizenship (Samuda 1990). Therefore, a systemic approach to assessment that goes beyond standardized testing to include informal curriculum- and instruction-based techniques should be adopted (Dunst, Trivette, and Deal 1988; Palinscar, Brown, and Campione 1991; Rueda and Garcia 1997).

The needs of immigrant and refugee deaf children are complex, and addressing these needs is equally complex. The need for a multidisciplinary team is never more pronounced than when serving these children. A systemic approach to assessment that goes beyond standardized testing is critical for understanding and responding to these needs. A thorough background history is essential, including information about previous schooling in other countries, learning strengths and weaknesses, and behavioral difficulties at home and school. Any documentation of the student's educational, medical, and mental health histories should be obtained. This information should be discussed with the team to further refine any referral questions. Appendix A contains sample interview protocols for gathering background information.

The role of assessment is an integral part of instruction, guided learning, and accountability. Assessment should be a process of gathering information about a student in order to identify learning strengths and needs and develop appropriate educational services (Cole 1991; 1996b). Concern about assessment practices for deaf children has centred largely on two major issues: (1) validity and reliability of the measures and (2) subsequent educational practices that encourage maximal achievement. It is axiomatic that verbal measures of intelligence are inappropriate to use with deaf and hard of hearing populations. These cautions were raised earlier with equal fervour in the multilingual and multicultural literature (Cummins 1994; Genesee and Hamayan 1994). Nevertheless, ongoing measures of language-related abilities (whether in signed or printed language) are necessary for formulating a comprehensive view of a deaf immigrant or refugee student (Akamatsu 1998; Marschark 1993), although finding appropriate methods for doing this is extremely difficult.

To add to the complexity of assessment, the practice of restricting the process to nonverbal measures in the early years of an immigrant or refugee child's experience can be problematic. For example, a child's performance on standardized nonverbal measures may be tainted by a lack of experience with the materials used in the assessment. It may be unreasonable to expect decontextualized problem solving (e.g., social problem solving based on hypothetical situations) based on experiences that are very different from the population on whom the measure was standardized. Deaf children may, as a population, have more neuropsychological impairments than normally hearing children. Given the degree of early deprivation, cultural background, and migration experience, the picture is understandably more complicated with deaf immigrant and refugee students. What holds true for assessing immigrant/refugee or language minority students may hold doubly true for immigrant/refugee deaf students.

The literature on deafness is fairly consistent about the disadvantage at which deaf students find themselves when faced with measures of ability that do not adequately differentiate between language-related difficulties and the actual level of knowledge or skill the students possess (Marschark 1993). Furthermore, differences in linguistic, social, and educational experiences affect native-born deaf students' performances on the various tasks that usually comprise tests of intelligence. It is therefore important not to misperceive linguistic deficits as deficits in ability since decontextualized language may present difficulties for children from culturally different homes. Moreover, Marschark (1993) notes that even when deaf and hearing children have equivalent nonverbal IQs, the academic achievement of the deaf students is several grade levels below that of their hearing peers. Vernon and Andrews (1990) also note that neurological damage associated with deafness (e.g., certain medical syndromes, prematurity, maternal rubella, and high fever during infancy) can also contribute to both greater variability and lower scores on tests of nonverbal intelligence within the deaf population. Therefore, one must exercise caution when interpreting the results of even nonverbal intelligence tests.

Educators and parents must be aware of lowered expectations for immigrant or refugee deaf students, either because of their migration experience or their hearing status. While actual levels of achievement, particularly in the early years, may not accurately reflect their abilities, ongoing dynamic assessment can aid in setting realistic goals for these students. Mayer, Akamatsu, and Stewart (in press) suggested that by examining videotaped classroom discourse, teachers and psychologists (or speech/language pathologists) can discuss how well a given student can "take up" the classroom discussion and apply his or her abilities to problem solving at hand.

Therefore, when assessing the academic achievement and social adjustment of deaf immigrant and refugee students, it might be useful to measure progress in four ways. First, how well has the individual student done academically and socially since arrival? Second, how does the student compare to others with similar immigrant or refugee backgrounds? Third, how does he or she compare with the general deaf population? Fourth, how does the student compare with normally hearing peers?

Alternative assessment procedures, such as portfolio-based assessment and the use of authentic or performance-based assessments, alone or in combination with culturally sensitive tests, have been advocated because they provide information that can be applied directly to instructional planning and incorporated into students' individual education plans (Cole 1996b; Estrin 1993; Gordon and Musser 1992). One practical and immediately applicable procedure is to perform dynamic assessments over a period of time, creating and analyzing portfolios of the student's work. For example, samples of the student's schoolwork can be collected. Changes in individual education plans can be documented. Standardized ability and achievement tests can be administered and compared across, say, a one-year time span. Diagnostic teaching and close observation of the student performing various tasks can be made, and different kinds of intervention offered. Where appropriate, the "test-teach-test" method will yield information to allow educators and parents to understand what the student can do without help. It can also help determine what kinds of intervention/teaching create the most learning for the student. Documentation of the kinds of interventions that seem to be most helpful can be made and discussed with the classroom teacher and parents.

Concerns have been raised, however, that such evaluations are not equally valid for all groups and may lead to unfair outcomes (Cole 1996a). Assessment continues to be emphasized in school systems as a legislated requirement and as a valued service by teachers and parents (Green 1998). Psychologists trained in both deafness and multicultural issues bring many skills and areas of knowledge to the assessment and consultation process (Cole 1991; Cole and Siegel 1990; Martin 1991; Vernon and Andrews 1990). Such skills include observation and interview skills, selection and evaluation of appropriate measures, and interpretation of the effects of language, culture, and personality on adjustment and performance. Knowledge domains include developmental, learning, and personality theories; individual differences; and multilingual education. This evolution toward comprehensive and equitable psychological assessment is timely in light of the diverse student population, the reform movement in education, and the re-evaluation of special education services. Through consultation and assessment, which provide a comprehensive picture about children, parents are likely to be reassured that in spite of their child's early history, significant and relevant gains in language and learning can be made by their child, and that favourable outcomes are possible.

In school, regular contact with a peer helper may be of help in dealing with both social and academic issues. Cooperative learning may help to facilitate the learning process by structuring groups so that students depend on one another (and not just on the teacher). Students can become valuable resources to each other and responsible for their own success and for the success of each group member. Cooperative learning also promotes active, hands-on learning rather than passive learning, and thus increases the motivation to learn.

Demonstration of self-initiative and assumption of responsibility in learning should be fully recognized and reinforced. The student should be encouraged to make decisions, such as by asking how he thinks he should begin his work, and so forth. Independent decision making and problem solving should be supported to help the student become more actively involved in the learning process.

A teacher could help the student to set up a "binder reminder," which the student carries everyday. In it, the student is expected to put down the materials he or she needs and the different work items he or she is expected to complete for the day. Step-by-step directions or an index card for routine procedures might be taped to the student's notebook. Responsibility for developing a "learning set" can be developed by encouraging the student to organize all materials needed for a particular task (e.g., books, pencils, erasers, etc.) before starting to work. Teaching organizational and time management strategies may be helpful, especially for developing effective work habits, study skills, and test-taking strategies. An orderly work plan might be provided to help the student manage his or her assignments and workload (Cole and Brown 1996; Cole and Siegel 1990).

It is expected that these students will initially make academic progress at a slower pace. In effect, they not only need to learn, in most cases, they need to learn how to learn. It is expected that students will grasp abstract concepts more easily if concrete or tangible materials are used for illustrations. Demonstration learning is a good avenue for these students. A spiral approach to the curriculum, with many repetitions and gradual introduction of new concepts will be best suited to the students' learning abilities. Teaching strategies that involve frequent repetition of instructions and a language-rich environment will provide maximum exposure to each concept being taught. The vocabulary of each subject of study will likely need to be taught. Teachers will need to ensure that the students know the terms and their meanings before further instruction with new concepts.

## SUMMARY

The education, health, and mental health service needs of deaf immigrant and refugee children are too complex to be addressed by one profession or by one system at a time. Instead, coordination must occur among the many systems with which the family comes into contact if effective, efficient, and culturally sensitive services are to be provided (Cole 1998). Service providers need to become familiar with the frames of reference of the families with whom they work (Turner 1996). Cultural values, in general and those specifically related to deafness, must be explored and understood. Without a cultural context and knowledge of deafness, factors related to age, gender, education, and family position may be misinterpreted, and professionals may incorrectly judge the behaviors of deaf children as symptoms of psychopathology (Pollard 1998). Giordano (1994) has offered helpful clinical guidelines for mental health professionals working in a multicultural milieu. His guidelines may be modified to include: (a) the assessment of behavior and learning in the context of cultural norms, the importance of ethnicity to the family, and the cultural implications of deafness to the family; (b) validating and strengthening the student's and family's ethnic identity and cultural background; (c) identifying and resolving family value conflicts, particularly around deafness and the use of sign language; (d) an evaluation of the teacher's own hearing status and ethnicity and its impact on the student's willingness to learn; and finally, (e) the teacher's ongoing self-assessment related to limits of knowledge about the impact of deafness in the context of the student's ethnic background. As we pointed out earlier, families from different cultures may view deafness not only as an inability to hear, but also as an inability to learn. Furthermore, a teacher who is also deaf may be viewed as less competent than a normally hearing teacher. On the other hand, the teacher may serve as a concrete role model for positive educational outcomes for a deaf child. Gender differences may also influence a family's perception of the teacher's competence. Families who do not have confidence in a teacher, for whatever reason, may undermine that teacher's attempts at teaching their deaf child. It is important for the school personnel to be aware of the impact of the particular hearing status, ethnic, and sometimes gender match between the teacher, student, and family.

Schools are often the first system recent immigrants learn about, but special education services, under whose auspices deaf and hard of hearing children receive education, may be uncharted territory. Parents may not realize that special education services are available in North America or not understand their rights and responsibilities with regard to receiving appropriate educational services for their children. Due to language, educational, and/or cultural barriers, they may be unable to advocate effectively for their children. A sample pre-interview protocol for gathering background information is presented in Appendix A.

Because schools are perceived to be a trusted environment that facilitates education and eventual access to North American society, parent outreach is vital at the point of contact with the education system. Given the ongoing emotional and social needs of immigrant and refugee children, it is important for schools to develop partnerships with external agencies and ethnic organizations. It is thus important for psychologists and social workers employed by school boards to develop multicultural and integrated service delivery models, which can facilitate the coordination of prevention and intervention functions (Cole 1996b).

One such vehicle for service delivery in many North American school boards is that of in-school multidisciplinary consultation teams, comprised of educators, school psychologists, and social workers (Cole 1992). Generally, these teams are designed to support teachers in providing appropriate interventions for students in need of assistance. Expanded team mandates can include consultative services to staff, parents, and community agencies, including ethnocultural groups. In their five-year follow-up study on school teams, Cole and Brown (1996) found that teams continue to be utilised for consultation about immigrant and refugee students, particularly around the common difficulties in coping with adjustment to a new language and culture. About a quarter of those surveyed saw refugee needs as an attribute that was most often related to student referral for team consultation. A sample pre-interview protocol for consultation with resource people is presented in Appendix B.

Consultation services in Canadian schools have been documented as providing valued services to educators (Sladeczek and Heath 1997). Siegel and Cole (1990) developed a consultation framework for organizing programs which link primary, secondary, and tertiary prevention initiatives. This model provides both for direct intervention by mental health professionals as well as for preventative programs delivered by teachers and other in-school staff. A schematic of this model, with examples for deaf children is presented in table 3. For example, primary prevention programs such as anti-racist education and self-esteem or social skills training can be provided by mental health staff in partnership with teachers. Given the severity of the problem, primary prevention programs could also include consultations with hospitals and ethnic community organizations that make referrals for deaf children. It is hoped that a broader role for mental health professionals in education will provide an avenue for advocacy about the provision of preventatively oriented services. Secondary prevention programs, formulated in consultation with schools, are directed toward students who are at-risk emotionally or socially. Tertiary prevention programs should be directed to students and families in crisis. Primary and secondary prevention programs might best be provided in a collaborative model, with one expert on refugee issues and one expert on deafness. Tertiary prevention (or active intervention) might best be accomplished by someone who has primary expertise in deafness, in consultation with informed others.

Substantive change in practice often takes several years to achieve. Cross-disciplinary participation among psychologists, social workers, teachers, public health nurses, and language/cultural interpreters is likely to stimulate shared understanding and new approaches to multicultural services. Educational options for newly arrived immigrants and refugees must be explored with individuals knowledgeable about both deafness and multicultural services. It would seem vital that when immigrant or refugee deaf students are identified, a multidisciplinary team should meet to evaluate the student's and family's history and expectations so that the parents are able to make an informed decision about special education services and placement. In line with the trend toward increased accountability in education and mental health, there is a growing need to address outcome-based measures for training and practice in the field. Ecological models for multicultural services require conceptual knowledge and skills training. This, however, will require knowledge of multicultural education, anti-racist policies and programs, social skills training, crisis management, and violence prevention. As Vygotsky (1997) once stated, "Education is

## TABLE 3
### Preventatively Oriented Interventions for Immigrant and Refugee Deaf Students

| Recipient and Level of Service | Primary Prevention | Secondary Prevention | Tertiary Prevention |
|---|---|---|---|
| | Identify resources, provide and analyze information; program for all deaf students | Program for deaf students "at risk" | Intervention with deaf students whose problems significantly interfere with their adaptation to school |
| School system | Present in-service workshop on deaf refugee/immigrant issues | Develop plan for identifying deaf students at risk for adjustment difficulties | Develop plan for responding to needs of deaf refugee students and their families |
| School staff | Invite community-based workers to consult on issues relevant to specific ethnocultural groups (e.g., cultural implications of deafness) | Discuss relevance of migration background of specific ethnocultural groups with teachers of deaf students | Liaise between school and community service providers to provide services for those in need |
| Students or parents, mediated service | Co-lead, with a teacher, a series of social skills workshops for an entire class | Consult with teachers on learning and emotional needs of newly arrived students | Consult with teacher prior to formal referral |
| Students or parents, direct service | Inform parents about local resources for deaf children and their families | Facilitate group for new immigrant and refugee students; liaise with ethnic community agency to co-lead a group | Conduct individual assessment and/or counselling |

a process of mutual and continuous adaptation of both camps, where sometimes it is guide or leader which represents the most active and the most original effective side, and sometimes those who are being led" (349). Effective change and exemplary practice will be developed best through the collaborative efforts of multidisciplinary teams.

## LITERATURE CITED

Ajduković, M., and D. Ajduković. 1993. Psychological well-being of refugee children. *Child Abuse and Neglect* 17: 843–54.

Akamatsu, C. T. 1998. Thinking with and without language: What is necessary and sufficient for school-based learning? In *Deaf education in the 1990s: International perspectives*, ed. A. Weisel, 27–40. Washington, D.C.: Gallaudet University Press.

Akamatsu, C. T., and E. Cole. 2000. Immigrant and refugee children who are deaf: Crisis equals danger plus opportunity. In *Deaf plus: A multicultural perspective*, ed. K. Christensen, 93–120. San Diego: DawnSignPress.

Alter, R. C. 1992. Parent-school communication: A selective review. *Canadian Journal of School Psychology* 8: 103–10.

Beiser, M., R. Dion, A. J. Gotowiec, and I. Huyman. 1995. Immigrant and refugee children in Canada. *Canadian Journal of Psychiatry* 40: 67–72.

Benard, B. 1993. Fostering resiliency in kids. *Educational Leadership* November: 44–48.

Bonkowski, N., J. Gavelek, and C. T. Akamatsu. 1991. Education and the social construction of mind. In *Advances in cognition, education and the deaf*, ed. D. Martin, 185–194. Washington, D.C.: Gallaudet University Press.

Branson, J., and D. Miller. 1998. Achieving human rights: Educating deaf immigrant students from non-English-speaking families in Australia. In *Issues unresolved: New perspectives on language and deaf education*, ed. A. Weisel, 88–100. Washington, D.C.: Gallaudet University Press.

Burke, M. A. 1992. Canada's immigrant children. *Canadian Social Trends* Spring: 15–20.

Calderon, R., and M. Greenberg. 1993. Considerations in the adaptation of families with school-aged deaf children. In *Psychological perspectives on deafness*, ed. M. Marschark and M. D. Clark, 27–47. Hillsdale, N.J.: Erlbaum.

Christensen, K., ed. 2000. *Deaf plus: A multicultural perspective*. San Diego: DawnSignPress.

Christensen, K., and G. Delgado. 1993. *Multicultural issues in deafness*. White Plains, N.Y.: Longman.

Coelho, E. 1994. Social integration of immigrant and refugee children. In *Educating second language children*, ed. F. Genesee. Cambridge: Cambridge University Press.

Cole, E. 1991. Multicultural psychological assessment: New challenges, improved methods. *International Journal of Dynamic Assessment and Instruction*, 2–10.

———. 1992. Characteristics of students referred to school teams: Implications for preventive psychological services. *Canadian Journal of School Psychology*, 8:2–38.

———. 1996a. Immigrant and refugee children and families: Supporting a new road travelled. In *Dynamic assessment for instruction: From theory to application*, ed. M. Luther, E. Cole, and P. Gamlin, 35–42. Toronto: Captus University Publications.

———. 1996b. An integrative perspective on school psychology. *Canadian Journal of School Psychology* 12:115–21.

———. 1998. Immigrant and refugee children: Challenges and opportunities for education and mental health services. *Canadian Journal of School Psychology* 14:36–50.

Cole, E., and R. Brown. 1996. Multidisciplinary school teams: A five-year follow-up study. *Canadian Journal of School Psychology* 12:155–68.

Cole, E., and J. Siegel. 1990. School psychology in a multicultural community: Responding to children's needs. In *Effective consultation in school psychology*, ed. E. Cole and J. Siegel, 141–69. Toronto: Hogrefe.

Corson, D. 1993. *Language, minority education and gender*. Clevedon, U.K.: Multilingual Matters.

Cummins, J. 1984. *Bilingualism and special education: Issues in assessment and pedagogy*. Clevedon, U.K.: Multilingual Matters.

———. 1991. Language development and academic learning. In *Language, culture and cognition*, ed. L. Malave and G. Duquette. Philadelphia: Multilingual Matters.

———. 1994. Knowledge, power, and identity in teaching English as a second language. In *Educating second language children*, ed. F. Genesee, 33–58. Cambridge: Cambridge University Press.

Cummins, J., M. Swain, K. Nakajima, D. Handscombe, D. Green, and C. Tran. 1984. Linguistic interdependence among Japanese and Vietnamese immigrant students. In *Communicative competence approaches to language proficiency assessment: Research and application*, ed. C. Rivera. Clevedon, U.K.: Multilingual Matters.

Dunst, C., C. Trivette, and A. Deal. 1988. *Enabling and empowering families: Principles and guidelines for practice*. Cambridge, Mass.: Brookline Books.

Edwards, G. J., and M. Beiser. 1994. Southeast Asian refugee youth in Canada: The determinants of competence and successful coping. *Canada's Mental Health* (Spring): 1–5.

Estrin, E. T. 1993. Alternative assessment: Issues in language, culture and equity. *Far West Lab for Education and Development Knowledge Brief* no. 11. San Francisco, California. ERIC 373082: 1–8.

Fischer, S. 1998. Critical periods for language acquisition: Consequences for deaf education. In *Deaf education in the 1990's: International perspectives*, ed. A. Weisel, 9–26. Washington, D.C.: Gallaudet University Press.

Genesee, F., and E. V. Hamayan. 1994. Classroom-based assessment. In *Educating second language children*, ed. F. Genesee. Cambridge: Cambridge University Press.

Gerner de Garcia, B. 2000. Meeting the needs of Hispanic/Latino deaf students. In *Deaf plus: A multicultural perspective*, ed. K. Christensen, 49–198. San Diego: DawnSignPress.

Giordano, J. 1994. Mental health and the melting pot. *American Journal of Orthopsychiatry* 64:342–45.

Gordon, E. W., and J. H. Musser. 1992. Implications of diversity in human characteristics for authentic assessment. *CSE Technical Report 341*. Los Angeles: Center for Research on Evaluation, Standards, and Student Testing. ERIC ED348381.

Grace, C. 1993. A model program for home-school communication and staff development. In *Multicultural issues in deafness*, ed. K. Christensen and G. Delgado, 29–42. White Plains, N.Y.: Longman.

Green, J. 1998. Constructing the way forward for all students. *Education Canada* 38:8–12.

Gregory, S. 1998. Deaf young people: Aspects of family and social life. In *Psychological perspectives on deafness*, ed. M. Marschark and M. D. Clark, 153–70. Hillsdale, N.J.: Erlbaum.

Hafner, A. L., and S. H. Ulanoff. 1994. Validity issues and concerns for assessing English learners. *Education and Urban Society* 26:367–89.

Lederburg, A. 1993. The impact of deafness on mother-child and peer relationships. In *Psychological perspectives on deafness*, ed. M. Marschark and M. D. Clark, 93–119. Hillsdale, N.J.: Erlbaum.

Lucas, C., and C. Valli. 1992. *Language contact in the American Deaf community*. Washington, D.C.: Gallaudet University Press.

Luetke-Stahlman, B., and D. C. Nielsen. 2003. The contribution of phonological awareness, and receptive and expressive English to the reading ability of deaf students exposed to grammatically accurate English. *Journal of Deaf Studies and Deaf Education* 8 (4): 46–84.

Marschark, M. 1993. *Psychological development of deaf children*. New York: Oxford University Press.

_____. 1997. *Raising and educating a deaf child.* New York: Oxford University Press.
Martin, D., ed. 1991. *Advances in cognition, education, and deafness.* Washington, D.C.: Gallaudet University Press.
Mayberry, R., and E. Eichen. 1991. The long-lasting advantage of learning sign language in childhood: Another look at the critical period for language acquisition. *Journal of Memory and Language* 30:486–512.
Mayer, C. 1999. Shaping at the point of utterance: An investigation of the composing processes of the deaf student writer. *Journal of Deaf Studies and Deaf Education* 4:37–49.
Mayer, C., and C. T. Akamatsu. 1999. Bilingual-bicultural models of literacy education for deaf students: Considering the claims. *Journal of Deaf Studies and Deaf Education* 4:1–8.
_____. 2000. Deaf children creating written texts: Contributions of American Sign Language and signed forms of English. *American Annals of the Deaf* 145(5): 394–403.
Mayer, C., C. T. Akamatsu, and D. Stewart. (in press). The case for situated assessment and evaluation in students who are deaf. *Deafness and Education International.*
Mayer, C., and G. Wells. 1996. Can the linguistic interdependence theory support a bilingual-bicultural model of literacy education for deaf students? *Journal of Deaf Studies and Deaf Education* 1:93–107.
Montanini Manfredi, M. 1993. The emotional development of deaf children. In *Psychological perspectives on deafness,* ed. M. Marschark and M. D. Clark, 49–63. Hillsdale, N.J.: Erlbaum.
Motta, R. W. 1995. Childhood post-traumatic stress disorder and the schools. *Canadian Journal of School Psychology* 11:65–78.
Mylander, C., and S. Goldin-Meadow. 1991. Home sign systems in deaf children: The development of morphology without a conventional language model. In *Theoretical issues in sign language research: Psychology,* ed. P. Siple and S. Fischer. Chicago: University of Chicago Press.
Newport, E. 1996. Sign language research in the Third Millennium. Paper presented at the Theoretical Issues in Sign Language Conference, 19–22 September, in Montreal, Canada.
Palinscar, A. S., A. Brown, and J. Campione. 1991. Dynamic assessment. In *Handbook on the assessment of learning disabilities,* ed. H. L. Swanson, 75–94. Austin, Texas: Pre-Ed.
Pollard, R. 1998. Psychopathology. In *Psychological perspectives on deafness,* vol. 2, ed. M. Marschark and M. D. Clark, 171–98. Mahwah, N.J.: Erlbaum.

Rueda, R., and E. Garcia. 1997. Do portfolios make a difference for diverse students? The influence on type of data on making instructional decisions. *Learning Disabilities Research and Practice* 12:114–22.

Samuda, R. J. 1990. *New approaches to assessment and placement of minority students.* Toronto: Ministry of Education.

Siegel, J., and E. Cole 1990. Role expansion for school psychologists: Challenges and future directions. In *Effective consultation in school psychology*, ed. E. Cole and J. Siegel, 3–17. Toronto: Hogrefe Publishers.

Sladeczek, I. E., and N. L. Heath. 1997. Consultation in Canada. *Canadian Journal of School Psychology*, 13:1–14.

Spencer, P., and M. Marschark. 2003. Cochlear implants: A review of linguistic, social and educational implications. In *The handbook of deaf studies, language, and education*, ed. M. Marschark and P. Spencer. New York: Oxford University Press.

Thomas, T. N. 1992. Psychoeducational adjustment of English-speaking Caribbean and Central American immigrant children in the United States. *School Psychology Review* 21:566–76.

Turner, S. 1996. Meeting the needs of children under five with sensorineural hearing loss from ethnic minority families. *Journal of the British Association of Teachers of the Deaf* 20:91–100.

United Nations High Commissioner for Refugees. 1994. *Refugee Children.* Geneva: UNHCR.

U.S. Census Bureau. 2000. Current Population Reports, P25-917 and P25-1095; and "Resident Population Estimates of the United States by Age and Sex: April 1, 1990 to July 1, 1999; with short-term projections to April 1, 2000"; published 24 May 2000.; http://www.census.gov/population/estimates/nation/intfile2-1.txt.

U.S. Committee for Refugees. Canada: World Refugee Survey 2003 Country Report. http://www.refugees.org/world/countryindex/canada.cfm.

———. United States: World Refugee Survey 2003 Country Report. http://www.refugees.org/world/countryindex/us.cfm.

———. Worldwide Refugee Information: Evolution of the Term "Refugee."http://www.refugees.org/news/fact_sheets/refugee_definition.htm.

Vernon, M., and J. Andrews. 1990. *The psychology of deafness.* New York: Longman.

Vygotsky, L. S. 1997. *Educational psychology.* Trans. R. Silverman. Boca Raton, Fla.: St. Lucie Press.

## APPENDIX A
## Sample Interview Protocol for Gathering Background Information
## (Adapted from Cole and Siegel 1990)

Country of birth:

Years in present country:

Number of countries prior to present:

Is there sufficient documentation to provide a profile of the student's educational experiences and social adaptation?
❏ Yes
❏ No   If not, what is still needed?

Previous formal educational experience:
Home language(s):
   (who speaks what?)

Student's preferred language/modality:

Past learning strengths and weaknesses:

| Country | Number of schools | Grade | Language | Special education? |
|---------|-------------------|-------|----------|--------------------|
|         |                   |       |          |                    |
|         |                   |       |          |                    |
|         |                   |       |          |                    |
|         |                   |       |          |                    |
|         |                   |       |          |                    |

Discrepancies between past and present evaluations of skills and/or social adjustment?

Previous mental health and/or educational assessments?

## APPENDIX B

| Date | Facility | Type of Assessment | Language |
|---|---|---|---|
|  |  |  |  |
|  |  |  |  |
|  |  |  |  |
|  |  |  |  |

**Sample Pre-Interview Protocol for Consultation with Resource People For Teachers' Use (Adapted from Cole and Siegel 1990)**

What is the symptomatic reason for referral?

❑ Academic:

❑ Behavioral:

❑ Socioemotional:

❑ Health/Physical:

Present level of instruction: Language          Math

What does an evaluation of daily work suggest about the student's academic functioning?

Does the student have the skills to complete assignments?
❑ Yes, independently
❑ Some, need support
❑ No, needs exensive support

### Student's learning style (circle all that apply)

Auditory   Visual   Tactile   Kinesthetic   Motoric

Good rote memory     Good thematic memory

Understands the large ideas     Surface/shallow
but gets lost in detail         understanding only

| Easily distracted | Maintains good attention | Good eye-hand coordination |

Impulsive    Reflective

Overly active    Overly passive

### Class participation

What motivates this student?

Interaction with teachers: ❑ good  ❑ satisfactory  ❑ poor

Interaction with peers: ❑ good  ❑ satisfactory  ❑ poor

Prefers company of children who are  ❑ older  ❑ younger  ❑ same age

School attendance:  ❑ regular  ❑ irregular

Nonacademic strengths:

Intervention strategies already tried:

| Strategy | Outcome |
| --- | --- |
|  |  |
|  |  |
|  |  |
|  |  |
|  |  |
|  |  |
|  |  |
|  |  |
|  |  |

**APPENDIX C**
**Outline for Immigrant Parent Group**

I. Introduction
   Roles of facilitators
   Role of interpreters
   Role of parent participants
II. Issues to address
   Communication within the family (direct vs. mediated)
   Communication with the deaf child (direct vs. mediated)
   What is misbehavior vs. what is the result of lack of understanding?
   Other stresses on the family
III. Temperament (yours and your child's)
   Types of temperament
   Match or mismatch?
IV. Reasonable expectations
   Limitations because of deafness
   Limitations because of age
   Limitations because of temperament
   Other limitations?
V. The school system
   Differences between Canada and your home system
   Your child's school experience
   Your rights (what you can expect from the school system)
   Your responsibilities (what the school system expects from you)

# Cultural and Linguistic Voice in the Deaf Bilingual Experience

## Lillian Buffalo Tompkins

Within the last decade, there has been an increasing dialogue and sharing between two previously disparate groups: those interested in bilingualism and those interested in raising and educating deaf individuals (Baker 2000). There is a growing conviction that "much of what has been written about bilinguals also applies to deaf children" (Baker 2000, 180). And yet, the fields of deaf studies and deaf education have only just begun to articulate the conditions and factors that socially, culturally, and linguistically comprise a "deaf model" of bilingualism and bilingual education. Perhaps the most valid parameters of the deaf bilingual model will be found in the narratives of deaf bilingual individuals who have lived the experience and can offer advice for the future, grounded upon their past successes and struggles.

What can we learn from the unique perspectives of deaf adults who recount their life experiences of becoming and being bilingual in American Sign Language (ASL) and English? In Tompkins (2001), I examined the notion of deaf bilingualism from the vantage point of achieved bilingual competence in deaf offspring of deaf parents (DD), mapping backward to discover through first-person insights how the six study participants characterized and explained their current ASL–English bilingualism.

---

This essay is distilled from: L. M. B. Tompkins. 2001. Deaf adults' perspectives on their bilingualism in American Sign Language and English. *Dissertation Abstracts International* 60 (12), 4651. (UMI 9999263)

In addition to inviting the participants' perspectives on bilingualism in the adult deaf experience, I asked them to describe how their own dual languages had developed across time in home and school settings. The participants responded to investigative instruments that included a background questionnaire, a videotaped semi-structured interview, e-mail responses to three rounds each of follow-up inquiries and reflective stimulus statements/questions, and additional personal artifacts submitted at the discretion of individual participants.

The six individuals—in this study called Eve, Mariel, Sydney, Ellen, Paul, and Karen—met three criteria: (1) they were in attendance at Gallaudet University or were recently graduated from the university within the six months prior to the study recruitment process; (2) they were prelingually and severely to profoundly deaf offspring of signing deaf parents, and their first language of memory was ASL; and (3) they were competent users of both ASL and English. At the time of recruitment into the study, the participants ranged in age from twenty-two years nine months to twenty-four years eleven months. All six had come into the American educational system when the Total Communication (TC) movement held sway and had, as elementary or high school students, witnessed the Deaf President Now (DPN) protest. The cultural and linguistic climate of the times provides an interesting historical backdrop to their narratives. Later in this essay, I will provide brief descriptive profiles of each participant and include excerpts from their narrative responses.

It had not been within the original scope and design of my study to pursue the notion of biculturalism or the sociocultural implications of deaf bilingualism. However, the overarching theme of finding one's cultural and linguistic "voice" in the sociocultural sense arose as a powerful element embedded across the categories of meaning that emerged from the participants' responses. The participants' narratives presented a compelling parallel between their experiences in the DEAF-WORLD and those of hearing world cultural and linguistic minority individuals who have portrayed their life events in narratives, or had them portrayed by others (see Anzaldúa 1990; Baker 1985; hooks 1990; Humphries 1996).[1]

Language use strongly influences who we are as a people and compels minority group members to seek out and/or to define for themselves their

---

1. DEAF-WORLD characterizes the life experiences of culturally deaf persons and their community. (See Lane, Hoffmeister, and Bahan 1996). Terms presented in small capital letters indicate sign glosses or the English equivalents of ASL concepts.

cultural and linguistic identity within the borderlands of larger communities (Anzaldúa 1990). As evident in the narratives of the six study participants, the need for self-definition was as strong for them as it has been for such minority voices as Frederick Douglass, bell hooks, and Gloria Anzaldúa. In the participants' progress through this study, they came to epiphanies about bilingualism in general and the paths to their own deaf bilingual identity specifically.

A shared aspect among deaf bilinguals and other bilingual or multilingual language minorities appears to be the common experience of having to virtually create their being out of nothingness (see Anzaldúa 1990; Baker 1985; hooks 1990). Baker considers the autobiographical account of Frederick Douglass to be one of the finest black American slave narratives available, in which the recovered past and the journey back were illustrative of the autobiographer's quest for being. There is a resonance in the shared journeys here in that the DD participants in this study, in retrospection, came to create for themselves a meaningful definition of deaf bilingualism where none had previously existed. They had grown up in and were living the condition of bilingualism in ASL and English during a time before the notion had formally entered the DEAF-WORLD milieu or been considered at all by the larger hearing community.

## THROUGH THE DEAF-EYE: DESCRIBING ASL–ENGLISH BILINGUALISM

In the unwritten deaf folklore of my generation, the term DEAF-EYE refers to the essentially visual nature of the deaf life-view, a perspective not intuitively understood by non-deaf individuals (Bahan, B., personal communication, 25 August 1999). In the following passages, we learn about deaf bilingualism from the vantage of the DEAF-EYE.

In a mosaic of narrative responses, the participants defined their deaf bilingualism this way: Possessing communicative competence in native ASL as well as in the additional language of English to degrees that allowed for effective conversational and academic applications of both languages. It should be noted that in the eyes of the participants, bilingual competence did not necessarily imply fluent mastery. Asked to rate their current language skills in ASL on a scale of 1 to 5, with 5 being highest, four of the six participants rated their competence as 5, and two gave themselves a rating of 4. In English competence, one participant self-rated as 5, one as "4 to 5," three as 4, and one as 3. Overall, each participant considered him- or herself to be at least competent in both languages—and had been deemed so in the study recruitment process—although only one claimed to have balanced skills at the highest rating; the rest conveyed some level of self-doubt, especially in English performance. This lack of self-confidence in linguistic performance appears to be not unusual in mainstream bilingual individuals (Grosjean 1992; 1996).

All six of the DD participants remarked that in their deaf homes, they had been strongly instilled with an early appreciation for both sign language and English. During the time of their growing-up and K–12 years—from the mid-1970s up until the DPN movement in 1988—the term *ASL* had not been in common use, at least not in their school programs. Regardless, the participants had intuitively recognized sign language as a foundation of their linguistic communication system, separate from but coupled with English.

All six participants named ASL as their first or native language because it was the primary language of their deaf homes and communities. However, they also claimed that their English was simultaneously or sequentially acquired and early in evidence through parental modeling and meaningful interactions with reading and writing activities that were observed or personally experienced in the home and community. Even in homes where parents were not competent users of English, the language was valued and used in a variety of ways. These interactions with English involved newspapers, magazines, and books; shopping lists and other note-writing; story-writing; and TTYs and closed captioning. Another source of English input at home and in the community was identified as contact signing, which incorporates aspects of ASL and English.

In several cases—through the influence of tutors, teachers, and school programs—"Signed English" (SE) or other English-based sign systems or their components were also used in deaf homes. One participant from a multi-generation deaf family reported that her parents were given dire warnings from an "English-centric" deaf education professional about the negative impact of ASL on deaf children's language development. Consequently, her mother attempted to use only SE when communicating through-the-air with the two deaf offspring in the family, although ASL was used between the parents and in view of the children.

Despite experiencing society's efforts to suppress ASL use in their deaf homes and/or schools, each participant remarked that it was impossible to imagine life without one or the other of their two languages.

Gloria Anzaldúa writes of the need to claim all of the tongues in which we communicate, to figuratively "make speech" of the many languages that give expression to the unique reality of a people (1990, 191). In Anzaldúa's narratives of life as a Chicana, I see a parallel with the linguistic reality of being deaf in two worlds, especially in terms of being able to claim rather than disparage the linguistic variations within the ASL-to-English spectrum of deaf bilingual usage.

As a defining feature of their bilingualism, Eve, Mariel, Sydney, Ellen, Paul, and Karen each emphasized their constant—differentiated from simultaneous—use of both ASL and English. This use varied according to situational and practical needs from the bilingual presence of both languages to the monolingual exercise of one or the other; but there was never a day when they did not function extensively in both.

Hooks wrote, "Individuals who speak languages other than English, who speak patois as well as standard English, find it a necessary aspect of self-affirmation not to feel compelled to choose one voice over another, not to claim one as more authentic, but rather to construct social realities that celebrate, acknowledge, and affirm differences, variety" (1990, 190). Participants credited the grounding in language they received in their homes for their ease from an early age in being able to intuitively switch codes or to adapt language usage within a range of ASL forms acceptable within their deaf community and an array of English modalities, depending on the communication partner's/-s' linguistic ability and situational circumstances. In fact, their relative linguistic sophistication meant that they were often called upon to accommodate or mediate in community and school situations that involved communication partners of mismatched linguistic ability.

Each of the six participants reported a strong and sustained inner motivation to learn the nuances of and to creatively use both of their languages. Participants identified the ability to "play" with either or both of their languages as one of several advantages of having come from deaf homes. Sydney, Paul, and Karen provided delightful examples of their creative language play: Sydney related how a deaf uncle had adapted the sign version of "I love you" to [ME] [L-O-5-E] [YOU], for emphasis replacing the fingerspelled /v/ with /5/; Paul mentioned the particular signed argot he used when in the company of his peer group of young deaf male African American athletes; and Karen told of a running competition to outdo her younger deaf brother in the use of colorful English adjectives, especially when trading insults. Karen also expressed a situational inclination to incorporate more fingerspelling into her ASL so that her carefully chosen vocabulary would be more explicit than if she were to use a sign with multiple possible interpretations.

## CULTURAL AND LINGUISTIC EXPERIENCES
## WITHIN THE DEAF EDUCATION ARENA

The social, political, and educational landscape of the deaf experience in the United States has been influenced by events that played out in the civil rights era of the 1960s and in the cultural, linguistic, and educational movements of the 1970s and 1980s (Humphries 1996; Padden 1996). From the 1960s, Stokoe's pioneering empirical work on ASL offered support for the linguistic validity, if not popular acceptance, of the unwritten face-to-face language of sign that was at the heart of the deaf community (Maher 1996). Additionally, a notion first posited by Croneberg at this time inspired national dialogue about the phenomenon that would later become known as deaf culture, for which the shared language of ASL was the cornerstone (see Stokoe, Casterline, and Croneberg 1965).

In the field of deaf education, a shift away from oral instructional methodologies in the sixties spurred research on the educational and social advantages of early "manual communication," evidenced in the positive findings in studies of signing DD children (e.g., Meadow 1968; Stuckless and Birch 1966; Vernon and Koh 1970). Such studies contributed to the theoretical foundation for future research efforts, particularly on the topic of the academic performance of DDs (e.g., Charrow and Fletcher 1974; Corson 1974). However, the positive findings of early studies showing successes in DD learners were consistently offset by persistent reports of the abominably low average reading achievement in deaf learners at the age of graduation from high school (see Allen and Schoem 1997; Moores 1996).

Influential research in the 1980s found that deaf children with early ASL access reached the same linguistic milestones in their native ASL acquisition and development as did their hearing counterparts in English (e.g., Caselli 1983; Newport and Meier 1985).

In 1989, Israelite and a committee of Canadian and U.S. research associates reviewed with favorable conclusions the literature on the use of native sign languages in the acquisition of majority languages, bolstering the body of evidence on the positive aspects of native ASL acquisition and development (Israelite et al. 1989). Johnson, Liddell, and Erting (1989) made similar claims for native sign language use in their document *Unlocking the Curriculum: Principles for Achieving Access in Deaf Education*. The widespread dissemination of the latter Gallaudet Research Institute report opened floodgates of inspection and introspection (Johnson 1990) about the crucial role of native sign language acquisition, and repositioned the burden of accountability for the success or failure of language instruction onto the educational system, rather than the deaf learner.

The publication of *Deaf in America: Voices from a Culture* (Padden and Humphries 1988) offered the world a revealing look at the cultural and linguistic lives of deaf persons as perceived from within and outside the deaf community. During the DPN protest on the campus of Gallaudet University in 1988, the deaf student body, with the support of their deaf community, asserted their right to be understood and represented by leaders who shared their language and culture (see Christiansen and Barnartt 1995; Gannon 1989); the protest inspired a growing deaf middle class to demand for itself new roles, from those of managers to CEOs (Padden 1996). DPN drew worldwide attention especially to the place and importance of ASL in deaf lives. The following year, The DEAF WAY international conference on deaf culture was held in Washington, D.C., showcasing the phenomenally rich linguistic diversity of the world's sign languages and the DEAF-WORLD's traditions of cultural literacy (Erting et al. 1994).

Although DPN and the publication of *Unlocking the Curriculum* were seen as culminating events in themselves, they were actually outcomes of a strong groundswell of ideas that preceded both events and entailed the deaf community's coming into its own voice, so to speak. In this process, they were moving to alter a long-standing perceived suppression in accord with the national discourse on culture and language that had begun in the 1970s (Humphries 1996). Prior to this time, deafness and the deaf experience had long been considered abnormal and disordered conditions. Deaf persons had been measured by the degree to which they could mold themselves or adapt to fit a "normal" and hearing model. In terms of language expectations, and in spite of mounting research evidence to the contrary, deaf persons were treated and educated as faulty monolingual users of English to be fixed by massive infusions of rule-based prescriptive grammar and speech lessons (Brueggemann 1999; Grushkin

1998; Livingston 1997). One need only witness the reluctance of deaf people to write to know that something very powerful had silenced them; something beyond the relative ease, for DD individuals at least, of learning to compose in English (Humphries, T. L., personal communication, 28 November 1999).

DPN and *Unlocking the Curriculum* were overt manifestations of change, at least in the way deaf persons viewed themselves and were viewed in relation to hearing others (Padden 1996). But outside the cultural arena, in the nation's classrooms, change was slow in coming. One long-reaching educational consequence of the stubborn belief that ASL had no effect on reading and writing development—and the argument by extension that ASL use by deaf children should be confined to social and not academic settings—was to remove ASL from the deaf classroom (Hoffmeister 2000). This nullification-by-default of the deaf learners' native language was, in effect, a form of suppression or oppression.

With the advent of TC in the mid- to late-1970s (Hoffmeister 2000; Lane, Hoffmeister, and Bahan 1996), rather than embracing ASL for classroom use with deaf learners, the educational establishment continued to favor the artificially created English-based Manually Coded English (MCE) systems that arose. Deaf-of-deaf learners may have been bilingual in the daily applications of their two languages, but their educational programs were not.

By the mid-1970s, the TC philosophy had become an entrenched fixture in most deaf classrooms, and in theory, allowed multiple approaches that alternated or combined the use of sign language, fingerspelling, speech, speechreading, auditory training, and writing "to ensure effective communication with and among hearing impaired persons" (Garretson 1976, quoted in Lou 1988, 91). While ASL was a viable and permissible component within TC, its use tended to be that of last resort by teachers unable to make a deaf child understand in any other way (Hoffmeister 2000; Strong 1988), a situation that Strong (1988) attributed, in part, to too few deaf teachers. Eventually, the use of TC became, in reality, that of simultaneous communication (SimCom) or signing with voice (called Sign Supported Speech [SSS] by Johnson, Liddell, and Erting 1989).

While, since the mid-1970s, there had been experimentation and rhetoric concerning conceptualizations of bilingual deaf education (e.g., Kannapell 1979), it was not until the mid-1980s that the construct of bilingualism began to emerge in some K–12 school systems, in reference to native ASL acquisition and the learning/teaching of English-as-second-language (ESL). Stewart (1985) made the observation that even in the mid-1980s, the concept of a bilingual education was relatively new in terms of deaf children.

Into the mid-1990s, MCE systems, rather than ASL, remained as the preferred communication mode in classroom use, especially by hearing teachers (Hoffmeister 2000), and only a handful of programs in deaf education claimed to be guided by a bilingual or bilingual-bicultural educational philosophy (Strong 1995). Grushkin (1998) asserted, however, that even into the present time, some so-called bilingual programs continue to ignore the strengths of the visually oriented deaf learner and teach English according to traditional and monolingual oral/aural methodologies.

The general education trend toward the monolingual primacy of English appears to have had far-reaching consequences on language instruction practices in the field of deaf education. From participant reports, the focus of language instruction in their K–12 years was largely that of an English skills-based prescriptive approach, particularly evident in speech and syntax drills. This emphasis on language over literacy translated into language arts lessons and activities that were largely devoid of meaning for the DD participants. The participants' early enthusiasm for reading and writing, grounded in their deaf home experiences, was often dulled and stifled by classroom practices that emphasized worksheets and repetitious book exercises. Teachers' responses to writing were generally corrective rather than explanatory, which participants found to be as ineffective as the worksheets and led participants to report that writing in school was boring and not fun.

Deaf signing families appear to have use of repertoires of effective strategies that establish in the motivated learner not only native ASL, but also the foundations for English literacy attainment. These repertoires include the use of fingerspelling, ways of combining sign and print, pointing, facial markings, and other visual strategies in patterns such as sandwiching and chaining (Blumenthal-Kelly 1995; Humphries and MacDougall 1999/2000; Kelly 1991; 1992; Padden and Ramsey 1998; 2000). It appears, however, that deaf classrooms and programs failed to give recognition to these strategies or to capitalize on the DD learners' early bilingual foundations.

Most of the participants described themselves as avid readers and writers from an early age, whose constant reading led to better writing outside of—and according to some participants, despite of—school settings and practices. Indeed, one of the most revealing, and possibly the most disturbing, of my realizations stemming from this study was that these six DD bilingual individuals had been able to sustain the cultural, linguistic, and literate impetus of their deaf homes and communities in the face of resistance emanating from the educational programs they attended.

Among the deaf signing homes, classrooms, and programs, there was a dissonance of beliefs, conditions, and practices. This incongruity reflects what Larson and Irvine (1999) call "reciprocal distancing," a discourse with negative consequences in which teachers and students "invoke existing sociohistorical and political distances between their communities in classroom interaction" (394). In the process of reciprocal distancing, educational systems or their representative individuals exhibit a devaluing of students' linguistic and sociocultural knowledge and abilities.

In most of their school experiences, the participants of this study—and their deaf peers—experienced a virtual nullification of ASL and a denial of recognition of an important part of their cultural and linguistic heritage. Consequently, their teachers' literacy practices often exhibited degrading beliefs about their students' language(s), backgrounds, and abilities. Mariel, Sydney, and Karen reported that in school, they had been conditioned to join with their teachers in belittling and devaluing their deaf peers who used less-than-proficient English. This raises concern and calls to mind cautionary words from Anzaldúa: "[B]ecause we internalize how our language has been used against us by the dominant culture, we use our language differences against each other" (1990, 207). Anzaldúa makes a powerful point: "So if you want to really hurt me, talk badly about my language. Ethnic identity is twin skin to linguistic identity—I am my language. Until I can take pride in my language, I cannot take pride in myself" (1990, 207). It is not surprising that in the narratives of several of the study participants, emotionally laden terms such as *suppression* and *oppression* surfaced.

## DEAF VOICES: EVE, MARIEL, SYDNEY, ELLEN, PAUL, AND KAREN

In 1990, bell hooks defined *voice* in several contexts: voice in the connotation of rebellion; "coming to voice" as a way of speaking for those who are oppressed and whose unrepresented voices need to be heard; and voice in the sense of an individual's distinctive style of expression (190). All of these meanings find resonance in the participants' narratives that follow.

The direct quotations attributed to the individual participants in this section were obtained in two ways: from my transcriptions of the videotaped interviews, which each participant read for accuracy, and from e-mailed communication between the researcher and the individuals. In the latter, the informal conversational nature of the electronic medium contributed to lapses in grammatical correctness or spelling accuracy. I edited these responses where necessary for clarity, but kept the editing to a minimum, and so some grammatical inaccuracies remain. (For more detailed within-case and cross-case descriptions, see Tompkins 2001.)

**Eve: Twenty-three years, eight months; severely deaf since eighteen months from chicken pox and high fever; older hard of hearing brother, no deaf extended family members**

In responding to a query regarding her development of ASL and English, Eve wrote, "I'm not sure where to begin. The first thing that comes to mind [is] that I have no doubt that I developed 'world knowledge' largely due to the fact that my family communicate[s] and interact[s] with me in ASL. Also, the interaction my parents [and I] had with other older friends taught me a lot. I still remember some of their conversations."

She remembered "reading a children's book every single night before going to bed. Without realizing it, I'm sure that I developed good writing skills because of the reading habits [I had] when I was young. Also, my parents sold the TV and didn't buy [another] one for a year. That's when my brother and I decided to start going to the public library to borrow books." At the library in her elementary day program, Eve enjoyed book-sharing sessions where the librarian would read children's books aloud, with an ASL interpreter to sign them.

Eve commented that when growing up, she never liked writing and did not do much of it. However, in her elementary day program, her teacher required "free writing," where the students could write anything they wanted about the stimulus pictures the teacher used. It became a classroom game to see who could write the most pages. After Eve's entry into a residential school, she experienced "zero writing," and lost interest in it. "We didn't do writing, just boring exercises and drills." By the time Eve was required to do creative writing in high school, she "didn't feel confident or creative enough."

**Mariel: Twenty-three years three months; severely (right ear) to profoundly (left ear) deaf at birth with a genetic etiology; deaf twin brother, deaf older sister, deaf younger half-brother, hearing younger half-sister, no deaf extended family members**

Mariel wrote, "I strongly value the richness of ASL [in which] I feel I can express totally and freely. There are no barriers that I've experienced using ASL. It's my first language and I feel completely confident using ASL." Although Mariel wrote in a preliminary background questionnaire that she recalled no barriers in using ASL, she later made a contrasting statement. In the interview, she said that school experiences were "always negative connected to language" and recounted a time when an elementary teacher at her residential school had told the students in Mariel's class that "ASL is animal talk." This teacher firmly rejected ASL and used what she called SEE because it was "more formal." Mariel added that it was only late in high school, after DPN in 1988, that she realized that ASL, too, was a "formal" language.

About English, Mariel wrote, "Even though the English language is not my best language, I still value it wholly. It is a key to success. With the ability to read and write well, I am capable of any profession."

**Sydney (female): Twenty-three years zero months; severely (left ear) to profoundly (right ear) deaf at birth with a genetic etiology; no siblings, deaf maternal grandparents and a number of deaf aunts, uncles, and cousins, some with whom she lived at times**

In responding to a query about memorable educational experiences, Sydney wrote, "All my life, I've known myself to be a very fluent ASL user. But in English, I don't recall when I first recognized that I was very good in writing English. I do know that I knew quotes or phrases known in general earlier than my classmates while growing up in a Deaf School. I've rarely had problems correcting my English except for being consistent with the past, present and future tenses when writing a story or whatever. Now, I pay more attention to that since I know it's my weakest area."

Sydney also said that she became very frustrated when a particular teacher would tell her that something she had written—and which she thought looked fine—was "wrong." Then the teacher would tell Sydney how she "preferred" to see it corrected. In contrast to this, Sydney, as well as several other participants, remarked that she learned best when a teacher would take the time to sit and discuss her writing with her and explain strategies of language usage. As with Eve and Mariel, Sydney's favorite teachers were deaf—they had the sign skills to be able to explain the intricacies of written English.

Sydney saw the tendency for some teachers to put so much emphasis on correcting English writing as an oppressive deaf–hearing issue, to which she responded, "My writing is my writing, leave it alone!"

**Ellen: Twenty-two years nine months (youngest in study); profoundly deaf at birth with a genetic etiology; deaf older sister, deaf older brother, deaf extended family members, and other deaf adult members of household**

Ellen was read to by her parents and also by a sister six years her senior. "I was the last baby in the family," she related, "so I guess my parents learned from their mistakes with the first two kids. I don't know. They gave me books to read, but with my sister and brother they did not do that. They gave them books, but they did not really expose them to that. For me, they read stories to me. I think that is really the key—signing, plus the book and pictures. I have many photos of me with books, one with me asleep in the crib with a book in my hands, covering my face. Pictures show that as a baby I had books."

Over the years, Ellen maintained an avid love of reading. Regarding writing, she recalled a time when she was about seven years old, when after seeing an uncaptioned movie in the theater, she went home and wrote a nine-page story about it. She remarked, however, that in school, she lost interest in writing and did not write much—writing was neither expected nor required of her.

**Paul: Twenty-four years six months; severe bilateral hearing loss discovered at age two months—adventitious condition of genetic etiology; deaf younger sister, hearing older and younger sisters, deaf grandmother, and deaf aunt living in the home**

Paul responded to a query about memorable educational experiences by writing that he fully used ASL at home from birth, but that "oralism came forcefully" into his life when he was enrolled in an oral preschool program. His mother observed him there in a room with a two-way mirror, and three months in that educational setting were "formidably enough" for him before she moved him to a public school with a sign-based program, where he was much happier.

In the latter program, he was "heavily exposed to fundamentals of reading and writing" and used "SEE II" and English, while continuing to use ASL and "contact sign" at home with his deaf family. Paul described how he would occasionally use an English-based sign at home, and if it "made sense" to his family, they might use it; otherwise, the sign would not show up again in home conversations.

After a family move, Paul was placed by his school district in a special school for "disabled" students where he remained from ages seven to nine. He remarked, "Luckily, the teacher [for the deaf students] was a Gallaudet graduate who happened to be superb. I used ASL, PSE, [and] SEE to communicate." He recalled that one of his hearing teachers with weak sign skills would persistently invent signs rather than fingerspell a word or ask the students for the acceptable sign. These inventions often produced disgusting results, Paul added.

In referring to his years at a residential deaf school (in grades 6–12), where he experienced more ASL and the reinforcement of his native language skills, Paul wrote, "There, I grew up the most and evolved into what I am today."

**Karen: Twenty-four years eleven months (oldest in the study); profoundly deaf at birth with a genetic etiology; deaf younger brother, multi-generational deaf family**

In a communication autobiography that Karen provided for the researcher, she wrote about an oral day program she attended for one year, before age six:

> I remember hating that school. I remember looking at the clock when other students filed out of the classroom, knowing I was being held back from the lunchroom yet again because I hadn't accurately pronounced the sound of the day. My classroom experience there consisted mainly of continuous speech therapy; my mother filled notebooks with tales of games my brother and I played, and I had to read the stories out loud to the speech therapist. My parents and I once ran into the speech therapist at the mall, and I refused to talk to her. Weekends were my time off, and I didn't have to obey her then! (One good thing came of all this, though—I believe this tiresome task [of reading aloud to the speech therapist] really developed my reading skills.)

In another passage of the autobiography, Karen reflected, "Not until recently did I realize that the young [Karen] felt her isolation at [the oral school] was perfectly normal, merely a part of the school day. 'They don't know what they're missing' runs through my mind every time I meet a student in a classroom without barrier-free communication. I understand what they understand, though—that their isolation is perfectly normal, school is always like that."

❖

Taken separately, it is unlikely that any of the above narratives or the participants' individual experiences and perspectives of the ASL–English bilingual condition will suggest new or particularly remarkable information. However, taken together, the voices of the six deaf-of-deaf participants offer a revealing body of cultural and linguistic discourse not previously available. Rose (1989), speaking of the urban neighborhood, wrote, "There are basic truths about the vulnerability and power of coming to know, about the way the world invites and denies language. This is what lies at the base of education—to be tapped or sealed over or distorted by others" (240).

The deaf experience of coming to know and coming to voice remains situated within a complex cultural, linguistic, and educational arena. It is up to us to tap into and invite the knowledge and power of language in deaf individuals and to be wary not to seal over or distort. Until the voices of lifelong users of both ASL and English receive respectful attention, until the world at large recognizes and understands the unique deaf bilingual condition, and until the educational establishment responds accordingly, Eve, Mariel, Sydney, Ellen, Paul, and Karen will continue to be voices from the borderland.

## LITERATURE CITED

Anzaldúa, G. 1990. How to tame a wild tongue. In *Out there: Marginalization and contemporary cultures*, ed. R. Ferguson, M. Gever, T. Minh-ha, and C. West, 203–11. New York: New Museum of Contemporary Art; Cambridge, Mass.: MIT Press.

Allen, T. E., and S. Schoem. 1997. Educating deaf and hard of hearing youth: What works best? Paper presented at the meeting of the Combined Otolarygological Meeting of the American Academy of Otolaryngology, Scottsdale, Arizona.

Baker, C. 2000. *A parents' and teachers' guide to biolingualism*. 2nd ed. Boston: Multilingual Matters.

Baker, H., Jr. 1985. Autobiographical acts and the voice of the southern slave. In *The slave's narrative*, ed. C. T. Davis and H. L. Gates, 242–61. New York: Oxford University Press.

Blumenthal-Kelly, A. 1995. Fingerspelling interaction: A set of deaf parents and their deaf daughter. In *Sociolinguistics in deaf communities*, ed. C. Lucas, 62–73. Washington, D.C.: Gallaudet University Press.

Brueggemann, B. J. 1999. *Lend me your ear: Rhetorical constructions of deafness*. Washington, D.C.: Gallaudet University Press.

Caselli, M. C. 1983. Communication to language: Deaf children's and hearing children's development compared. *Sign Language Studies* 39: 113–44.

Charrow, V. R., and J. D. Fletcher. 1974. English as a second language of deaf children. *Developmental Psychology* 10(4): 463–70.

Christiansen, J., and S. Barnartt. 1995. *Deaf president now! The revolution at Gallaudet University*. Washington, D.C.: Gallaudet University Press.

Corson, H. 1974. Comparing deaf children of oral deaf parents and deaf parents using manual communication with children of hearing parents on academic, social, and communication functioning. *Dissertation Abstracts International* 34 (10): 6480. (University Microfilms No. AAT 7408454).

Erting, C. J., R. C. Johnson, D. L. Smith, and B. D. Snider, eds. 1994. *The DEAF WAY: Perspectives from the international conference on Deaf culture*. Washington, D.C.: Gallaudet University Press.

Gannon, J. 1989. *The week the world heard Gallaudet*. Washington, D.C.: Gallaudet University Press.

Grosjean, F. 1992. The bilingual and the bicultural person in the hearing and in the deaf world. *Sign Language Studies* 77:307–20.

———. 1996. Living with two languages and two cultures. In *Cultural and language diversity and the deaf experience*, ed. I. Parasnis, 20–37. New York: Cambridge University Press.

Grushkin, D. 1998. Why shouldn't Sam read? Toward a new paradigm for literacy and the deaf. *Journal of Deaf Studies and Deaf Education* 3(3): 179–204.

Hoffmeister, R. J. 2000. A piece of the puzzle: ASL and reading comprehension in deaf children. In *Language acquisition by eye*, ed. C. Chamberlain, J. P. Morford, and R. I. Mayberry, 143–63. Mahwah, N.J.: Erlbaum.

hooks, b. 1990. "When I was a young soldier for the revolution": Coming to voice. In *Democracy, a project by Group Material*, ed. B. Wallis, 189–98. Seattle, Wash.: Bay Press.

Humphries, T. 1996. Of deaf-mutes, the *strange*, and the modern deaf self. In *Culturally affirmative psychotherapy with deaf persons*, ed. N. S. Glickman, and M. A. Harvey, 99–114. Mahwah, N.J.: Erlbaum.

Humphries, T., and MacDougall, F. 1999/2000. "Chaining" and other links: making connections between American Sign Language and

English in two types of school settings. *Visual Anthropology Review* 15(2): 84–94.

Israelite, N., C. Ewoldt, R. Hoffmeister, J. Greenwald, A. Wilber-Leach, M. Brown, R. Crettien, M. French, B. Bahan, K. Bishop, L. Macauley, J. Kowal, and B. Kjiersdam. 1989. *A review of the literature on the effective use of native sign language on the acquisition of a majority language by hearing impaired students*. Ontario, Canada: Minister of Education.

Johnson, R. C. 1990. The publication and aftermath of unlocking the curriculum. *Sign Language Studies* 69: 295–325.

Johnson, R., S. Liddell, and C. Erting. 1989. *Unlocking the curriculum: Principles for achieving access in deaf education*. Gallaudet Research Institute, Working Paper 89–93. Washington, D.C.: Gallaudet University Press.

Kannapell, B. 1979. Bilingualism: A new direction in the education of the deaf. *Deaf American* 9–15.

Kelly, A. B. 1991. Fingerspelling use among the deaf senior citizens of Baltimore. In *School of Communication Student Forum*, ed. E. A. Winston, 90–98. Washington, D.C.: Gallaudet University School of Communication.

———. 1992. Fingerspelling analysis: Baltimore's deaf senior citizens. Poster session presented at the Theoretical Issues in Sign Language Research Conference, August, San Diego, California.

Lane, H., R. Hoffmeister, and B. Bahan. 1996. *A journey into the* DEAF-WORLD. San Diego: DawnSign Press.

Larson, J., and P. D. Irvine. 1999. "We call him Dr. King": Reciprocal distancing in urban classrooms. *Language Arts* 76(5): 393–400.

Livingston, S. 1997. *Rethinking the education of deaf students: Theory and practice from a teacher's perspective*. Portsmouth, N.H.: Heinemann.

Lou, M. W. 1988. The history of language use in the education of the deaf in the United States. In *Language learning and deafness*, ed. Strong, M., 175–98. New York: Cambridge University Press.

Maher, J. 1996. *Seeing language in sign: The work of William C. Stokoe*. Washington, D.C.: Gallaudet University Press.

Meadow, K. 1968. Early manual communication in relation to the deaf child's intellectual, social and communicative functioning. *American Annals of the Deaf* 113(1): 29–41.

Moores, D. F. 1996. *Educating the deaf: Psychology, principles, and practices*, 4th ed. Boston: Houghton Mifflin Company.

Newport, E., and R. Meier. 1985. Acquisition of American Sign Language. In *The cross-linguistic study of language acquisition*. Vol. 1, ed. D. Slobin, 881–938. Hillsdale, N.J.: Erlbaum.

Padden, C. A. 1996. From the cultural to the bilingual: The modern deaf community. In *Cultural diversity and the deaf experience*, ed. I. Parasnis, 79–98. New York: Cambridge University Press.

Padden, C., and T. Humphries. 1988. *Deaf in America: Voices from a culture*. Cambridge, Mass.: Harvard University Press.

Padden C., and C. Ramsey. 1998. Reading ability in signing deaf children. *Topics in language disorders*, 18(4): 30–46.

———. 2000. American Sign Language and reading ability in deaf children. In *Language acquisition by eye*, ed. C. Chamberlain, J. P. Morford, and R. I. Mayberry, 65–189. Mahwah, N.J.: Erlbaum.

Rose, M. 1989. *Lives on the boundary*. New York: Penguin Books.

Stewart, D. 1985. Language dominance in deaf students. *Sign Language Studies*, 49:375–85.

Stokoe, W., D. Casterline, and C. Croneberg. 1965. *A dictionary of American Sign Language on linguistic principles*. Washington, D.C.: Gallaudet College Press.

Strong, M. 1988. A bilingual approach to educating deaf children: ASL and English. In *Language learning and deafness*, ed. M. Strong, 113–29. New York: Cambridge University Press.

Strong, M. 1995. A review of bilingual/bicultural programs for deaf children in North America. *American Annals of the Deaf* 140:84–94.

Stuckless, R., and Birch, J. 1966. The influence of early manual communication on the linguistic development of deaf children. *American Annals of the Deaf* 111(2): 452–60; 499–504.

Tompkins, L. M. B. 2001. Deaf adults' perspectives on their bilingualism in American Sign Language and English. Ph.D diss., Gallaudet University, 2000. Abstract in *Dissertation Abstracts International*, publ. nr. AAT9999263, DAI-B 61/12 (June 2001): 4651.

Vernon, M., and H. Koh. 1970. The influence of early manual communication on the linguistic development of deaf children. *American Annals of the Deaf* 115(5): 527–36.

# Struggling for a Voice:
# An Interactionist View of Language and Literacy in Deaf Education

## Sherman Wilcox

### UNDERSTANDING DEAFNESS

We can understand deafness in two ways: as a disabling condition, or as a unique way of perceiving and understanding the world. According to the first view, the essential feature of deafness is the physical condition of not being able to hear. Deaf students are disabled compared to "normal" students—they are hearing-impaired. Under this pathological view, deafness is seen as a potential barrier to students' development into normal, hearing adults. The goal of education is to intervene as early as possible with effective techniques to remediate this condition. Parents, teachers, and other professionals must be prepared to identify social, cognitive, and language difficulties that might arise because of impaired hearing. Specialists are then brought in to treat these disorders.

According to the alternative, cultural view, deaf students are not impaired hearing students any more than Hispanics and blacks are "impaired" Anglos. They are instead people with a different but equally valid view of the world.[1] According to the cultural view, the goal of education is to facilitate

---

This chapter was originally published in *Sociocultural Approaches to Language and Literacy: An Interactionist Perspective*, ed. V. John-Steiner, C. P. Panofsky, and L. W. Smith (Cambridge: Cambridge University Press, 1994), 109–38, © 1994 by Cambridge University Press. All rights reserved. Reprinted by permission of the publisher.

157

deaf students' development into multilingual, multicultural, Deaf[2] adults. Teachers, parents, and others must be alert to situations in which obstacles, misunderstandings, and misinterpretations might arise because of differing views of the world. These become the topics for discussion and learning.

The cultural view does not deny that deaf students experience difficulties. The task is not merely, however, to identify and label these problems but to appropriately interpret their significance. In order to accomplish this, we must first understand the process by which knowledge is acquired.

On one hand, as John Dewey (1916:335) put it, knowledge seems to be

> the sum total of what is known, as that is handed down by books and learned men. It is something external, an accumulation of cognitions as one might store material commodities in a warehouse. Truth exists ready-made somewhere. Study is then the process by which an individual draws on what is in storage.

The acquisition of knowledge is understood as a passive, receptive affair. Dewey believed that this notion was mistaken and led to teaching that was lacking "in any fruitful connection with the ongoing experience of the students" (342).

Instead, Dewey (1916:3,44) believed that:

> Knowledge is not just something which we are now conscious of, but consists of the dispositions we consciously use in understanding what now happens. Knowledge as an act is bringing some of our dispositions to consciousness with a view to straightening out a perplexity, by conceiving the connection between ourselves and the world in which we live.

Knowledge is actively created by people in interaction with their world. "Education," Dewey wrote, "is not an affair of 'telling' and being told, but an active and constructive process" (38).

## TOWARD A DEAF EPISTEMOLOGY

If we accept the pathological view of deafness and also believe that knowledge is external to a person, then it is natural to ascribe the source of deaf students' difficulties to their physical condition. Deafness clearly imposes a barrier between a mind waiting to be filled and the external source of knowledge. The result in education is domestication of the Deaf student. "Education for domestication is an act of transferring 'knowledge'" (Freire, 1985:102).

If we believe, however, that deafness can enable people to view the world differently and that knowledge is actively constructed, then we will expect that deaf people might arrive at a different understanding of the world than hearing people do. "If one changes the tools of thinking available to a child, his mind will have a radically different structure" (Vygotsky, 1978:126). The result in education is education for freedom. "Education for freedom is an act of knowledge and a process of transforming action. . . . Obviously learners are not seen as 'empty vessels,' mere recipients of an educator's words. Since they are not marginal beings who need to be 'restored to health' or 'saved,' learners are viewed as members of the large family of the oppressed. Answers for their situation do not reside in their learning to read alienating stories, but in their making history that will actualize their lives" (Freire, 1985:102–103).

The interaction of these two themes—the pathological versus the cultural view of deafness, and the conception of knowledge as actively created versus passively received—will form the basis for the exploration of language and literacy in the remainder of this chapter. As they impact on schooling, the two themes lead to two pedagogies of deaf education. The results of these two pedagogies—disabling and empowering—on the major issues in deaf education are shown in Table 1.

## BREAKING THROUGH THE CULTURE OF SILENCE

In order to start our exploration we need a better understanding of the Deaf experience. One way to do this is to listen to the voices of Deaf writers. I start with an excerpt from a poem by the Deaf poet Ella Mae Lentz.

We were simply talking
in our language of signs
When stormed by anthem driven soldiers
Pitched a fever by the score of their regime.
They cuffed our hands, strangled us with iron reins.
"Follow me! Line up! Now sit!"
The captain, whip in hand,
Inflicts his sentence with this command:
Speak!

**TABLE 1**
**Disabling and Empowering Pedagogies in Deaf Education**

| Issues | Disabling | Empowering |
|---|---|---|
| Where is the problem? | Inside the student Deafness | Interaction of dominated and dominant groups |
| View of Deafness | Pathological | Cultural |
| Educational practices | Effective methods Students as patients | Transformative action Students as agents |
| Student's relation to knowledge | Passive recipient Depositing | Active creator Creating and exploring |
| What should happen in the classroom? | "Fixing and filling" | "Dialoguing and exploring" |
| What is the role of the teacher? | Clinician/technician | Transformative intellectual |
| Effect on students | "The culture of silence," which leads from boredom through inaction to unconsciousness | "The struggle for voice," which leads from reflection through action to critical consciousness |
| What about reality? | Reality is given—student accommodates | Reality is opaque but can be illuminated—students transform reality |

"Sh–?"
Speak!
"–i–?"
Speak!
"–t?"
Damn your chains!
We'll pronounce our own deliverance
And articulate our message loud and clear.
And for the width of a breath
We grant each other asylum
Talking in our language of signs.
When they pound, pound, pound.
"Don't answer. Don't open. It's bad, don't."
The thunder rolls again.
"But I want to. I want to see.
Well maybe. I just want to see."
So step by step we succumb
Our silent agreement undone.

Come out of your dark and silent world
And join us in our bright and lovely world.
Look! Those whose ears work are signing!
Yes, but such queer speech they shape.
What waits out there?
To be fair we should see more.
Could it be they've rearranged the score?
And one by one
We go down the corridor of their sterile syntax,
Not knowing . . . [3]

Ella Lentz has clearly won the struggle to acquire a voice. Unfortunately, the majority of deaf students lose this battle. Deaf students are rarely in a position to write their own words, to construct their own sentences, or to author their own world. Deaf education most often inflicts sentences upon deaf students.

One form this infliction takes is defining Deaf students as those with an affliction. The Deaf world is not considered to be a separate but equal world. It is seen as a partial world, a "dark and silent world" of limited experience and false knowledge. Deaf education has made little effort to understand and incorporate the Deaf experience into the school curriculum. Instead, it has considered Deaf students as objects to be turned into images of the dominant, Hearing society. In such an atmosphere, the only reality for a Deaf student "is to be like, and to be like is to be like the oppressor" (Freire, 1970:33). The effect on students is what Freire has called the culture of silence, which leads from boredom to inaction to a state of unconsciousness. Bernard Bragg, one of the founders of the National Theater of the Deaf, has told of his experience in grade school.

> Spontaneous outbursts of laughter in the classroom were often stilled by scornful reprimands from our ... teacher not so much because they were impolite or erupted at inappropriate times as because he said they sounded disgustedly unpleasant or irritating—even animalistic. Young and uncomprehending as we were, we were given long lectures on the importance of being consistently aware of what our laughter sounded like to those who could hear.... Compliments were often lavished upon those who came up with forced but perfectly controlled laughter—and glares were given to those who failed to laugh "properly" or didn't sound like a "normal" person. Some of us have since then forgotten how to

laugh the way we had been taught. And there are two or three from our group who have chosen to laugh silently for the rest of their lives (reported in Gannon, 1981:355–356).

## BITTER WORDS FROM THE SILENCED

Freire (1985:192) asks, "What happens when the dominated people finally realize their culture is not ugly as the dominators say? What happens when they see that their values are not so deplorable, that their presence in the world is not as despicable as the dominators say?"

For those willing to listen, another Deaf voice, Lex Lohman, has broken through the culture of silence in answer.

Bitterweed
Beware the dark eyes on you in the street
And the impersonal glances
Of those who pass you by—
They have no love for you, though you be their brother;
Though you should cry for pity, there would be none.
Growing in alien soil, the strange plant dies
From rocks that press too hard, that block its root,
Sent underground for nourishment in earth
That holds no sustenance for such as come
Unbidden through the tunnel of rain.
Wherever you may go, the word shall pass
That you are stranger there, and you shall know
The unreceptive ground and fierce sunlight
In the press of hostile faces: they will shout
In a bitter voice the wisdom of the old,
Who have no will to live nor strength to die
And speak the blind prejudice of the stone,
And close the shadowy door.
Only the bitterweed can sink its root
Into the powerful rancor of the soil
And blossom forth in strong integrity,
Undaunted by a hatred. You must send
Your anger forth to rend the strangling rock
And with your strength build shelter from the sun;
And send them also

A word as bitter as theirs, as filled with hatred:
Then only will they let you pass in peace.[4]

Deaf education is conceived as "education of the disabled" (see Cummins, 1986, for a similar account of minority education). The goal is to help the students overcome their pathology, their deafness—and join hearing people in our "bright and lovely world." Teachers are seen as clinicians who must cure their patients before they can fill their heads. What do Deaf people think of this approach? Guie C. Cooke provides a humorous but insightful glimpse in the poem, "Pests to Exterminate."

There is a pest we can't endure:
He is the one who has a cure,
And comes around with this or that.
Politely, we pass him his hat.
(If there's a cure we'd like to try
It's socking him upon the eye!)

There is a sense, though, in which Deaf education is truly education of the "disabled." The source of disablement is not within Deaf students. It is not the result of their deafness. Deaf students are rendered disabled by their interactions and struggles with the educational establishment. Myths—linguistic and cultural—are imposed on Deaf people's lives. Their struggle for consciousness is the struggle to illuminate these myths by questioning them, to shape their world by speaking their own words. The character Alice in Gilbert Eastman's play *Sign Me Alice II* says, "The hearing people do not treat me right. . . . Their ideas are false. They are hypocrites. They mold deaf people's lives. Not mine. Not my soul. I won't let them reshape me. . . . Deep in my body there is a flame."

Deaf education does not have to be disabling. There is an empowering alternative (Cummins, 1986). Bilingual, bicultural approaches to Deaf education can fan the flame by incorporating "knowledge and social relations that dignify one's own history, language, and cultural traditions" (Giroux & McLaren, 1986:221). Such an approach to Deaf education can empower students. It can enable them to question false ideas, to transform the world, and to mold their own reality.

In order to begin empowering Deaf students we must understand a simple fact: Deaf students do make sense of the world. If it looks like they do not, it is because our understanding has been mystified in two ways. Teachers often are not aware of what Deaf students are doing.

Once we choose to ignore the Deaf experience, we lose our link to making sense of the sense the student makes. Teachers are also often unaware of what they are doing, especially in their language-mediated, finely tuned interactions (or, as is too often the case, out-of-tune interactions) with Deaf students.

## MAKING SENSE OF THE WORLD

By listening to the voices of Deaf people we can also gain a glimpse of what the world looks like through their eyes. Ethnography is ideally suited to this task. The ethnographer assumes that the only way to discover how people understand the world is to accept the validity of their knowledge, "to grasp the native's point of view, his relation to life, to realize his vision of his world" (Malinowski, 1922:25). The point of this is not to "become Deaf" but to better understand what Deaf people are doing, how they make sense of their world. As Geertz (1983:58) explained:

> The trick is not to get yourself into some inner correspondence of spirit with your informants. Preferring, like the rest of us, to call their souls their own, they are not going to be altogether keen about such an effort anyway. The trick is to figure out what the devil they think they are up to.

In the sections that follow, I recount the experiences of a young Deaf child with the goal of discovering how she makes sense of her world (Wilcox & Corwin, 1990).

BoMee was born in Kang Won-do, Korea on March 26, 1984. She was born eight weeks prematurely, but apparently responded to sound as a neonate. Her lungs were not completely formed when she was born, and consequently BoMee developed chronic pneumonia. She was given streptomycin as an antibiotic during this time; the medication, as well as her premature birth and subsequent illness, are possible factors in the etiology of her deafness. BoMee is profoundly deaf with a 110 dB sensorineural loss in both ears.

BoMee was assigned to a foster family in Korea when her health returned at age 0;6. She stayed with this family until she was adopted. BoMee arrived in the United States on August 23, 1986, at age 2;5. She immediately started attending the local preschool for the deaf.

BoMee's adoptive mother, Joanne, teaches special education for the local school district, specializing in working with communicatively disordered, hearing children. Joanne has taken a few sign language classes and primarily signs English.

BoMee's adoptive father, Kim, is Korean and also was adopted by an American family. Kim holds a baccalaureate degree in sign language interpreting. He is a certified interpreter and employed as a classroom interpreter. Kim is fluent in American Sign Language (ASL) as well as signed English.[5] BoMee was 4;3.

BoMee's parents decided to provide as rich and healthy a learning environment for her as they could. They knew before she arrived that BoMee was deaf; because of their backgrounds—their knowledge of ASL and their acquaintance with deaf people and Deaf culture—they decided that they would make every effort to raise BoMee in a multilingual, multicultural environment. What does it mean to provide such an environment to a young deaf child? For Joanne and Kim, it meant the following.

BoMee is exposed to a wide variety of signing. Kim signs primarily ASL to her, and Joanne signs primarily English (typically using simultaneous communication, or speech and voice at the same time). When Micah was born, Joanne and Kim decided to sign to him also, not only so he would naturally acquire signed language but also so BoMee would see her parents signing to other children. Grandparents, aunts, uncles, nieces, and nephews all either took sign language classes or learned basic vocabulary from Kim and Joanne. One of BoMee's relatives was already a student in a local sign language interpreter program.

In addition, Kim and Joanne attempted to provide BoMee with a wide variety of models of Deaf adult signing. They routinely ask Deaf adults to visit and encourage them to talk with BoMee, tell her stories in ASL, and read to her by signing from children's storybooks. BoMee has many videotapes of Deaf adults telling stories in ASL.

BoMee is encouraged to recognize her multicultural background. She is exposed to Deaf culture and allowed to see this as a positive part of her cultural heritage. She also is exposed to and told about Hearing culture (the ways and values of hearing people).

BoMee's encounters with the Deaf community have been structured so that she can learn the ways and values of many different adults: educated, uneducated; professionals, workers; oral, signing; ASL users, signed English users, and so forth. Deaf adults are invited to take BoMee on short trips to parks or shopping, giving her the chance to talk with Deaf people and to see them interacting with hearing people.

Korean culture was an important part of BoMee's early life and remains so in her new home. Both parents are familiar with Korean culture and incorporate it into their home life (e.g., Korean holidays, food, customs, language, and stories).

## FINDING AN IDENTITY

BoMee's multilingual, multicultural environment has had an influence on her social and cultural development in at least two ways. It has provided her with an environment in which clear and easy communication can take place with family, adults, and peers; and, it has provided her with a secure sense of who she is and where she fits into the world. Young children clearly need free and easy communication to develop the finely tuned interactions so important to language development (Bruner, 1983). They also need it to resolve conflicts, to establish healthy relations with others, and to ease the ever-present fears of childhood (Meadow, 1968; Schlesinger & Meadow, 1972). This was especially true for BoMee.

Once, for example, BoMee was unable to go to sleep at her normal bedtime. She continued to jump out of bed, ask for water, horseplay, and do the various things a five-year-old does when avoiding sleep. Kim and Joanne were becoming rather irritated, so Joanne went into the bedroom to talk to BoMee. BoMee told her mother that at first she was postponing going to sleep because she had felt afraid of the dark. Later, she explained, as her parents became more and more irritated with her behavior, she found it even more difficult to relax and go to sleep because of the anxiety she felt trying to force herself to sleep quickly so that her parents would not become more upset.

Without the ability to communicate freely and easily with her parents, this situation would never have been discussed in such rich detail. Instead, BoMee's fear and anxiety would have gone unexpressed, and her parents would have had little or no insight into the cause of their daughter's behavior.

Deaf children often grow up not knowing what will become of them as adults. Since they rarely see deaf adults, they often assume that they will die or be killed before they become adults (Fletcher, 1987) or that they will suddenly become hearing since the world seems to be populated only by hearing adults.

BoMee had a similar misconception, related not to her deafness but to her adoption experience. One day, BoMee and Joanne were driving by the airport. BoMee asked, THAT'S THE AIRPORT WHERE I ARRIVED, RIGHT? Joanne said, YES, THAT'S RIGHT. Then BoMee asked with a very gloomy expression, IS IT TIME YET? Joanne, not understanding what BoMee was talking about, asked, IS IT TIME FOR WHAT? BoMee replied, TO PUT MICAH ON A PLANE AND SEND HIM AWAY. BoMee remembered arriving at the airport on a plane when her Korean foster family sent her to the United States. She also knew, from stories that Kim had told her, that he too had arrived on a plane when he was adopted. BoMee was under the impression that parents must send their children away when they reach a certain age. This misconception was easy for Joanne to clear up. Clearly, though, the resolution of this misconception depended critically on fluent and easy communication between Joanne and BoMee.

Because of her exposure to a wide variety of Deaf adults, BoMee has a firm understanding of what it means to be a Deaf person; of the appropriate way to behave when associating with Deaf people; and of how she, as a Deaf person, can interact in a healthy and appropriate way with hearing people. An encounter with a hearing woman in a grocery store demonstrates her bicultural competence.

Hearing adults are easily attracted to BoMee; she is a cute, deaf girl who talks with her hands to her parents. Frequently, strangers want to pick her up, play with her, and give her candy or gum. Joanne has tried to teach BoMee that she doesn't have to let people touch her just because she is deaf, and that she should not accept candy or food from strangers. Once, in a grocery store, an older woman noticed BoMee and Joanne signing in the checkout line. "Oh, she's so cute," the woman bubbled. Then, she offered BoMee a stick of gum. Turning to Joanne, BoMee said, MOM, TELL HER 'NO THANK YOU—I'M DEAF, I'M NOT POOR.'

BoMee has a strong, positive sense of self-identity as a Deaf person. There is no indication that BoMee is confused or self-conscious about what it means to be deaf. On the contrary, she seems to think that being deaf is something that anyone could be proud of.

When he was 0;10, Micah had chronic ear infections and subsequently had to have grommets or "tubes" put in his ears. Before this surgery the mass of fluid in his ears had become adhesive, allowing little or no sound conduction to take place. Once, during this time, BoMee called to Micah, and he did not respond. Joanne explained to BoMee that because of the fluid in Micah's ears, he was temporarily "deaf." MICAH'S DEAF? BoMee asked incredulously. She ran to Micah and signed, GOOD BOY, MICAH!

## WATCHING OTHERS THINK

L. S. Vygotsky (1978:57) noted that thinking is a social activity. The roots of the higher cognitive functions begin in our interactions with others:

All the higher functions originate as actual relations between human individuals. . . . Every function in the child's cultural development appears twice: first, on the social level, and later, on the individual level; first, between people (interpsychological), and then inside the child (intrapsychological).

In a natural language setting, children have access to all the language that is in their environment—not only talk that is directed to them, but also talk from adults to other children, from children to adults, from adults to adults, and the private or problem-solving speech of adults and children.

Educators often cite the need for access to this environmental talk as an advantage of total communication (Pahz & Pahz, 1978). In the experience of many Deaf people, however, total communication rarely lives up to its name (Bahan, 1989a). Parents and teachers frequently do not sign everything they say or sign it in such a way that it cannot be understood (Johnson, Liddell, & Erting, 1989; Marmor & Petitto, 1979). One type of speech that is especially likely not to be signed is speech that is clearly not intended for the deaf child: adult's problem-solving speech.

The Corwins sign all of their verbal interactions with BoMee. They also try, as much as possible, to sign their interactions with others when BoMee is present. About a month. after BoMee arrived, they also decided to sign their private speech. Every time they were talking to themselves or verbally problem solving, they would sign "aloud." Some examples are: GEE, WHAT GOES NEXT IN THIS RECIPE? I WONDER WHERE KIM IS. MAYBE HE HAD A MEETING. Every morning when they looked for their shoes they would sign to themselves, WHERE ARE MY SHOES? In about a week, they noticed BoMee in her bedroom signing to herself, WHERE MY SHOES WHERE ("Where are my shoes?").[6]

This private speech continued to progress as BoMee's ASL developed. Soon, BoMee was signing her own private speech while she solved problems. Some examples are:

(Trying a dress on a doll. The dress is just a little too small): HMMM. WRONG ME. THIS DRESS FIT HERE? THINK NOT. HMMM. FOR OTHER DOLL HERE. ("Hmmm. I'm wrong. Does this dress go on this doll? I don't think so. Hmmm. It goes on this other doll.")

(Looking for her shoes): WHERE SHOES MINE WHERE? HMMM. THINK LEFF MY ROOM THERE MAYBE. NO, NO. KNOW, KNOW, KNOW. BEHIND CHAIR, KNOW. ("Where are my shoes? I think I might have left them in my room. No, no. I know, I know! They're behind the chair.")

The effects of her early exposure to interpersonal and problem-solving speech can be seen in BoMee's later problem solving. One day BoMee told a lie. Since she had started doing this fairly frequently, her parents decided this required a family meeting. They sat down with her and told her that they knew that she understood what she had done was inappropriate, and that they wanted to discuss with her what the consequences of this behavior should be. WELL, she signed in ASL, IN MY OPINION YOU HAVE THREE CHOICES. YOU CAN EITHER TAKE AWAY MY TOYS, GIVE ME A SPANKING (BUT I DON'T THINK THAT'S A GOOD IDEA), OR GIVE ME TIME OUT. OF COURSE, IT'S YOUR DECISION. She was so sophisticated and serious in her manner that BoMee was given time out so that her parents could go into the other room and laugh.

## USING THE TOOLS AT HAND

BoMee's early life was not conducive to language development. Her Korean foster family did not know any sign language, and BoMee received no special schooling or therapy. The extent of her language development during her first two and a half years was reflected in the "home signs" that her Korean foster family used with her. These were gestures that this particular family used to identify BoMee's basic needs (potty, food) and to name items (animal). She arrived in the United States with no more than five of these home signs.

Many professionals in deafness might assume that the use of home signs is a harmful practice since they are not part of a formal linguistic system. The Corwins feel, however, that this signed input served the useful function of making BoMee aware at an early age that motions of the hands can be meaningful. They allowed BoMee to learn that words (signs) can represent things in the environment. They served much the same function that phonetically consistent forms or protowords serve for young hearing children (see, e.g., Berko-Gleason, 1985:50, 72).

We have seen other deaf children who come to school without any idea of what words are for. This becomes an obstacle in their language and cognitive development. Perhaps because of the few home signs that

BoMee had, she began to learn words for concrete objects fairly soon after she arrived in the United States. The first evening, for example, she learned DADDY, MILK, and KISS.

The family spends much time talking about language. They talk about ASL, English, signing, and speech; about why some deaf people speak and others don't; about when deaf people should use their voice and when they should not. At one point, BoMee was concerned with whether she would learn to speak like hearing people. At another, she wanted to know why all hearing people don't sign. All this talk has made BoMee quite aware of language in its signed, spoken, and written manifestations.

One indication of BoMee's metalinguistic awareness is her interactions with Micah. BoMee signs motherese to Micah. She works on expanding his language and its complexity in a natural way. One evening at the dinner table Micah signed MORE. YOU WANT MORE? signed BoMee, emphasizing MORE to reinforce his attempt. HERE'S SOME MORE. THIS IS RICE. YOU WANT MORE RICE? THAT'S RIGHT!

BoMee's awareness of sociolinguistic variation extends to adults. She knows that some people talk and others sign; she also knows that some people sign and understand ASL while others only sign and understand English. As early as age 3;2 she recognized the variation in her home linguistic environment: she signed the game THIS LITTLE PIGGY in ASL to Kim and in English to Joanne.

BoMee seemed to develop an early affinity for ASL. We are not able to say why this occurred. Perhaps it is because ASL is a more "natural" language, one that is better suited to the visual modality (Supalla, 1986). It is also possible, however, that BoMee preferred ASL because of the early bond that developed between her and her father. Whatever the reason, BoMee went through a phase when, after her mother would sign something to her, she would turn to her father and say, SAY IT THE RIGHT WAY.

BoMee's awareness of sociolinguistic variation is now quite refined. Once, watching a videotape of the deaf actress and storyteller, Linda Bove, BoMee commented to Joanne, THAT WOMAN SIGNS PRETTY GOOD. I THINK SHE'S DEAF. The same tape featured a hearing woman who signed a story. THAT OTHER WOMAN, BoMee continued, DOESN'T SIGN THAT GOOD. SHE'S PROBABLY HEARING.

BoMee is also quite adept at dealing with sociolinguistic variation at school. She knows that the teachers prefer English and speech to ASL.[7] She understands the idiosyncratic signs that deaf children with limited ASL or English vocabularies use, and she uses them with her deaf peers but not, for example, her parents. One day when Joanne was visiting the preschool, a young deaf boy ran up to BoMee and signed a word; it was clearly not an ASL or signed English word. Later, Joanne asked BoMee what the boy had said. HE SAID LET'S PLAY THE GAME WHERE WE CHASE EACH OTHER AROUND THE PLAYGROUND, she explained. Puzzled, Joanne asked BoMee how she knew that the boy had meant that. BECAUSE THAT'S WHAT HE SAID, was BoMee's matter-of-fact reply.

Deaf parents fingerspell to their deaf children. Hearing parents are often advised against this because it is assumed that deaf children who are unable to read and write lack the skills to make fingerspelling meaningful. ASL researchers have noted, however, that deaf children may make sense of fingerspelling not as a letter-handshape correspondence, but as a primary signed system (Akamatsu, 1985; Padden & LeMaster, 1985; Wilcox, 1992). In other words, deaf children may comprehend fingerspelling as a gestalt just as hearing children perceive speech as a gestalt in the early stages of language development (Peters, 1983).

Joanne at first accepted the common wisdom that fingerspelling depends on spelling and was concerned when Kim began fingerspelling to BoMee. She had little formal language, much less any letter recognition. Within the first month, however, BoMee was fingerspelling her first word, B-U-S. It seems that BoMee understood this simply as a complex sign, because she could not read the word "bus" or say which letters were in B-U-S. Later, though, when she started reading, these fingerspelled words quickly became sight vocabulary for BoMee.

BoMee has enjoyed stories and books since she was three years old, but the actual process of reading as it pertains to phonological symbols was often perplexing to her. Initially, she started reading words in context. "Don't Walk," "Open," "McDonald's," and "No Parking Any Time" were some of her favorites. Her family also helped her to read environmental print in the home such as "milk" and "cat food." Words for which she had some visual association seemed to come easily, but she still was not able to read even the shortest of stories.

One of the most remarkable events in BoMee's language development was her discovery of how to use the phonology of ASL to solve the problems she faced learning to read.

By about the age of five, BoMee was reading simple books. As Joanne would read to her and BoMee would pick out the words she knew, Joanne noticed that BoMee had difficulty remembering some words: "that," "not," and "and" gave her particular problems.

Joanne tried using Dolch word cards with BoMee with minimal success. Just as Joanne began looking for other ideas, she noticed that BoMee was reading these words on her own.

In order to understand BoMee's solution, it is necessary to have a basic understanding of the phonology of ASL.[8] Signed words, like spoken words, are composed of minimal contrasting units—phonemes. As is true for spoken languages, ASL phonemes are composed of contrasting units called distinctive features.

Just as a hearing child first reads out loud, BoMee "signs out loud" when she reads. One day, Joanne was watching BoMee read and noticed that when she came to the word 'that' BoMee made the Y handshape (a phoneme of the ASL word THAT) with her right hand. With her left hand, BoMee moved the fingerspelled letter T from her thumb to her pinky finger. When Joanne asked what this meant, BoMee replied, SEE, IT LOOKS LIKE "THAT." T AND T, SEE? (see figure 1).

The feature [+spread] is a feature of the Y handshape and other handshapes such as horn-Y (as in the sign MOCK). In the Y handshape, [+spread] is realized as the extension of the thumb and pinky finger. What BoMee had done was establish a relationship between this feature of the Y phoneme and the fact that in English orthography "that" is spelled with a "t" at the beginning and the end. The two extended digits of the Y phoneme represented for BoMee the English grapheme "t" at the beginning and end of "that." She had created a three-way link between the visual phonetics of signed language (the Y phoneme and its feature [+spread]), fingerspelling (the handshape T), and English orthography.

BoMee also showed Joanne the word NOT. NOT is produced with an open-A handshape. The open-A handshape shares the feature [ +spread]

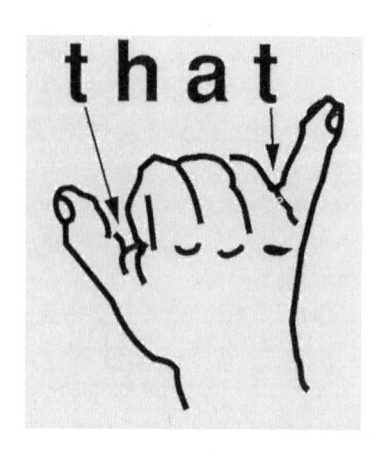

**FIGURE 1**

with Y. It contrasts with the regular A handshape used in fingerspelling and in signs such as WITH.[9] BoMee demonstrated that the closed fingers of NOT can represent the English graphemes "n" and V and the thumb can represent "t." Again, for BoMee the extended thumb represented the English grapheme "t."

Finally, BoMee showed her mother how she remembered the English word "and." She explained, BECAUSE IT LOOKS LIKE "AND," SEE THE A, N, AND DT? BoMee demonstrated how the shape of the hand in forming the word AND resembles the shape of the word "and" in print by fingerspelling A, N, and D starting at the tips of the handshape and extending to the base of the palm (see figure 2). Indeed, in print, the letters A, N, and D increase from left to right, just as does the final handshape (flat-0) in the ASL word AND.

Eventually these words became sight words for BoMee and she discontinued using the phonological cues she had created for herself. She has not, however, discontinued using this strategy with new words. She had found a way to use her knowledge of the phonology of her preferred mode of communication, signing, to facilitate acquisition of her second language, written English.

## QUEER SPEECH

The previous example showed how BoMee used the structure of signed language to facilitate her acquisition of English. Sometimes, however, what

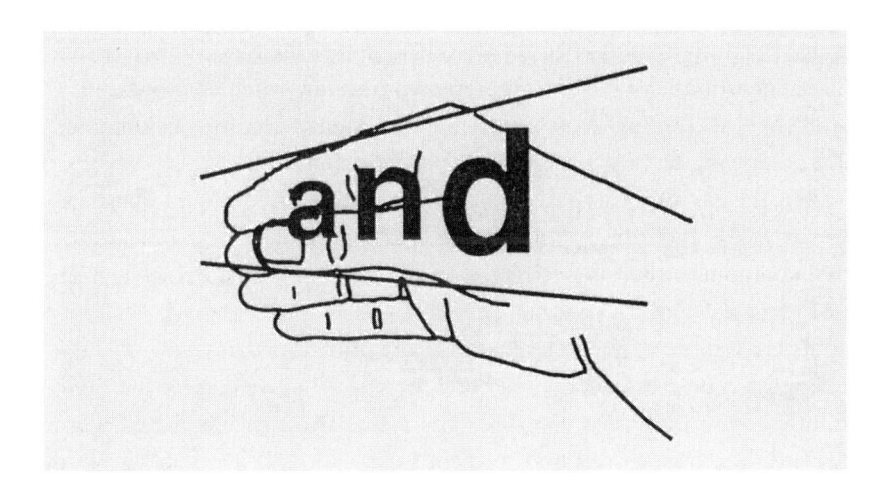

**FIGURE 2**

BoMee was taught about signed and spoken languages impeded her acquisition of English.

BoMee was introduced to the present progressive signed English suffix, -ING, in school. BoMee was already producing present progressive in ASL (verb plus head nod), as well as other verbal tense and aspect forms. She knew that in ASL, the tense marker is often placed at the beginning of a sentence: FINISH ME EAT ME, "I ate." It was no surprise to her parents when BoMee started producing sentences like -ING ME EAT ME, "I am eating."

It makes perfect sense. It follows the grammar of ASL. It expresses a concept that was obviously in BoMee's zone of proximal development. More important to her teachers, however, was the fact that BoMee used -ING as a free morpheme, a word. It was, in this sense, ungrammatical English, a language problem to be explained.

Teachers inflict the command to "Speak" but they also accept that students should sign. "Those whose ears work" are signing in Deaf education more and more. As Ella Lentz noticed, however, it is often "queer speech they shape."

This queer speech is called Manually Coded English (MCE). In an earlier section I suggested that teachers are often not aware of what they are doing. A critical gap in their awareness is their own language behavior, their signing. Teachers have very little idea about what these coded English systems that they rely on really are, how they are constructed, and what they accomplish.

These systems are inventions, engineered languages designed to represent natural language from one modality in another modality—spoken English becomes signed English (Wilcox & Wilcox, 1991). Thus, they are analogous to writing systems, which likewise represent spoken language in another modality. Like writing systems, MCE must answer two design questions: what will be represented (sounds, syllables, words, etc.), and where will the symbols (written marks, signed gestures) be obtained (by borrowing from existing systems or by invention)?

For the example at hand, the solution to these two design questions is that words and affixes will be signed—as opposed, for example, to the two component sounds in -ING. The sign for EAT was borrowed (from ASL) and the sign for -ING was invented.

There is more to the story of -ING. The present progressive inflection in English is unstressed: "eat-ing" not "eat-ing." Notice that for the MCE solution the situation is reversed. The visual stress in the signed word EAT+ING does not correspond to the acoustic stress of the spoken word "eat-ing." When the -ING marker is added to a word in MCE, the stress shifts from the root word to the suffix: EAT-ING.

Hearing teachers are little aware of this subtle but critical difference. As hearing people, they rely more on the acoustic stress than the visual stress. We know that stress and intonation play an important role in young hearing children's language acquisition (Cruttendon, 1986; Peters, 1983). Should we expect otherwise for Deaf children? The only difference is that they are surely more attuned to the visual stress. From there, they take the ball and run, right into -ING ME EAT ME.

The teachers at BoMee's school took note of this language behavior. Their conclusion was that Deaf children always have difficulty with English present progressive. It is, they declared, a particular characteristic of the abnormal language development of deaf children.

## LEGITIMIZING THE DISABILITY: WHOSE WORLD IS IT?

Others also took note of the situation. About this time, Joanne took BoMee to be evaluated at the local school district. The diagnostician asked whether BoMee was using present progressive. Joanne replied "Yes." "You mean BoMee consistently signs -ING," the diagnostician asked. Joanne told her that BoMee was not yet consistently using present progressive in English, but was using it quite regularly and properly in ASL. The diagnostician's assessment, duly entered into BoMee's permanent record: "Child has not acquired present progressive." Thus, BoMee was transformed from a creative language user to a disabled child with a developmental language disorder.

Deaf students do not come to school as passive, empty containers waiting to be fixed and filled. They are, like their hearing peers, active, critical learners. In spite of diagnosticians' assessments to the contrary, lack of hearing leads to neither lack of knowledge nor inability to learn. It may, as we have seen, lead to different knowledge. This different knowledge may then lead the Deaf student, using her critical, constructive thinking, to arrive at a different understanding—of English grammar, for instance—from her hearing peers or from the hearing teacher. Finally, this different learning experience most certainly will be differently valued. But this is clearly a socially, culturally, and politically constructed accomplishment. It is, as Foucault (1980) understood, a matter of power, of determining who is charged with saying what counts as true knowledge.

It seems that BoMee has the world at her fingertips. But whose world is it (Bahan, 1989b)? From the hearing perspective—especially those such as teachers and diagnosticians who are in positions of authority to say what counts as right and wrong, normal and abnormal—there is but one reality. It is a hearing world, and deaf children must learn to live in it. In fact, the world is neither hearing nor deaf. It is as we create it, given our own unique perceptions, dispositions, and active, constructive minds. "The effective environment of any organism is never merely the objective situation in which he finds himself, but rather the product of an interaction between his unique organismic characteristics and whatever opportunities for experience his objective surroundings may provide" (John-Steiner & Souberman, 1978:125).

## STRAIGHTENING OUT PERPLEXITIES

"Children solve practical tasks with the help of their speech, as well as their eyes and their hands" (Vygotsky, 1978:26). This is profoundly true for BoMee, especially when we consider that for her, speech is signed language. With regard to the practical task of reading, BoMee's solution is informative for at least three reasons.

First, it was BoMee's invention, not an outsider's intervention. Using the tools at hand, Deaf children can devise effective solutions to meaningful problems. For Deaf as well as hearing students, learning need not be an affair of being told but an active, constructive process.

Second, the strategy depended on BoMee's knowledge of ASL. The case is often made that ASL is detrimental, or at least of no help, to the acquisition of English by deaf children. This clearly was not true for BoMee. Her knowledge of ASL was critical to her literacy development.

Finally, it was a visual strategy. The relation between speech and writing, phoneme and grapheme, depends on sound. As hearing people, we may not think it is possible to use the structure of a language unrelated to English—a language in which phonemes are produced with the hands and perceived with the eyes—to establish a phoneme-grapheme connection. Indeed, there is no historical connection between ASL handshape phonemes such as Y, open-A, and flat-O and English graphemes. To BoMee, however, this was a natural way to bring her unique "dispositions to consciousness with a view to straightening out a perplexity" (Dewey, 1916:334). It was a stunning glimpse at a tiny spark of critical consciousness. [10]

## EMPOWERING TEACHERS AND STUDENTS

The story of -ING suggests that teachers frequently are not critically aware of the impact of what they are doing, especially in their language-mediated interactions with Deaf students. For this, we must lay responsibility with teacher education and teacher accreditation. It is not only Deaf students who "go down the corridor . . . not knowing." Educators, whether they are hearing or deaf, must also struggle against the mystifications that are provided to them through the official curriculum, history, and their own unexamined beliefs. Just as education has disempowered Deaf students, teacher training programs continue to withhold knowledge from future teachers that would enable them to engage in active, critical dialogue with their Deaf students. Those few who are capable of doing this have become what Giroux and McLaren (1986:217; see also Giroux, 1988) call transformative intellectuals, "capable of articulating emancipatory possibilities and working towards their realization. [They] . . . treat students as critical agents, question how knowledge is produced and distributed, utilize dialogue, and make knowledge meaningful, critical, and ultimately emancipatory."

What can be done about this situation? How can Deaf education empower Deaf students? How can teacher training programs turn out Deaf educators who are capable of acting as transformative intellectuals?

First, we must reexamine the role of the Deaf community in Deaf education. As Elsasser and John-Steiner (1977:356) have remarked, "A student's sense of personal power and control emerges largely as a result of the increasing movement of his or her social group towards self-determination. In the absence of such movement educational intervention is most often futile." The Deaf community, the Deaf experience, Deaf culture, and Deaf history must become a part of the official school curriculum.

Second, we must examine and restructure teacher training programs and accreditation requirements. This movement is already under way in a limited way. Harlan Lane (1988) has pointed the way in his recommendations to the Commission on Education of the Deaf on restructuring Deaf education teacher preparation. Until the macrostructure of Deaf education requires it, though, we will continue to produce teachers of the Deaf who know more about vocal-fold physiology than they do about Deaf culture or ASL.

Third, we must all—Deaf and hearing, teacher and student—become critically aware of the language situation in Deaf education. Vygotsky

(1978) tells us that language is a tool for thought. It is time to examine our tools—all of them: ASL, MCE, spoken English, written English, and whatever languages are being used in the Deaf student's home and community.

Bakhtin (1981:295–296) describes the importance to illiterate Russian peasants of becoming critically aware of their own complex language situation; the insight is equally applicable to Deaf students.

> Thus an illiterate peasant, miles away from any urban center, naively immersed in an unmoving and for him unshakable everyday world, nevertheless lived in several language systems: he prayed to God in one language (Church Slavonic), sang songs in another, spoke to his family in a third, and, when he began to dictate petitions to the local authorities through a scribe, he tried speaking yet a fourth language (the official-literate language, "paper" language). All these are different languages. . . . But these languages were not dialogically coordinated in the linguistic consciousness of the peasant; he passed from one to the other without thinking, automatically: each was indisputably in its own place, and the place of each was indisputable. He was not yet able to regard one language (and the verbal world corresponding to it) through the eyes of another language (that is, the language of everyday life and the everyday world with the language of prayer or song, or vice versa). As soon as a critical interanimation of languages began to occur in the consciousness of our peasant, as soon as it became clear that these were not only various different languages but even internally variegated languages, that the ideological systems and approaches to the world that were indissolubly connected with these languages contradicted each other and in no way could live in peace and quiet with one another—then the inviolability and predetermined quality of these languages came to an end, and the necessity of actively choosing one's orientation among them began.

Approaches to Deaf education which impose others' solutions, concepts, and truths on the student—not only old-fashioned, fix-and-fill, "banking concept" (Freire, 1970) approaches but also some bilingual/bicultural programs—are doomed to failure. The path to critical consciousness does not begin from without, but from within the Deaf student. The first step is true dialogue between teachers and students, which allows students to act not as patients but as agents in the discovery and transformation of their inner world of knowledge and outer world of sociocultural relations.

The educator's role is to propose problems about the codified existential situations in order to help learners arrive at a more and more critical view of their reality. . . . He can never be a mere memorizer, but a person constantly readjusting his knowledge who calls forth knowledge from his students. For him, education is a pedagogy of knowing. The educator whose approach is mere memorization is antidialogical; his act of transmitting knowledge is inalterable. For the educator who experiences the act of knowing together with his students, in contrast, dialogue is the sign of the act of knowing. (Freire, 1985:55)

## DISCOURSES OF POWER AND TRUTH

The interaction of language and culture in Deaf education is shown in figure 3. The critical factors of language and culture are considered as they impact the Deaf student on a macro level (e.g., in pedagogy and ideology; teacher talk about Deaf students' language; culturally transmitted myths about deafness) and on a microlevel (students' and teachers' bilingual/bimodal competence; the daily interactions between Deaf students, teachers, parents, and others and hearing teachers, administrators, diagnosticians, and others).

Interactions of language and culture on the macrolevel are called "discourses of power and truth." They include scenarios such as described here in which BoMee was labeled a language-disordered child by a diagnostician charged with "saying what counts as true knowledge." Interactions at the microlevel are called "interpersonal interactions." Many of them contribute not only to the moment-to-moment disablement of Deaf students

| Language | | Culture | |
|---|---|---|---|
| Talk about language and literacy | ◄── Discourses of Power and Truth ──► | Ideology and cultural myths | Macro |
| Bilingualism Bimodalism | ◄── Interpersonal Interactions ──► | Daily lived Interactions | Micro |

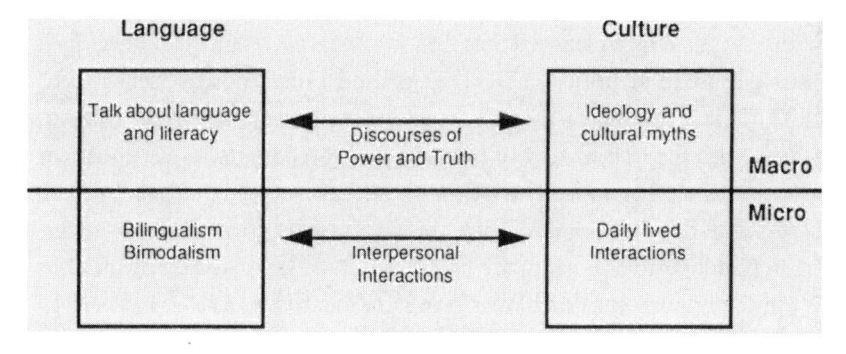

**FIGURE 3**

but also to the creation of the "historical-cultural configuration we have called the culture of silence" (Freire, 1985:72). Giroux (1981) elaborates:

> Culture . . . [is] defined not simply as experiences functioning within the context of historical structures and social formations, but as "lived antagonistic relations" situated within a complex of sociopolitical institutions and social forms that limit as well as enable human action. . . . It is a complex realm of antagonistic experiences mediated by power and struggle. . . . To rethink the concept of culture is thus to attempt to articulate not only the experiences and practices that are distinctive to a specific group or class, but also to link those experiences to the power exercised by the dominant class.

Clearly, ASL must play a much more active role in Deaf education. Students should be receiving formal classroom instruction not only in ASL but also about ASL. Students and teachers together must explore and discuss the languages of the community. This is occurring in only a limited way in very few experimental or proposed programs (Humphries, Coye, & Martin, 1989; Johnson et al., 1989; Strong, 1988).

That such an approach empowers disenfranchised communities is clear (Elsasser & Irvine, 1985; Freire, 1985; Shor & Freire, 1987). The reports of the people themselves are remarkably univocal. A Nicaraguan writer reports, "I realized that in order to study what I wanted I had to begin by studying my own language. I had to begin all over again. It was hard, but little by little I began with the Spanish and as I went along I discovered that it's a beautiful thing to study one's own language; I was beginning to understand so many things" (Randall, 1984:187). Mervin Garretson, a Deaf writer, expresses the same sentiment: "To know, once and for all, that our 'primitive' and 'ideographic' gestures are really a formal language on a par with all other languages of the world is a step towards pride and liberation" (in Gannon, 1984:367). Barbara Kannapell, a Deaf sociolinguist, says, "Once I learned that ASL is my native language, I developed a strong sense of identity as a Deaf person and a more positive self-image" (ibid.: 372). A speaker of Virgin Island Creole pleads that, "as we strive to identify with the rich history of our enslaved foreparents, as we endeavor to become more patriotic, let us learn to cherish everything that belongs to us; this includes our Creoles. They are works of art created by our ancestors in bondage and, as such, are precious gifts to be treasured by all of us here in the English-speaking West Indies" (Richardson, 1985). In his 1913 film, *Preservation of the Sign Language*, George Veditz, a Deaf teacher and president of the National Association of the Deaf, offered the same plea.

"A new race of Pharaohs that knew not Joseph" are taking over the land and many of our American schools. They do not understand signs, for they cannot sign. They proclaim that signs are worthless and of no help to the Deaf. Enemies of the sign language, they are enemies of the true welfare of the Deaf. . . . As long as we have Deaf people on earth, we will have signs. . . . It is my hope that we all will love and guard our beautiful sign language as the noblest gift God has given to Deaf people. (in Padden & Humphries, 1988:36)

Critical bilingual/bicultural education—in ASL and English, by Deaf and hearing teachers—must become the accepted method in Deaf education. Only in this way will educators cease to inflict sentences and instead enable Deaf students to discover and pronounce their own.

## WRITING OUR OWN WORDS

Such an approach to education not only empowers language users, it also empowers and strengthens the suppressed language. Freire (1985:185) recognized this when he wrote, "A language can only develop when it is practiced in all domains and given opportunity to do so." In this regard, it is important to realize the effect that a writing system can have on a language. In the specific instance of Virgin Island Creole, Carrington (1981) has noted that "The . . . opportunity for the use of creole by the development of a writing system breaks the barrier that has shut out from information transfer, from 'language-hood' and from confidence, large numbers of people over several hundred years in this society, has shut them out from full communication within their society. . . . There is a need, a very deep need, for communication tools that allow people to share in the development of their society."

It is important not to underestimate the importance of writing to the integrity of languages and their users. Literacy is a double-edged sword (Coulmas, 1989:5):

To those who cannot read and write, a book or any other written document manifestly demonstrates their own ignorance and powerlessness; of which fact the educated few can and, of course, do take advantage. One of the crucial consequences of the invention of writing becomes apparent here: it is a powerful instrument of social control.

Writing also "greatly enlarges the range of communication and, consequently, power" (ibid.:7). Some of the functions that writing affords in addition to those provided by spoken or signed language are (Coulmas, 1989):

1. *Mnemonic function:* writing can aid in preserving individuals' memory (e.g., lists) and a peoples' memory. "History becomes possible thanks to the mnemonic function of writing, as well as the accumulation of knowledge" (ibid.:12). Although they probably overstate the case when they claim that "prehistory is the study of peoples without writing, whereas history is the study of people who possess written texts" (Stuart & Houston, 1989:82), there is a sense in which literacy allows people to create their own histories, to "transform the world with their work and create their own world. This world, created by the transformation of another world they did not create and that now restrains them, is the cultured world that stretches out into the world of history" (Freire, 1985:14–15).

2. *Distancing function:* "writing is a distancing medium not only with respect to sender and receiver, but also as regards the sender and the message" (ibid.).

3. *Reifying function:* "The spoken word is ephemeral and spontaneous in its very essence. In writing, on the other hand, words become stable and tangible. As objects in their own right they become, moreover, depersonalized" (ibid.). In spoken and signed utterances the focus is on what the person means. In written works, the focus is more likely to be on what the words mean, independent of the author. This opens the avenue for users of the language to record and analyze it in ways otherwise quite difficult. "Writing provides the means of analyzing language because it turns language into an object" (ibid.: 15).

4. *Social control function:* by committing words to writing we gain the potential for regulating social conduct by means of laws, policies, regulations, wills, and so forth. It is no accident that the words author and authority are etymologically related.

5. *Interactional function:* We usually think of speech or sign as the more interactional medium of communication. Writing, however, affords the possibility of a different type of interaction such as "instruction manuals, recipes, style sheets, etc., directed at an

unspecified readership" (ibid.: 14). In another sense writing is interactional because it allows the reader to review previous words and paragraphs. Videotapes of signed language and audiotapes of spoken language are only marginally interactive in this way.

6. *Aesthetic function:* While the notion of literature does not depend on writing (Frishberg, 1988), writing certainly makes possible new genres such as novels and certain types of poetry. It would be hard to imagine, for example, the poetry of E. E. Cummings without the written word and its layout on a page. An entire area of specialization, including typography and the graphic arts, has developed around the specialized aesthetic function that writing affords.

The question of writing signed languages, particularly ASL, has been a thorny one for many years. Many people, both advocates and opponents of the Deaf way, have noted the powerful potential of writing ASL. A. G. Bell (1883:217), for instance, believed that certain conditions were leading toward the production of a "defective race of human beings." One condition was the growth of a Deaf community. A second was the spread of American Sign Language, "a different language from that of the people at large . . . a language as different from English as French or German or Russian." Bell foresaw the power of writing ASL: "Another method of consolidating the deaf and dumb into a distinct class in the community would be to reduce the sign-language to writing, so that the deaf-mutes would have a common literature from the rest of the world" (Bell, 1883:219). Bell's evaluation of such a move was decidedly negative, even racist (Bahan, 1989c). My own belief is that Bell got his observation right but his conclusion wrong. Written ASL does hold the potential for empowering Deaf people, and this is precisely what we need. Why should the only avenue to literacy for Deaf people be through English?

The case is often made that for ASL, videotape is the equivalent of writing. Videotape certainly provides some of the functions of writing, such as the distancing and aesthetic functions. It allows people to preserve their words and to distribute some types of literature. Preserving spoken words on audiotape also serves many useful purposes, but it is not writing.

Those opposed to writing ASL counter that writing does not preserve the eloquence of ASL as it is signed by a Deaf person. This is true, but is hardly an indictment of writing ASL. Written English likewise does not preserve the eloquence of performance. Anyone who has ever heard Dylan Thomas perform his poem, "And Death Shall Have No Dominion," and compared that with the written words on the page of a book will attest to this fact. This is not a fault of writing, it is a potential that authors and performers of English literature utilize to their advantage. ASL authors and performers, it seems to me, should be afforded the same opportunities.

Consider a simple example. Literacy is not just something taught in classroom lessons. Children often incorporate written English into their games and personal lives. Why do we insist on denying Deaf children these experiences with their own language? Why must literacy for Deaf students mean English literacy?

## CHOOSING OUR OWN LANGUAGE

The word in language is half someone else's. It becomes "one's own" only when the speaker populates it with his own intentions, his own accent, when he appropriates the word, adapting it to his own semantic and expression intention. Prior to this moment of appropriation, the word does not exist in a neutral and impersonal language (it is not, after all, out of a dictionary that the speaker gets his words!), but rather it exists in other people's mouths, in other people's contexts, serving other people's intentions: it is from there that one must take the word, and make it one's own. . . . Consciousness finds itself inevitably facing the necessity of having to choose a language. (Bakhtin, 1981:293–294, 295)

The choice is clear—for many Deaf people, the language of consciousness is ASL. But it is also impossible to overestimate the importance of writing our own words. Here too, the lesson is clear—literacy is not the problem, it is the solution. It is time for those concerned with Deaf students' struggles to find a voice to realize the importance of ASL literacy. ASL is a beautiful language. It captures and expresses the pride, the history, and the identity of Deaf people. But it is still an unwritten language. This does not diminish ASL as a language. It is an untapped potential. We need an accepted ASL writing system, and we need to explore its use in Deaf education.[11]

The movement to empower Deaf students to "pronounce their own deliverance and articulate their message loud and clear" is long overdue in Deaf education. We can only hope that one day, Deaf writers will also be able to spell out the terms of their liberation and write their stories in their own language. Maybe then the hearing, literate, educational establishment will begin to listen and see.

# Postscript

## BoMee

Dr. Sherman Wilcox asked me to write a postscript to this chapter. I am happy to do so. Dr. Wilcox (whom I will refer to as "Sherman" for the remainder of this postscript since that is what I called him while I was growing up, and I find it difficult to do otherwise now) wrote a chapter in the book *Sociocultural Approaches to Language and Literacy: An Interactionist Perspective*. This book was originally published in 1994. In the chapter Sherman wrote, "Struggling for a Voice: An Interactionist view of Language and Literacy in Deaf Education," he described my early language and cultural upbringing. Much of the information in that chapter is the same as that found in another article that Sherman and my mom wrote, entitled "The Enculturation of BoMee: Looking at the World through Deaf Eyes."

When I was about ten or eleven years old, I remember reading "The Enculturation of BoMee: Looking at the World through Deaf Eyes." I was completely unimpressed, except that it was fun to see my name in print so many times. Over the years, I have had many people within the field of deafness recognize my name and ask me if I was, in fact, the BoMee that had been "enculturated." I could see that they wondered how I was doing. I guess at the time the article was written, it was unusual to talk about or think about raising a child bilingually and biculturally. I have been under the impression through the years that some people thought my bilingual/bicultural upbringing would somehow leave me cognitively and emotionally scarred or at least with overt ticks. Actually, I think quite the opposite has been true. I have fared pretty well so far. It is now the middle of 2003. I am nineteen years old and a student at Gallaudet University. I am happy. I love my family and feel very close to them. I look back fondly on the times we have spent together, which includes all of the language and cultural experiences we have shared.

This brings me back to the idea of a postscript. I liken this postscript to the end of a movie. I'm sure all of us have watched a movie and at the end, while the credits are rolling, the audience is told what happened to the main characters. I think that is what Sherman wanted you to know. I'm glad he asked for a postscript and not the outtakes of my life so far.

The most common question that I have been asked about my bilingual upbringing relates to my ability to read and write in English. I think this is looking at a very small part of who I am as a whole person, but because it seems to be a concern in regard to bilingual education, I will respond. I enjoy reading and writing. I enjoy English. It is a wonderful and rich language. I also enjoy American Sign Language (ASL). It is a wonderful and rich language with the added benefit of making every aspect of my environment visually accessible to me. With the many terrific technological advancements made in the last fifteen to twenty years related to computers, instant messaging, two-way text pagers, real-time captioning, and digital hearing aids—advancements all intended to provide more and better access to information—none of these have come close to or have in anyway replaced the accessibility provided through American Sign Language. ASL is still, as George Veditz said many years ago, "the noblest gift God has given to deaf people."

So is there anything I would have changed in my bilingual/bicultural upbringing, other than having my parents buy me a Porsche? Absolutely. I would wish for every child to have as much language as soon as possible. I was adopted by my parents at the age of two and a half years old. I began to learn both English and ASL the very day that I arrived in my adoptive home, but the age of two and a half is too late. A deaf child, like every child, deserves language from the second they are born. Writing in English can still sometimes be a slow process for me. I am a competent writer, but I need to edit and re-edit my work. It can be slow work. I sometimes feel like deaf and hearing people who have had access to language since birth are traveling on the neuropathway freeway while I am taking the long road through the woods to get to the same place. So, I would not in any way change my exposure to two languages. I would have just wanted this exposure sooner.

Roll credits. Ten years after "Struggling for a Voice: An Interactionist View of Language and Literacy in Deaf Education" was published, BoMee Corwin has survived her freshman year at Gallaudet University with academic honors. She is planning to major in deaf education and buy a car. And she is grateful that her parents provided her with two languages and two cultures. With these resources, she is planning to be happy for the rest of her life. Fade to black.

## NOTES

1. See Baker & Cokely (1980), Padden & Humphries (1988), Woodward (1989), Wilcox (1989a, 1989b), and Wilcox & Wilcox (1991) for further discussion of the pathological and cultural views of deafness.

2. Following the commonly accepted convention proposed by Woodward (1972), I use the lowercase deaf to refer to the condition of not being able to hear and uppercase Deaf to refer to a group of people who share the same language, ASL, and culture.

3. This poem was originally conceived in American Sign Language; the text presented here is a transcription by the author of an English translation from the videotape, "American Culture: The Deaf Perspective (Literature)," produced by Susan D. Rutherford for the San Francisco Public Library, 1984.

4. All poems with the exception of Lentz (see n. 3) appear in Gannon (1981).

5. See Baker & Cokely (1980) and Wilcox & Wilcox (1991) for further discussion of signed English and ASL.

6. ASL words are glossed as small capitalized English words; fingerspelled letters are given in all small capitals with the letters in fingerspelled words separated by hyphens; English words and English translations are given in double quotes.

7. The implications of BoMee's sociolinguistic competence are profound. Not only does BoMee recognize others' preferred language and level of competence; she also adjusts her language accordingly. Hearing teachers and diagnosticians frequently are not proficient signers. BoMee recognizes this and adapts. This presents a dilemma: how is it possible for these professionals to know whether they are observing BoMee's language proficiency or a reflection of their own?

8. See Liddell (1984), Liddell & Johnson (1989), Padden & Perlmutter (1987), and Wilbur (1987) for further discussion of ASL phonology.

9. As a matter of fact, substituting the A for the open-A handshape (e.g., in the ASL classifier for upright objects) is a mispronunciation common among adult, hearing signers.

10. This confirms the reports of Deaf persons that deafness has little to do with their sense of identity; a more appropriate description, according to Bahan (1989d), would be "seeing persons." See also Mather (1989) for an ethnographic description of how one teacher—a Deaf,

native signer of ASL—used visually oriented strategies to help deaf children acquire communicative competence.

11. A proposal for such an ASL orthography is given in McIntire et al. (1987).

## REFERENCES

Akamatsu, C. T. 1985. "Fingerspelling formulae: A word is more or less than the sum of its letters." In W. Stokoe & V. Volterra (eds.), *SLR '83: Sign Language Research*. Silver Spring, MD: Linstok Press.

Bahan, B. 1989a. "Total communication: A total farce." In S. Wilcox (ed.), *American Deaf culture*. Silver Spring, MD: Linstok Press.

Bahan, B. 1989b. "It's our world too!" In S. Wilcox (ed.), *American Deaf culture*. Silver Spring, MD: Linstok Press.

Bahan, B. 1989c. "What if . . . Alexander Graham Bell had gotten his way?" In S. Wilcox (ed.), *American Deaf culture*. Silver Spring, MD: Linstok Press.

Bahan, B. 1989d. "Notes from a 'seeing' person." In S. Wilcox (ed.), *American Deaf culture*. Silver Spring, MD: Linstok Press.

Baker, C., & D. Cokely. 1980. *American Sign Language: A teacher's resource text on grammar and culture*. Silver Spring, MD: T. J. Publishers.

Bakhtin, M. M. 1981. *The dialogic imagination*. (Edited by M. Holquist, translated by C. Emerson & M. Holquist.) Austin: University of Texas Press.

Bell, A. G. 1883. *Upon the formation of a deaf variety of the human race*. New Haven, CT: National Academy of Sciences.

Berko-Gleason, J. 1985. *The development of language*. Columbus, Ohio: Charles E. Merrill.

Bruner, J. 1983. *Child's talk: Learning to use language*. New York: W. W. Norton.

Carrington, L. D. 1981. A seminar on orthography for St. Lucian Creole, January 29–31. In *Language and development: The St. Lucian context*. Castries, St. Lucia: Folk Research Centre and Caribbean Research Centre.

Coulmas, F. 1989. *The writing systems of the world*. Oxford: Basil Blackwell.

Cruttendon, A. 1986. *Intonation*. Cambridge: Cambridge University Press.

Cummins, J. 1986. Empowering minority students: A framework for intervention. *Harvard Education Review*, 56(1), 18–36.

Dewey, J. 1916. *Democracy and education.* New York: Macmillan. (1966 Free Press paperback edition).
Eastman, G. 1983. *Sign me Alice II.* Washington, DC: Gallaudet College Press.
Elsasser, N., & P. Irvine. 1985. English and Creole: The dialectics of choice in a college writing program. *Harvard Educational Review,* 55(4), 399–415.
Elsasser, N., & V. John-Steiner. 1977. An interactionist approach to advancing literacy. *Harvard Educational Review,* 47(3), 355–369.
Fletcher, L. 1987. *Ben's story: A deaf child's right to sign.* Washington, DC: Gallaudet University Press.
Foucault, M. 1980. *Power/knowledge: Selected interviews and other writings, 1972–1977.* New York: Pantheon.
Freire, P. 1970. *Pedagogy of the oppressed.* New York: Seabury Press.
Freire, P. 1985. *The politics of education.* Granby, MA: Bergin & Garvey.
Frishberg, N. 1988. Signers of tales: The case for literary status of an unwritten language. *Sign Language Studies,* 59, 149–169.
Gannon, J. R. 1981. *Deaf heritage: A narrative history of Deaf America.* Silver Spring, MD: National Association of the Deaf.
Geertz, C. 1983. "From the native's point of view: On the nature of anthropological understanding." In C. Geertz, *Local knowledge.* New York: Basic Books.
Giroux, H. A. 1981. *Ideology, culture, and the process of schooling.* Philadelphia: Temple University Press.
Giroux, H. A. 1988. *Teachers as intellectuals: Towards a critical pedagogy of learning* Granby, MA: Bergin & Garvey.
Giroux, H. A., & P. McLaren. 1986. Teacher education and the politics of engagement: The case for democratic schooling. *Harvard Educational Review,* 56(3), 213–238.
Humphries, T., T. Coye, & B. Martin. 1989. A bilingual, bicultural approach to teaching English, or How two hearies and a deafie got together to teach English. In S. Wilcox (ed.), *American Deaf culture.* Silver Spring, MD: Linstok Press.
John-Steiner, V., & E. Souberman. 1978. Afterward to L. S. Vygotsky, *Mind in society: The development of higher psychological processes.* Cambridge, MA: Harvard University Press.
Johnson, R. E., S. K. Liddell, & C. J. Erting. 1989. *Unlocking the curriculum: Principles for achieving access in deaf education.* Gallaudet Research Institute Working Paper 89-3. Washington, DC: Gallaudet University.

Lane, H. 1988. Educating the American Sign Language speaking minority in the United States. *Sign Language Studies*, 59, 221–230.
Liddell, S. K. 1984. THINK and BELIEVE: Sequentiality in American Sign Language signs. *Language*, 60, 372–399.
Liddell, S. K., & R. E. Johnson. 1989. American Sign Language: The phonological base. *Sign Language Studies*, 64, 195–277.
Malinowski, B. 1922. *Argonauts of the Western Pacific*. London: Routledge.
Marmor, G., & L. Petitto. 1979. Simultaneous communication in the classroom: How well is English grammar represented? *Sign Language Studies*, 23, 99–136.
Mather, S. A. 1989. "Visually oriented teaching strategies with deaf preschool children." In C. Lucas (ed.), *The sociolinguistics of the Deaf community*. San Diego, CA: Academic Press.
McIntire, M., D. Newkirk, S. Hutchins, & H. Poizner. 1987. Hands and faces: A preliminary inventory for written ASL. *Sign Language Studies*, 56, 197–241.
Meadow, K. 1968. Early manual communication in relation to the deaf child's intellectual, social, and communicative functioning. *American Annals of the Deaf*, 113, 29–41.
Padden, C., & T. Humphries. 1988. *Deaf in America: Voices from a culture*. Cambridge, MA: Harvard University Press.
Padden, C., & B. LeMaster. 1985. An alphabet on hand: Acquisition of fingerspelling in deaf children. *Sign Language Studies*, 47, 161–172.
Padden, C., & D. Perlmutter. 1987. American Sign Language and the architecture of grammatical theory. *Natural Language and Linguistic Theory*, 5(3), 335–375.
Pahz, J. A., & C. S. Pahz. 1978. *Total communication*. Springfield, IL: Charles C. Thomas.
Peters, A. 1983. *The units of language acquisition*. Cambridge: Cambridge University Press.
Randall, M. 1984. *Risking a somersault in the air: Conversations with Nicaraguan writers*. San Francisco: Solidarity Publications.
Richardson, S. 1985. A gift to be treasured. Manuscript submitted for publication.
Schlesinger, H. S., & K. P. Meadow. 1972. *Sound and sign*. Berkeley: University of California Press.
Shor, I., & P. Freire. 1987. *A pedagogy for liberation: Dialogues on transforming education*. Granby, MA: Bergin & Garvey.

Strong, M. 1988. A bilingual approach to the education of young deaf children. In M. Strong (ed.), *Language, learning and deafness*. Cambridge: Cambridge University Press.

Stuart, D., & S. D. Houston. 1989. Maya writing. *Scientific American*, 261(2), 82–89.

Supalla, S. 1986. Manually Coded English: The modality question in signed language development. Master's thesis, University of Illinois at Champaign-Urbana.

Vygotsky, L. S. 1978. *Mind in society: The development of higher psychological processes*. Cambridge, MA: Harvard University Press.

Wilbur, R. B. 1987. *American Sign Language: Linguistic and applied dimensions*. Boston: Little Brown.

Wilcox, S. (Ed.). 1989a. *American Deaf culture*. Silver Spring, MD: Linstok Press.

Wilcox, S. 1989b. "Breaking through the culture of silence." In S. Wilcox (ed.), *American Deaf culture*. Silver Spring, MD: Linstok Press.

Wilcox, S. 1992. The phonetics of fingerspelling. Amsterdam: John Benjamins. Wilcox, S., & J. Corwin. 1990. The enculturation of BoMee: Looking at the world through Deaf eyes. *Journal of Childhood Communication Disorders*, 13(l), 63–71.

Wilcox, S., & P. Wilcox. 1991. *Learning to see: American Sign Language as a second language*. Englewood Cliffs, NJ: Prentice-Hall Regents (a publication of Center for Applied Linguistics).

Woodward, J. 1972. Implications for sociolinguistics research among the deaf. *Sign Language Studies*, 1, 1–17.

Woodward, J. 1989. "How you gonna get to heaven if you can't talk with Jesus? The educational establishment vs. the deaf community." In S. Wilcox (ed.), *American Deaf Culture*. Silver Spring, MD: Linstok Press.

# English Literacy in the Life Stories of Deaf College Undergraduates

## Kathleen M. Wood

There are as many literacy identities as there are students studying the ways of being literate in the various languages and cultures they study. This paper is a discussion of how Deaf undergraduate English majors portray literate identities outside of the cultural identities promoted in school, or more exactly, in the Deaf Education English Literacy System (DEELS). The DEELS is the public and ratified center of education for Deaf students: the schools, the staff, the curricula, the teacher preparation programs, and so forth.

### LITERACY LIFE STORIES

Literacy life stories are a rich source of information about Deaf students' literate identities and about the DEELS itself. What are literacy life stories and how are identities revealed in these narratives? If narratives and life stories have the power to simultaneously reveal individuals' identities and information about the surrounding social structures of these stories, as Bruner (1996) suggests, then one excellent site for the examination of this dual function of life stories is one particular type, the literacy life story. Literacy life stories provide an opportunity to examine the "models and agency" allowed in this specific community of practice.

Researchers in the field of literary criticism have popularized the use of literacy life stories as sites for the revelation of identities and for examining the nature of literacies. Using two terms interchangeably, Soliday explains that literacy *narratives* and literacy *stories* focus on "those moments when the self is on the threshold of possible intellectual, social, and emotional development" (1994, 511). She explains that "literacy narratives become sites of self-translation where writers can articulate the meanings and the consequences of their passages between language worlds" (511). Literacy life stories portray this travel within and beyond the literacies available to the students in the social institution of literacy.

How is the social institution of literacy translated for a Deaf individual's use? Or more specifically, how do tellers of life stories narrate their lives in relation to the surrounding social institution of literacy? And what is the relationship of sociocultural contexts (in this case, the DEELS) to the discursive production of the literate Deaf individual? These are the questions addressed in this essay.

## DEAF STUDENTS TELLING LITERACY LIFE STORIES

My interest in the literacy life stories of Deaf students began the semester that I had a dual appointment, teaching English majors and teaching students taking the noncredit, basic English courses. In a study (Wood 1998), both groups of students told me their literacy life stories after I asked them, "What was it like growing up learning to read and write?" After videotaping, transcribing, and conducting an extensive discourse analyses of these stories (Wood 1998), the following literate identity themes emerged:

- Against all odds, I succeeded.
- There was a turning point event or person who helped.
- I learned by living the culture and by being exposed to English everyday.
- I learned nothing in school.
- I never understood what was going on in English classes.
- I learned everything on my own.
- It was my family who helped me learn English.
- I learned English from my friends.

Although these themes are likely common to both Deaf and hearing students learning English as a second language (ESL), Deaf students tell their stories in ways that are very different from their hearing counterparts. The selection of some narratives over others, the foregrounding and backgrounding of related experiences, the positioning of themselves in relation to dominant ideologies, and the understanding of what those dominant ideologies are—all of these strategies make this telling a very different experience for Deaf undergraduates, because these stories are embedded in the DEELS. Their stories differ from those of hearing students because Deaf students rely on "systems of coherence" (Linde 1993) that are represented in and which permeate the DEELS.

In other words, when hearing ESL students tell literacy life stories, they draw upon an ESL-student literacy system, which includes an implicit assumption that its participants can eventually succeed. Deaf students, on the other hand, tell their stories, drawing on the DEELS, *from within a system that does not assume their eventual success.*

Hearing students are expected (by teachers, their families, and society) to become fully literate, while high-achieving Deaf undergraduates are more likely to experience comments like "you have really good writing/speaking/reading skills *for a Deaf person.*" Thus, Deaf undergraduates who tell literacy life stories create themselves and contend with the dominant themes promoted in a system that typically does not assume their success at literacy.

## SOCIAL SYSTEMS PROMOTED IN LITERACY LIFE STORIES

The relationship of language to identity is not a straightforward mapping of what is signed, spoken, or written to its social significance. And my discussion here is an argument against essentializing Deaf students' literacy life stories or suggesting that they are very different in form from any other self-transformation story, such as gay, lesbian, bisexual, and transgender peoples' coming-out stories (cf. Wood 1999) or religious conversion tales (cf. Stromberg 1993). Deaf students' literacy life stories, like all self-transformation stories, reveal the tellers' identities, which are the result of those tellers contending with the social context in which the stories are told and the "systems of logic" (Linde 1993) and hegemonies that contribute to the shape of these stories.

In his discussion of "languaculture," Agar (1994) suggests that conversationalists do more than reproduce or co-negotiate an immutable set of stereotypes, cultural models, or social facts. He explains that once speakers are in control of the language and culture of a community of practice, they can begin to see languaculture as a set of resources (as opposed to constraints) through which one "can create, improvise, criticize, or struggle against, as you please" (1994, 236). Textual identities are recognizable, and thus coherent, because they evoke some truth about the order of things in a given system. When the truth is a socially ratified truth, it is said to represent hegemony. Hegemony is the social nucleus to which tellers of life stories may connect with or transgress in order to reveal recognizable and acceptable identities. Likewise, even though Deaf students telling literacy life stories are constrained by the linguistic resources which utilize dominant and counter hegemonic ideologies, these constraints also provide them with the opportunity to resist and create themselves coherently, albeit in opposition to, the systemic DEELS notions of Deaf, English-literate people.

Writing in the 1930s, Albert Ballin (1998, 44), a Deaf man educated in the DEELS and an alumnus of Gallaudet University, commented on the state of Deaf education and explained, "Like most children, they learn more from one another in five minutes than they do in a whole week from their teachers." We know of his low opinion of the DEELS, not because he stated it directly, but because of his use of the underlying assumption: Students learn in schools. His statement reveals a fundamental stance toward the DEELS. I suggest that Ballin's life and the literacy he describes in his writings transgressed the literacies promoted in the DEELS at the time of his schooling; he reveals a literate identity despite the DEELS by contending with narrative hegemonies (Ballin 1998).

The collective narrative stances toward hegemony revealed in a life story produce the literate identity that is created with prevailing hegemonies or despite them. That is, identities are revealed in texts when tellers create narrative stances toward hegemony. And they accomplish this, in part, by using various systems of logic. Literate identities are created at the narrative intersection of dominant ideologies of who is and who can be literate and Deaf students' counter hegemonic stories of achievement. The narrative stances that these students take toward hegemony reveal their identities. By narrative stance, I am referring to the intertextual relationship of the narrative self to the possible selves available, in this case, the self in the DEELS and the self outside of the DEELS.

Lane et al. (1996) discuss the "Deaf-world" and what is means to be a part of that community. They explain that knowledge of the Deaf world comes through its clubs, schools, and individual members. Thus, as in all cultures, the narrative logics of the Deaf world are passed through the stories of that culture. What are the ways of being or systems of logic, connected to English literacy, that the DEELS promotes and how do these compare to the systems of logic promoted outside the DEELS and in the Deaf world? What are the English literacies promoted in the DEELS?

## ENGLISH LITERACIES PROMOTED IN THE DEELS

It has been suggested that the foundation of Deaf education rests on a deficit model, common in all of special education (cf., Wrigley 1996; Carver 1989; Jankowski 1997; Lane et al. 1996), in which Deaf people are people who cannot hear. As such, one significant focus in Deaf education has been on medical remediation, speech and auditory training, and a frantic push to get students to be able to function in the hearing world.

The DEELS, a subset of the larger Deaf education system, is the system of English literacy to which U.S. Deaf students are apprenticed. What do these students learn? Who do they become? Is there any connection between the literacies the system promotes and the literacies that its students eventually realize? To search for this connection, I studied several texts of the system, including curricula, letters to the editor of a major newspaper, reports, studies, program review summaries, and a student handbook (Wood 1998).

The DEELS is a social world. And as Fairclough (1989) points out, social worlds are built on assumptions and expectations, which control both the actions of members of a society and their interpretation of the actions of others. Such assumptions and expectations are implicit, backgrounded, taken for granted, thought to be common sense, and are usually not things that people are consciously aware of; they are rarely explicitly formulated, examined, or questioned. The common sense of discourse is a salient part of this picture. The effectiveness of ideology depends to a considerable degree on it being merged with this commonsense background to discourse and forms of social action.

Certainly, it is not possible to summarize all of the literacies that are promoted in the social world of the DEELS. Nor is it wise to suggest that there is a single kind of literacy promoted therein. However, there are patterns that emerge when some of the underlying assumptions and beliefs are studied and then summarized and some of these patterns end up making their way into the students' stories.

To organize the themes that emerged when analyzing these public documents, I adapted (by adding the word *reading* to each one and the headings) the NCTE Position Statement on Teaching Composition (NCTE 2003): The Acts of Reading and Writing; The Purposes for Reading and Writing; The Scenes for Reading and Writing; The Teachers for Reading and Writing; and The Means of Reading and Writing Instruction. Below is a discussion of these DEELS texts in relation to the adapted NCTE categories.

First of all, what does the DEELS say about "The Acts of Reading and Writing"? In other words, according to the DEELS, what is the nature of literacy? Of the acts of becoming literate? Here are some of the ways "The Acts of Reading and Writing" are portrayed in the DEELS.

1. Literacy is a quantity of skills.
2. Literacy is a hierarchy of skills.
3. Reading and writing are outgrowths or extensions of speech.
4. Speaking is the precursor to reading and writing a language.

The "Purposes for Reading and Writing" are also revealed in these texts. Is literacy promoted as a means to critical thinking, or is it promoted as something more functional, like a means to an end (e.g., getting good jobs, getting into graduate school)? The purposes of DEELS reading and writing seem to be to acquire the hierarchy of skills associated with literate behavior. The DEELS, at least in part, promotes a literacy that is a means to an end.

According to the DEELS, what are "The Scenes for Reading and Writing and The Means for Instruction"? What should the classroom be like? Is the classroom the only place for learning? How can classrooms be transformed into scenes for literacy? And how should reading and writing be taught? Again, the documents reveal that the DEELS has much to say about the scenes and means of instruction of Deaf students.

5. Basic college preparatory courses should focus on the one discourse form: the written message.
6. Because good speaking skill predicts success with print, speech shall be taught before or at least concurrently with reading and writing.
7. Reading and writing are best taught by focusing on sentences, not on words.

8. The literacy instruction for Deaf students means working through a sentence-based curriculum beginning with the learning of the five sentence patterns.
9. Students learn languages by using them interactively.
10. Using typed English on networked computers is equal to using it in its aural/oral form; that is, computer networking provides users with natural exposure to English. And natural exposure to language leads to language learning.
11. Educational approaches used with Deaf students, e.g., computer networking, should cater, at least in some ways, to the needs of teachers who lack fluency in ASL.
12. The purpose of Deaf education is to serve Deaf education, not Deaf students.
13. There are two sides to the literacy issue for Deaf students: those who support ASL to the exclusion of English and those who support English with ASL as a recreational supplement.
14. Teaching English to Deaf adults is an impossible task.
15. Students learn languages by using them interactively.</>

One can see that the DEELS, at least in some ways, promotes a literacy instruction based on hearing-student language acquisition research, on aural-oral methodologies, essay-text literacy, and prescriptionist grammar principles.

From these public texts, some of the roles and actions of "Teachers of Reading and Writing" in the DEELS become clear:

16. The teachers of literacy to Deaf students are special educators, who are trained to work with children who have a variety of physical and mental disabilities.
17. The teachers of English literacy for Deaf students need not be Deaf or fluent in ASL.
18. In the literacy education of Deaf students, the fact that teachers do not communicate well with Deaf students is of equal significance to the fact that Deaf students do not know English very well.
19. One means of instruction, computer communication, is an attempt to solve the problem that teachers cannot sign well and students cannot read and write well.

20. The struggle that Deaf students have with English has nothing to do with the fact that their teachers cannot communicate clearly with them.

And finally, what do the documents of the DEELS say about "The Students Who Study Reading and Writing," the students of the DEELS?

21. Deaf people do not read well because they have not been exposed to English. Exposure to English equals aural-oral exposure to English.
22. Deaf students who are skilled lip readers and who have intelligible speech are likely to be successful with written forms of English.
23. Deaf people are handicapped people, just as physically disabled and mentally handicapped people are.
24. If a child passes the critical age of language learning, there is little hope of that child ever learning the target language.
25. Deaf people can't read and write well because they cannot hear well.
26. Since reading and writing success is tied to hearing level, students with more hearing will be more literate than students who are more Deaf.

This list of twenty-six systems of logic points to at least one of the major kinds of literacies promoted in the DEELS: an essay-text, hierarchical, aural-oral based, deficit-focused, fatalistic conception.

This DEELS-sanctioned literacy is a major resource that students necessarily reproduce or transgress in their literacy life stories. The literacy life stories of Deaf students are necessarily told through the literacies promoted by the DEELS. That is, as members of the DEELS, students necessarily access these same systems of logic. For example, when a Deaf student explains, "She was Deaf, but she had really good English," she is accessing the assumption that hearing loss equals poor literacy skills, an assumption that reverberates in the documents of the DEELS.

Elliot (1996, 696) illuminates this echo effect when she describes the "double vision," of seeing oneself as others do, a phenomenon first described by W.E.B. DuBois (1973, 3):

> It is a peculiar sensation, this double-consciousness, this sense of always looking at one's self through the eyes of others, of measuring

one's soul by the tape of a world that looks on in amused contempt and pity.

All-pervasive, this double-vision logic about what is right and legitimate, and thus what is most appropriate, consequently ends up making its way into the discourses of the community; both mainstream and marginalized members of a society are constrained by dominant ideologies and have identities that are realized in relation to hegemony. That is, Deaf students, as members of the DEELS, often come to see themselves through the same ideological lens that authorities in the DEELS see them—and they must realize English-literate identities with, or despite, this lens.

## "SUCCESSFUL" DEAF STUDENTS TELLING LITERACY LIFE STORIES

One study (Wood 1998) shows that when a group of Deaf, English-major undergraduates told their life stories, they accessed three general themes, all of which indicate a departure from the themes promoted in the DEELS:

1. Hearing people as resource to English literacy
2. Struggle to success with English literacy
3. Literacy as personal achievement

Taken together, these themes add up to a literacy that is very different from the literacies promoted in the DEELS.

If Deaf English majors who told their literacy life stories portray this alternative literacy, what might be a literacy theme of the Deaf world, a Deaf English literacy? Ben Bahan (personal communication, 12 May 1998) suggests that Deaf folklore is a good site for examining themes of the Deaf world. Bahan's performed folktale of the Deaf hunter winning the hunting contest exemplifies the very common theme of hearing people as resource (but in this case, the "hearing person" is a horse).

> One day a deaf man tried to enter a deer-hunting contest in the hills of Tennessee. The contest referee explained he could not allow a deaf man to be in the contest because everyone knows that the best deer hunters hunt by listening to the Deere movement through the brush. But the deaf man prevailed explaining the he could beat any hearing man for miles around. The judge conceded and let the deaf man enter. Sure enough, at the end of the day, as the men lined up with the deer they had shot that day, the deaf man rode up on

his horse, towing what was clearly the largest buck. Everyone was amazed and puzzled as to how he managed to do it. "It was simple," he explained, "I'm deaf but my horse isn't. So the two of us sat quietly in the woods and when I saw the horse's ears move in the direction of a noise, I fired off a shot. And everyone knows that horses have a more keen sense of hearing than men do. My horse heard that deer from farther off than any of you ever could!"

This story repeats a common theme of the Deaf world—that hearing people, among other things, are resources for getting around in the hearing-centric world. In the case of this story, the "hearing" other is a horse. And the hearing horse is the resource the Deaf man accessed to win the contest.

It is not difficult to recognize this theme in the literacy life stories of Deaf undergraduates, especially the students whom the system has suggested are the successes—the English majors. Following are two excerpts from one of these stories in which the theme of *hearing people as resource* is accessed. In this excerpt, the student has just finished explaining that many of his teachers in hearing schools told him that his writing was very good. But finally, he explains, he got a teacher who told the truth, explaining what he needed to do to improve his writing.

**Excerpt 1 English Major: Hearing People as Resource**

So I wrote a story and gave it to my teacher.
The teacher said, "oh, good creativity, good imagination, good plot. They're all good, but the grammar is bad. It's broken English.
So he waved for me to sit down next to him and discuss my story.
I asked him, "why?"
And he explained.
And I said, "OK, great, I understand. . ."
And that's the way I improved.

This English major viewed his teacher as a resource for getting clear information about the difficulties in his writing.

In a second excerpt from the same story, he describes his experience in an ASL/English mentoring program language exchange program where he teamed up with a hearing professor who needed tutoring to improve her ASL skills.[1] In exchange, he got tutoring on his writing.

---

1. This is a project that was headed by Anne Marie Baer of the ASL Literacy Center at Gallaudet.

### Excerpt 2 English Major: Hearing People as Resource

One thing I'd like to add about last semester is that I joined the ASL/English Mentoring project. It's a Gallaudet program.

I was asked to work with a hearing teacher—to teach ASL and to help that person practice reading signs. In return, that teacher would help me with my English. I really liked that program. We worked on how to say things in different ways, like how to say things in a hearing way or in the more simple, direct, Deaf way.

Well that's my opinion. That it's more simple and direct. And we discussed more elevated registers of communication—more professional English and things like that.

I learned a lot and really enjoyed last semester. And as a result, I decided to really get into writing.

In this excerpt, he sees his language exchange partner, a hearing man, as a resource for understanding register and other aspects of writing.

The second theme that is quite prevalent in the stories of Deaf English majors is the *struggle-to-success* theme. According to Bahan (personal communication, 12 May 1998), this theme is also quite prevalent in the conversations, drama, and stories of the Deaf world. Moreover, there is currently widespread use of a sign, PAH, glossed as SUCCESS.[2] In fact, it is common in informal conversations, e-mail messages, and TTY conversations to see the word PAH used as a substitute for AND I FINALLY SUCCEEDED or SUCCESS.

And in every single literacy life story of the Deaf English majors, the *struggle-to-success* theme is replicated. Each student narrates a life from illiteracy to their success at becoming English majors, the ratified literate. This theme necessarily requires a change in narrative trajectory, reflecting the change in the course of real-world events. In other words, the change from failure/illiteracy/struggle must be somehow signaled. In life stories, this turn of events resembles what Luborsky (1994) calls the *signal event*. He suggests that signal events point to scenes of significant importance in the life of the storyteller.

For example, in the following excerpt, the student explains first how she overcame her dread of writing, and later overcame her frustration with it. In this case, her story takes us through the struggle to eventual success.

---

2. The ASL sign called PAH gets its name from the ASL mouth movement that accompanies the sign. The unvoiced, but sometimes aspirated mouth movement, like the pronounced PAH.

## Excerpt 3 English Major: Struggle to Success

I just hated writing until sixth grade. It was in sixth grade when I had one teacher who is still teaching at that school, I think. She was so patient! Before me, she had already taught my two older sisters and Lisa too. She really knew deaf people! And she worked with me, explaining that I really could learn English.

I learned a lot but I was still frustrated. I wanted to transfer back to the state school for the deaf but I still couldn't. Until finally in the seventh grade, they admitted me back. And I was really excited about reading because for me reading was easy, but it was the rules of writing that gave me trouble.

And it seemed like I was way above the other seventh graders— so they gave me a private tutorial with a teacher who worked with me on creative writing.

Wow, I really liked that! We did all kinds of different kinds of writing, using different techniques. And we did dialogue journals. I wrote like four stories during that time.

I still sometimes look back on the stuff I wrote and I remember how much I liked it—drawing illustrations and putting the books together. I really enjoyed that class.

This segment can be divided in two: (1) the student's "hate" of writing, to her encounter with the "patient" teacher who eventually helped her "learn a lot" and (2) the student's frustration and eventual enjoyment of reading with her private tutor. This excerpt shows the narrative movement from struggle with literacy to success, and it is also representative of a majority of English majors' stories in my study.

In the next excerpt, the student describes feeling frustration toward a teacher who did not explain things clearly. Later in the story, the student describes a more recent experience in which the teacher very clearly told the student what she needed to do to improve her writing.

## Excerpt 4 English Major: Struggle to Success

Once I remember in the gifted and talented program at the (residential Deaf school) we went to different museums. We had to choose one exhibit and write about that exhibit. My earliest memory of starting to write was when I wrote, "Once upon a time we went to the museum." And the teacher looked at me and said, "no, that's wrong." And I looked at her and wondered why it was wrong.

So I threw the paper away and started again. I thought that obviously she didn't want "we went to the museum." So I started with, "once upon a time." And the teacher looked at me and said, "That's wrong."

I looked at her like "what do you want?" I struggled with it and I wrote the same beginning again and again—The teacher never did tell me why it was wrong.

She never said anything about that kind of writing. She just kept saying, "it's wrong, it's wrong."

That got me very frustrated. I'll never forget that experience.

Now, this year, composition (course number) under (English professor's name)

I'd turn in a paper and get it back immediately—having to revise it.

She said, "and the ideas are all good, but the way you say it is wrong."

And I thought to myself, "oh, that's what writing is about." I always thought it was about sentence structure—that's all.

So I said, "fine, ok, I will," and took back the paper and revised it.

I enjoyed learning much more from that class than from any other.

That's it for writing.

This excerpt follows a three-part discursive pattern: (1) State of Struggle ("That got me very frustrated"), (2) Signal Event Interrupting the Struggle ("Now this year in [our course number]") and (3) State of Success ("I learned much more from that class than from any other"). This three-part discursive pattern is also prevalent in the literacy life stories of the English majors.

The third and final theme accessed in the English majors' literacy life stories is "Literacy as Personal Discovery." In one story, the student describes how she first got interested in reading. She was alone and reading a book when she first noticed a bad word, which led her to believe that books were the entrance to a world beyond her home environment where things like bad words were forbidden.

**Excerpt 5 English Major: Literacy as Personal Discovery**

Until much later when I was about nine and a half, near age ten, when I picked up a book and opened it up, read a little of it and thought to myself, "so?!"

And then I turned the page and it jumped out at me!
There it was!
A bad word!
That was it!
I was completely fascinated.

You see, in my house at the time, bad words were forbidden. I could speak—a long time ago I was just hard of hearing and I could talk. So anytime I was mad, or in an intense discussion I was always super tempted to blast out some dirty word but I couldn't.

So that book, like talked to me! I liked it. It really fit! So I kept reading and turning the pages and finally got it! That the words all had a purpose and had meaning. Even the bad words.

So that was the first novel I ever read. When I was nine.

In this excerpt, we can see that the student describes one reading event that had a very big impact on her—she realized that books had language and words that were forbidden in her everyday life. She, literally as a Personal Discovery Story, discovered the freedom that literacy would afford her. In another, the student explains how (in kindergarten) he got turned on to reading because of the book corner that the teacher had set up.

**Excerpt 6 English Major: Literacy as Personal Discovery**

I remember that in kindergarten we had a book corner, where the books were lined up. And there were picture books—Oh, I really enjoyed that so much. I'd read things all the way through without stopping. I think it was then that I fell in love with reading—And I have been ever since.

Closer examination of the systems of logic accessed by the English majors reveals the following list of *logics* that were indexed:

1. One way to literacy is with hearing people.
2. Hearing people obstruct the way to literacy.
3. Persistent struggles to literacy lead to eventual success.
4. Literacy is a state of mind, a state of knowing.
5. Literacy is achieved by personal involvement.
6. Literacy is an incremental process.
7. Literacy is the means to know the world, one's place in that world, and of worlds beyond the ones we are in.

Collectively, these logics portray an English literacy in which Deaf people are agents toward a state of being that has multiple routes and multiple realizations. However, this literacy significantly contrasts with the English literacy promoted in the documents of the DEELS: an essay-text, hierarchical, aural-oral, deficit-focused, fatalistic view of a set of skills.

## INCLUDING THE TELLING OF LIFE STORIES IN THE CURRICULA

Stromberg (1993), in his book on Christian conversion narratives, explains how the telling of transformation narratives constitutes more than a reflexive act, more than a referential retelling of that which has already occurred. He explains that the telling indexes the event, therefore becoming the event itself.

> Equally important in the creation of meaning are processes of indexing; language is meaningful to speakers in part because it may reflect a situation beyond the event of speech, but also because it creates a situation in the event of speech . . . for it is through language that the conversion occurred in the first place and also through language that the conversion is now re-lived as the convert tells his tale. (2–3)

For Deaf college students, telling literacy stories becomes the site to reflexivize themselves—to reflect on the past and to create a current, personal, and public personae, as well as an identity. My intent has been to show how some Deaf students of the DEELS realized literate identities through, yet *despite* the systems of logic perpetuated in the DEELS.

Why then should Deaf students be encouraged to tell (or write) literacy narratives? Besides the usual and expected benefits of raising students' personal awareness of their own literacy situation, there are other benefits and curricular shifts that can occur. When students and teachers sign and write their literacy life stories:

1. Teachers find out what students think worked and what did not work from their pasts. This can help plan curricula.
2. Students can "engage in a broader critical dialogue with each other and with well-known texts such as Richard Rodriquez's *Hunger of Memory* (Soliday 1994, 512).
3. Teachers learn about what Bruner (1996) calls the "models of identity" that are available to Deaf students for being literate in English.

4. Teachers and students will see that the literate identities promoted in the "Deaf world" (Lane, Hoffmeister, and Bahan 1997) include strong models for the English-literate selves and are linked to strong Deaf identities.
5. Students benefit from the power of narrating the self—of creating a break in the narrative trajectory of failure.
6. Students engage critically with their stories, classmates' stories, and other literary narratives (e.g., Frederick Douglass, Emmanuelle Laborit, Mike Rose in Anne Raimes, Susan Stocker in Karen Ogulnick, Margie English in Karen Ogulnick, Albert Ballin, and ESL Students in Taking Charge of My Life).

But perhaps the most important effect of asking the question and encouraging the writing and telling of the literacy life story is the creation of a bridge from individual literacies across the abyss of the DEELS and to the banks of a literacy that has room for diverse languages, cultures, and a variety of successes—as they make use of English literacy in order to transgress the literacies promoted in the DEELS. When Deaf students tell literacy life stories, they can narrate themselves alongside the ratified literates of the system—or better yet, they can narrate themselves even beyond those literates and the system that rarely acknowledges their existence.

## LITERATURE CITED

Agar, M. 1994. *Language shock*. New York: Morrow.
Ballin, A. 1998. *A deaf mute howls*. Washington, D.C.: Gallaudet University Press.
Bruner, J. 1996. *The culture of education*. Cambridge, Mass: Harvard University Press.
Carver, R. 1989. Deaf illiteracy: A genuine educational puzzle or an instrument of oppression? A critical review. Master's thesis, University of Alberta.
Commission on Composition. 2003. Teaching composition: A position statement. (online). National Council of English Teachers 2003 (cited 14 May 2003) (Available at http://www.ncte.org/positons/teaching_composition.shtml).
Douglass, F. 1999. *Narrative of the life of Frederick Douglass*. Cambridge, Mass.: Harvard University Press.

DuBois, W. E. B. 1973. *The souls of black folks.*
Elliot, M. 1996. Coming out in the classroom: A return to the hard place. *College English* 58 (6): 693–708.
Fairclough, N. 1989. *Language and power.* New York: Longman.
Jankowski, K. 1997. *Deaf empowerment.* Washington, D.C.: Gallaudet University Press.
Laborit, E. 2000. *The cry of the gull.* Washington, D.C.: Gallaudet University Press.
Lane, H., R. Hoffmeister, and B. Bahan. 1996. *A journey into the Deaf-World.* San Diego: DawnSign.
Linde, C. 1993. *Life Stories.* New York: Oxford University Press.
Luborsky, M. 1994. The identification and analysis of themes and patterns. In *Qualitative methods in aging research*, ed. J. Gubrium and A. Sankar, 189–210. Thousand Oaks, Calif.: Sage.
Ogulnick, K. 2000. *Language crossings.* New York: Teachers College Press.
Raimes, A. 1996. *Identities.* Boston: Houghton Mifflin.
Soliday, M. 1994. Translating self and difference through literacy narratives. *College English* 56 (September): 511–26.
Stromberg, P. 1993. *Language and self-transformation.* Cambridge, Mass.: Cambridge University Press.
*Taking charge of my life: Personal essays by today's college students.* 1993. Marlton, N.J.: Townsend Press.
Wood, K. M. 1998. *Undergraduates' life stories in the deaf education English literacy system: Revealing discursive identities with coherence resources.* Ph.D. diss., Georgetown University.
———. 1999. Coherent identities and heterosexist ideologies: Deaf and hearing lesbians coming-out stories. In *Reinventing identities*, ed. M. Bucholtz, A. C. Laing, and L. A. Sutton, 46–63. New York: Oxford University Press.
Wrigley, O. 1996. *The politics of deafness.* Washington D.C.: Gallaudet University Press.

# Contributors

C. TANE AKAMATSU is a psychologist with the Toronto District School Board, a highly multicultural school board, where she serves both hearing and deaf children. Her interests include assessment practices with deaf and multicultural children, classroom use of sign language, and effective teaching through dialogic inquiry.

BRENDA JO BRUEGGEMANN is Associate Professor of English at the Ohio State University; and an Associate Faculty member in Women's Studies and Comparative Studies. She is the author of *Lend Me Your Ear: Rhetorical Constructions of Deafness* (Gallaudet University Press 1999) and the coeditor of *Disability Studies: Enabling the Humanities* (Modern Language Association 2002). She was awarded Ohio State's Distinguished Diversity Enhancement Award in 2001 for her development of an interdisciplinary disability studies minor and an American Sign Language program.

SUSAN BURCH is Associate Professor of History at Gallaudet University in Washington D.C. She is the author of *Signs of Resistance: American Deaf Cultural History, 1900 to World War II* (New York University Press 2002). Her areas of expertise include American and Soviet Deaf history, women's history, and Disability history. She was awarded a Fulbright scholarship to the Czech Republic (for Spring 2004).

ESTER COLE is a psychologist in private practice. Previously, she supervised teams of school psychologists at the Toronto Board of Education for sixteen years. She also taught for two decades at O.I.S.E. She has coauthored and written numerous books and articles, and has lectured internationally on models of school psychology and services in inclusive societies. She is the current president of the Ontario Psychological Association.

BOMEE CORWIN has been deaf all her life. She was born in Kang Wondo South Korea in 1984 and adopted by a family from the United States in 1986. She graduated from a mainstream high school with honors in 2001 and is currently a sophomore at Gallaudet University in Washington D.C.

ELIZABETH ENGEN is an educational linguist, formerly of the Rhode Island School for the Deaf. Her field is language assessment, test development, and research on the language of children with hearing loss.

TRYGG ENGEN is Professor Emeritus at Brown University where he taught psychological testing and psychometric theory with emphasis on scaling and the definition and measurement of individual differences.

TOM HUMPHRIES is Associate Director of the Teacher Education Program and is on the faculty of the Department of Communication at the University of California, San Diego.

CLAIRE RAMSEY is a faculty member in the Teacher Education Program at the University of California San Diego. She is currently applying her training in linguistics and sociolinguistics to the community of elderly signers in Mexico City, and the consequences of Mexico's fully integration special education policy on Mexican Sign Language.

LILLIAN BUFFALO TOMPKINS is Associate Professor in the Department of Education at Gallaudet University. Her professional and research interests lie primarily in literacy, especially writing development in deaf and hard of hearing learners, and in creating a deaf-centric model of bilingual education.

SHERMAN WILCOX is Professor of Linguistics at the University of New Mexico. His main research interests are the theoretical and applied study of signed languages. His theoretical work focuses on iconicity, gesture, and typological studies of signed languages. He is widely recognized as an advocate for academic acceptance of American Sign Language in universities in the United States. He also has taught signed language interpreting for many years, and most recently has begun to demonstrate the application of cognitive linguistics to interpreting theory. He is the author of several books and articles, including *The Phonetics of Fingerspelling* (1992), *Gesture and the Nature of Language* (1994, with David F. Armstrong and William C. Stokoe), *Learning to See: Teaching American Sign Language as a Second Language* (1997, with Phyllis Perrin Wilcox), and several edited collections.

KATHLEEN M. WOOD has been teaching English to Deaf and hearing children and adults for twenty years. She is currently working with faculty and staff who work with Deaf children—studying and integrating learning technologies into the language arts classrooms and revising reading/writing curricula to reflect current theory and that work within the curricular confines of the NCLB legislation.

# Index

**Boldface pages** indicate figures or tables.

*A Dictionary of American Sign Language on Linguistic Principles* (Stokoe, Casterline, and Croneberg), 17
Addams, Jane, 62
aesthetic function: of writing, in Deaf education, 183
Agar, M., 194–95
American Association for the Promotion and Teaching of Speech for the Deaf (AAPTSD), 61
*American Deaf Citizen*, 64–65
American School for the Deaf (ASD), 59
American Sign Language (ASL), 17, 30, 38, 44, 117–19, 142–43, 144, 146, 148, 163–64, 180, 183; acquisition and development of, 145; written form of, 183–84
Andersson, Yerker, 22
Annual Conference on Issues of Language and Deafness (Fifteenth), 4
Anzaldúa, Gloria, 16, 141, 143, 148
ASL-deaf bilingualism, 139, 141; creative language play, 143; English input at deaf homes, 142; six first-person narratives on, 148–52
assessment: alternative assessment procedures, 124; of language-related abilities in deaf immigrant and refugee children, 121–25; psychological assessment, 124-25
autobiographics, 11, 76

Bahan, Ben, 200, 202
Bahktin, M. M., 178
Baker, C., 141
Balin, Albert, 195
Bauerle, Anna Joy, 67
Bednar, Lisa, 2
Beiser, M., 115
Belenky et al., 11
Belenky, M. F., 75, 84
Bell, Alexander Graham, 60, 183
bilingualism, 34, 39–41, **40**, 42, 139, 179–81; ASL-deaf bilingualism, 139, 141, 142, 143, 148–52; creative language play in, 143; first-person narratives on, 148–52; social implications of, 141–44
Bilingualism and Literacy in Deaf Children (Norwegian study), 91, 92, 108n1, 108n2; aim of research, 92, 93–94; language categories organized by language, mode, and mixtures of language and mode, **98**; the language milieu, 94–100; list of language categories, **95**; literacy assessments, 100–4; questions regarding language competence, 97; questions

*211*

Bilingualism and Literacy in Deaf
Children *(continued)*:
regarding language use, 97;
relationships between literacy
assessments and language
milieu, 102–4, **102**; results
and conclusions of, 104–8
Bolander, Anne, 10, 85–86
BoMee (case study), 18–20,
164–76, 185–87; awareness
of sociolinguistic variations,
170–71, 187n7; English
acquisition via signed language, 170–73; family background of, 164–66; language
development of, 169–73;
Manually Coded English,
173–75; multilingual and
multicultural influences on
BoMee's development,
166–67;
Bragg, Bernard, 18, 161–62
Brueggemann, B. J., 5, 10–11
Bruner, J., 13, 207
Burch, Susan, 5, 8–10
Burke, Kenneth, 74

Canada: immigration and,
110–13, **111, 112**, 128. *See
also* deaf immigrant and
refugee children
Carrington, L. D., 181
Cartagena, Teresa de, 10, 80–85,
81, 86
chaining, 6, 42–43, 44
Cixous, Helene, 11, 80, 85
Clarke School for the Deaf
(Massachusetts), 61, 62,
70n3

Clerc, Laurent, 59
cochlear implants, 113, 114
code mixing: in Norwegian study,
96, **98**, 99, 100
Cole, M., 53, 54, 56
Cole and Brown, 127–28
constructed knower, 11, 76, 84
Cooke, Guie C., 163
cooperative learning, 125
Croneberg, C., 144
*Cry of the Gull, The*
(Laborit), 10, 72, 77–80, **78**
cultural transmission: Deaf children and, 52–54; Deaf education and, 47–49; Deaf
people and, 51–52; evolution of, 49–50, 51
culture, 47–49; Cole's garden
metaphor, 53, 56; evolution
and transmission of, 7–8,
49–50, 51; interaction of
language and, in Deaf education, 179–81. *See also*
Deaf culture
culture of silence, 161, 180
Cummins, J., 117

deaf children of deaf parents
(DD), 16, 35, 139, 142,
144, 147
deaf children: cultural transmission and, 52–54; development of, vs. hearing children,
35; educational placement
considerations for, 115–16;
family's cultural views of
deafness and perception of
deaf child's needs, 114–15;
language acquisition and,

53–54; stereotyping of, 106–7
Deaf community: role in deaf education, 177
Deaf culture, 31; economic imperatives, 33–34; educational imperatives, 34; emergence of a self-conscious discourse on, 38–39; linguistic studies on, by hearing persons, 37–38; political activism, 33; spread of American, 59–60; themes of modern Deaf life, 32–34
*Deaf Digest*, 64–65
Deaf Education English Literacy System (DEELS), 20–21, 193, 194, 195–96, 206–7; definition of, 192, 196; literacy life stories promoted in the DEELS, 196–200; twenty-six systems of logic in the, 21, 197–99
Deaf education: ASL writing system and, 183–84; awareness of language situation in, 177–78; cooperative learning, 125; cultural transmission and, 47–49; culture of silence in, 161, 180; Deaf community's role in, 177; demonstration learning, 126; peer helper, 125; *disabling* and *empowering* pedagogies in, 159, **159**, 163–64; educator's role in, 177–79; functions of writing in, 181–84; influx of female teachers, 60–61, 69; informed by the Deaf community, 30, 34; interaction of language and culture in, 179–81, **179**; men in teaching profession and, 63–64, 69; oralism and, 60; oralism vs. manualism, 144; the pathological vs. the cultural view of deafness and, 157–59, 163–64; socio-cultural-political influences on, 144–48; teaching self-initiative strategies, 125; teacher training programs and accreditation requirements, 177; women and, 63–64, 69; writing and, 181–84. *See also* bilingual education
Deaf hunter folktale, 200–201
deaf immigrant and refugee children: 110, 112; assessing academic achievement and social adjustment in, 15–16; assessment of language-related abilities of, 121–25; in Canada, 119; challenge of first-language acquisition for, 116–19; cooperative learning, 16; multicultural services and programs, 128–29, **129**; cooperative learning and, 125–26; educational placement considerations for, 115–16; family's perception of teachers' competence, 126–27; home-school communication, 120; interpreters and relay interpreters, 121; language

deaf immigrant and refugee children *(continued)*:
competency, 14–15; language milieu of, 14–15; parents interaction with children and schools, 113, 119–21; peer helper(s), 16; schools as agents of change for, 115–21; self-initiatives, 16; study skills and parental guidance of, 119–21; unrealistic expectations of parents, 113
*See also* multicultural deaf individuals
*Deaf in America: Voices from a Culture* (Padden and Humphries), 17, 145
Deaf Lives series, 73
*Deaf-mute*, 30, 31
Deaf President Now (DPN) protest, 17, 33, 140, 142, 145, 146
Deaf residential schools, 59
Deaf teachers: effects of school setting on teachers' signing behavior, 44; use of ASL and English in classroom, 42–44
Deaf/deaf, use of, 1–2n, 187n2
DEAF-EYE: definition of, 141; describing ASL-English bilingualism through the, 141–44
deaf-mute, 5
deafness: cultural views of, 18, 115–16; the pathological vs. the cultural view of, 18, 157–59
DEAF-WAY international conference, 17, 145
DEAF-WORLD, 140, 140n, 141, 145, 161, 195–96, 207

decoding: in Norwegian study, 101, 105, 106, 107
Derrida, Jacques, 85
developmental time (ontogenetic): cultural evolution and transmission, 50, 54
Dewey, John: on the acquisition of knowledge, 158
distancing function: of writing, in Deaf education, 182
double-vision logic: in literacy life stories, 199–200
Douglass, Frederick, 16, 141
Du Bois, W. E. B., 199–200
dual inheritance: 51

Eastman, Gilbert, 163
education. *See* Deaf education
Egan, Susanna, 76, 79, 82, 84
Elliot, M., 199
English as a second language (ESL), 194
English-initialized signs, 6
Erd, Mary Williamson, 10, 66
eugenics, 68, 69
evolution of culture: dual inheritance and, 51; three critical features of, 49–50

Fairclough, N., 196
fingerspelling, 6, 42, 43
first-language acquisition, 39–40, 53
Foucault, M., 175
Freire, P., 161, 162, 180, 181

Gaillard, Henri, 66
Gallaudet, Edward Miner, 62, 63
Gallaudet College: creation of, 59; reaction to the feminization

of teaching at, 62; Normal (hearing) Department at, 62; oralism and, 62; women's admission to, 63
Gallaudet Research Institute, 145
Gallaudet University, 17, 20, 33, 73, 71n6, 145
garden metaphor, 53, 56
Garretson, Mervin, 180
Geertz, C., 164
gender, 9–10
Gilmore, Leigh, 11, 76, 79, 82, 84
Giordano, J., 126
Giroux, H. A., 177, 180
*Groves of the Infirm* (Cartagena), 10, 80, 81, 82–83, 84
Grushkin, D., 147

Halliday, M. A. K., 13
hearing child development vs. Deaf child development, 35
"hearing people as resource" theme (in literacy life stories), 21, 200–202
hearing teachers: effects of school setting on teachers' signing behavior, 44; use of ASL and English in classroom, 42–44
Heckman, Helen, 10, 65, 66
hegemony: literacy life stories and, 195
historic time, 7; cultural evolution and transmission, 50, 54
hooks, bell, 16, 141, 143, 148
Humphries, Tom, 4, 5, 6, 7
*Hunger of Memory* (Rodriguez), 206
hyper-American, 10, 64

in-school multidisciplinary consultation teams, 127–28
interactional function: of writing, in Deaf education, 183
internalized language, 40
interpreters: as links between school and family of deaf child, 121
interpreting services: Deaf participation in economic activities in U.S. and, 33–34
Israelite, N., 144
*I Was Number 87* (Bolander), 10, 85–86

Johnson, Liddell, and Erting, 17, 145
Jordan, I. King, 13–14, 106
Julian of Norwich, 80

Kannapell, Barbara, 180
Keller, Helen, 84
Kempe, Margery, 80
knowledge: acquisition of, 158; actively created vs. passively received, 158–59; the pathological vs. the cultural view of deafness and, 157–59

Laborit, Emmanuelle, 10, 72, 77–80, **78**
Lane, Harlan, 177, 195
languaculture, 194–95
language: cultural view of deafness, 18; pathological view of deafness, 18
language acquisition, 40, 53–54; early linguistic experiences and, 93; interaction of deaf child and parents, 93; three prerequisites for, 93

language competency: among deaf immigrant and refugee children in the U.S. and Canada, 14–15; among Norwegian deaf children, 12–13
language milieu: among deaf immigrant and refugee children in the U.S. and Canada, 14–15; among Norwegian deaf children, 12–13
Langue Signes des Quebeçois (LSQ), 117n
Larson and Irvine, 148
*Laugh of the Medusa, The* (Cixous), 80
Lentz, Ella Mae, 159–61, 187n3
Linguistic Interpendence theory, 117
literacy: cultural view of deafness, 18; future research questions, 22–23; pathological view of deafness, 18
literacy assessment: of academic achievement and social adjustment in deaf immigrant and refugee children, 15–16
literacy life stories, 20–21, 192–93; Deaf folklore in, 200; Deaf hunter folktale, 200–201; English literacies promoted in the DEELS, 196–200; identity themes in, 193; hearing ESL students' vs. deaf students', 194; hegemony and, 195; six reasons why Deaf students should be encouraged to write, 206–7; social systems promoted in, 194–96; themes promoted by Deaf, college undergraduates, 200–206
"literacy as personal achievement" theme (in literacy life stories), 21, 200, 204–6
Little Paper Family (LPF), 71n7
Lohman, Lex, 162–63
Luborsky, M., 202
*Lying* (Slater), 86

manual communication, 60, 144
Manually Coded English (MCE), 146, 147, 173–75
Marschark, M., 15, 123
Martin, David S., 3
Mayer and Akamatsu, 118, 119
Mayer, Akamatsu, and Stewart, 123–24
Mayer and Wells, 118
Meadow-Orlans, Kathryn P., 1, 3
media: view of link between Deaf women's normalcy and physical beauty in the, 64–66, 67
men: feminization of teaching and, 9, 69; teaching profession and, 61, 62–63
middle-class: rise of a Deaf middle class, 31
mirror talk, 11, 76–77, 79
*Mirror Talk: Genres of Crisis in Contemporary Autobiography* (Egan), 76
Miss Deaf America Pageant, 67
mnemonic function: of writing, in Deaf education, 182

modern Deaf self, 5–6, 8, 30–31, 32; dominant themes of, 32–33; dual views of self, 31; Deaf people's models of, 32; emergence of a self-conscious discourse, 38–39; hearing people's models of, 32
Moeller, Mary Pat, 4n
Moores, Donald F., 1, 2, 3
multicultural deaf individuals: migration, acculturation, and implications for, 113–14. *See also* deaf immigrant and refugee children

National Association of the Deaf (NAD), 67; sign language masters' films, 10, 66
National Council of Teacher of English (NCTE) Position Statement on Teaching Composition, 20–21, 197
National Fraternal Society for the Deaf (NFSD), 67
natural language setting, 168
natural sign systems, 118
New Jersey Association of the Deaf, 67
New York Institution, 60
Nielsen and Luetke-Stahlman, 118
nondiscrimination legislation: Deaf participation in economic activities in U.S. and, 33–34
nonverbal intelligence tests, 123
normalcy, 60, 64, 68, 145, 157, 161; culture and, 56; Deaf women's physical beauty and, 10, 64–66, 69; literate normalcy, 10; notions of Deaf, 36–37; marriage to hearing partner and, 69
Norsk (Norwegian) Gallup, 92
Norway: study on bilingualism and literacy in deaf children, 11–14. *See also* Bilingualism and Literacy in Deaf Children
Norwegian Sign Language (NSL), 12, 13, 92, 95, 99, 103, 104, 107

ontogenetic time, 7
oralism, 9; advocacy of, 60; gender connotations and, 68–69; in Norwegian schools, 91–92; popularity of, 61, 63–64; print media coverage of Deaf women and, 66

Padden, Carol, 3, 17
PAH: glossed as success, 202, 202n
Pearson product moment correlation coefficient, 102
peer helper, 125
Pennsylvania Society for the Advancement for the Deaf, 67
phylogenetic time (biological inheritance), 7; cultural evolution and transmission, 50, 54
physical beauty: media's view of Deaf women's bodies, 64–66, 67
Plato, 84–85
*Preservation of the Sign Language* (film), 180–81

public school setting: effects on teachers' signing behavior, 44

Ramsey, Claire, 1, 4, 5, 6–8
reading comprehension: in Norwegian study, 101, 105, 107
Reagan, Timothy, 1
reciprocal distancing, 148
refugee: definition of, 111
reifying function: of writing, in Deaf education, 182
Research Program in Language and Literacy at the University of California, San Diego: study on "teacher talk", 42
residential deaf schools: effects on teachers' signing behavior at, 44; oral education at, 60, 61
Rhode Island Test of Language Structure, 100
Rodriguez, Richard, 206
Rose, M., 153

second-language development, 39
self-determination movement, 33
Siegel and Cole, 128
*Sign Me Alice II* (Eastman), 163
Sign Supported Speech (SSS). *See* signing with voice
Signed English (SE), 142
signing with voice support (SSS, Sign Supported Speech), 17, 146
*Silent Worker*, 64–65
simultaneous communication (SimCom), 17, 146
Skavian, Sigvald, 91
Slater, Lauren, 86

Slaughten, S. S., 70n1
Smith, Sidonie, 82
Smith College, 62
social control function: of writing, in Deaf education, 182
Soliday, M., 193
SSS (Signed Supported Speech). *See* signing with voice support
Stewart, D., 147
Stokoe, W., 144
Stokoe, Casterline, and Croneberg, 17
Stromberg, P., 206
Strong, M., 146
"struggle to success" theme (in literacy life stories), 21, 200, 202–4
SUCCESS: PAH glossed as, 202, 202n
syntactic structures, 103, 105, 107; similarities in results between English and Norwegian tests, 100-101
syntax test, 100

teachers of deaf education: accreditation of, 177; cooperative learning, 125; demonstration learning, 126; factors affecting parents' perception of teachers' competence, 127; feminization of, 9, 69; peer helper, 125; teaching self-initiative strategies, 125; working in multicultural milieu, 126–27
teacher talk, 5, 6, 42
teacher training programs, 177
telephone relay systems: Deaf participation in economic activities in U.S. and, 33–34

time: cultural evolution and transmission and, 7–8, 50, 52, 54–55
Tomasello: evolution of culture, 49–50, 51
Tompkins, L. M. B., 139
Total Communication (TC), 17, 34, 39, 42, 140, 146, 168; definition of, 146; in Norwegian schools, 92
transformative intellectuals, 177
Trondheim, Norway, 91

United States: immigration and, 110–13, **111**, **112**. *See also* deaf immigrant and refugee children
*Unlocking the Curriculum: Principles for Achieving Access in Deaf Education* (Johnson, Liddell, and Erting), 17, 145, 146
U.S. Committee for Refugees, 111, 112

Veditz, George, 66, 181, 186
Vernon and Andrews, 123
Virgin Island Creole, 180, 181

*voice:* as defined by bell hooks, 148
*Volta Review,* 64
Vygotsky, L. S., 129, 168, 177–78

Walker, N. F., 60
Watson, Julia, 82
Winzer, Margret, 1, 11, 70n2
women: beauty contests, 67, 68; Deaf community's image of, 67–68; education and, 10; feminization of teaching and, 9, 69; literate normalcy and the female body, 10; in teaching profession, 60–61, 62, 63; media's view of normalcy and physical beauty of Deaf women, 64–66
*Wonder at the Works of God* (Cartagena), 10, 82, 83, 84
writing: ASL writing system in Deaf education, 183–84; Deaf education and, 181–84; functions of, 182–83

Yale, Caroline, 61, 62, 70n3